Praise for Bartending For Dummies

"Convivial Bartender-Publisher Ray Foley offers tested advice and tips, with experience and authority, as only a man can who professionally has served thousands behind the bar."
> — LeRoy Neiman, Artist

"Ray Foley is the bartender's bartender. Leave it to him to take the mystery out of mixology! *Bartending For Dummies* is the one ingredient no bar should be without."
> — Michel Roux, President and CEO, Carillon Importers Ltd.

"Who better than Ray Foley of *BARTENDER* magazine to write about the art of mixology!"
> — Clint Rodenberg, SVP of Marketing, Schieffelin &
> Somerset Co.

"Whether you are planning a small cocktail party at your home or planning to start a new career, this book offers a wonderful place to start your education."
> — Harry Knowles, Proprietor, The Manor, Highlawn Pavilion,
> Pleasantdale Chateau, and Rams Head Inn

"*Bartending For Dummies* is a must for all the 'do-it-yourself' bartenders."
> — Charles Chop, United States Bartender's Guild,
> International Bartenders Association

"Ray and Jaclyn Foley are the absolute best thing to happen to bartenders since the repeal of the Volstead Act that ended Prohibition."
> — Richard Lewis, TBWA Chiat/Day

"Who better to write *Bartending For Dummies* than America's best known and funniest bartender, Ray Foley."
> — Bill Samuels Jr., President of Maker's Mark Distillery, Inc.

"There are five original members of the Baseball Hall of Fame: Ty Cobb, Babe Ruth, Walter Johnson, Christy Mathewson, and Honus Wagner. There is only one original member of the Bartenders Hall of Fame: Ray Foley. Need I say more!"
> — Bob Suffredini, Vice President/Division Manager, Hiram
> Walker, Allied Domecq Spirits & Wine USA, Inc.

TM

References for the Rest of Us!™

BESTSELLING BOOK SERIES

Do you find that traditional reference books are overloaded with technical details and advice you'll never use? Do you postpone important life decisions because you just don't want to deal with them? Then our *...For Dummies*® business and general reference book series is for you.

...For Dummies business and general reference books are written for those frustrated and hard-working souls who know they aren't dumb, but find that the myriad of personal and business issues and the accompanying horror stories make them feel helpless. *...For Dummies* books use a lighthearted approach, a down-to-earth style, and even cartoons and humorous icons to dispel fears and build confidence. Lighthearted but not lightweight, these books are perfect survival guides to solve your everyday personal and business problems.

> *"More than a publishing phenomenon, 'Dummies' is a sign of the times."*
>
> — *The New York Times*

> *"...you won't go wrong buying them."*
>
> — *Walter Mossberg, Wall Street Journal, on IDG Books' ...For Dummies books*

> *"A world of detailed and authoritative information is packed into them..."*
>
> — *U.S. News and World Report*

Already, millions of satisfied readers agree. They have made *...For Dummies* the #1 introductory level computer book series and a best-selling business book series. They have written asking for more. So, if you're looking for the best and easiest way to learn about business and other general reference topics, look to *...For Dummies* to give you a helping hand.

BARTENDING
FOR
DUMMIES®

by Ray Foley

IDG
BOOKS
WORLDWIDE
IDG Books Worldwide, Inc.
An International Data Group Company

Foster City, CA ♦ Chicago, IL ♦ Indianapolis, IN ♦ New York, NY

Bartending For Dummies®

Published by
IDG Books Worldwide, Inc.
An International Data Group Company
919 E. Hillsdale Blvd.
Suite 400
Foster City, CA 94404
www.idgbooks.com (IDG Books Worldwide Web site)
www.dummies.com (Dummies Press Web site)

Library of Congress Catalog Card No.: 97-80177

ISBN: 0-7645-5051-9

Printed in the United States of America

10 9 8 7 6

1P/RV/QS/ZZ/IN

Distributed in the United States by IDG Books Worldwide, Inc.

Distributed by Macmillan Canada for Canada; by Transworld Publishers Limited in the United Kingdom; by IDG Norge Books for Norway; by IDG Sweden Books for Sweden; by Woodslane Pty. Ltd. for Australia; by Woodslane (NZ) Ltd. for New Zealand; by Addison Wesley Longman Singapore Pte Ltd. for Singapore, Malaysia, Thailand, and Indonesia; by Norma Comunicaciones S.A. for Colombia; by Intersoft for South Africa; by International Thomson Publishing for Germany, Austria and Switzerland; by Distribuidora Cuspide for Argentina; by Livraria Cultura for Brazil; by Ediciencia S.A. for Ecuador; by Ediciones ZETA S.C.R. Ltda. for Peru; by WS Computer Publishing Corporation, Inc., for the Philippines; by Contemporanea de Ediciones for Venezuela; by Express Computer Distributors for the Caribbean and West Indies; by Micronesia Media Distributor, Inc. for Micronesia; by Grupo Editorial Norma S.A. for Guatemala; by Chips Computadoras S.A. de C.V. for Mexico; by Editorial Norma de Panama S.A. for Panama; by Wouters Import for Belgium; by American Bookshops for Finland. Authorized Sales Agent: Anthony Rudkin Associates for the Middle East and North Africa.

For general information on IDG Books Worldwide's books in the U.S., please call our Consumer Customer Service department at 800-762-2974. For reseller information, including discounts and premium sales, please call our Reseller Customer Service department at 800-434-3422.

For information on where to purchase IDG Books Worldwide's books outside the U.S., please contact our International Sales department at 317-596-5530 or fax 317-596-5692.

For information on foreign language translations, please contact our Foreign & Subsidiary Rights department at 650-655-3021 or fax 650-655-3281.

For sales inquiries and special prices for bulk quantities, please contact our Sales department at 650-655-3200 or write to the address above.

For information on using IDG Books Worldwide's books in the classroom or for ordering examination copies, please contact our Educational Sales department at 800-434-2086 or fax 317-596-5499.

For press review copies, author interviews, or other publicity information, please contact our Public Relations department at 650-655-3000 or fax 650-655-3299.

For authorization to photocopy items for corporate, personal, or educational use, please contact Copyright Clearance Center, 222 Rosewood Drive, Danvers, MA 01923, or fax 978-750-4470.

is a trademark under exclusive license to IDG Books Worldwide, Inc., from International Data Group, Inc.

About the Author

Ray Foley, a former Marine with over 20 years of bartending and restaurant experience, is the founder and publisher of *BARTENDER* Magazine, the only magazine in the world specifically geared towards bartenders and one of the very few primarily designed for servers of alcohol. *BARTENDER* Magazine is enjoying its 18th year and currently has a growing circulation of over 150,000.

Ray has been published in numerous articles throughout the country and has appeared on many TV and radio shows, including David Susskind, ABC-TV News, CBS News, NBC News, *Good Morning America,* Joe Franklin, Patricia McCann, WOR-TV, and *Live with Regis and Kathy Lee.* Ray has also been featured in major magazines, including *Forbes* and *Playboy.*

Ray is the founder of the Bartender Hall of Fame, which honors the best bartenders throughout the United States not only for their abilities as mixologists but for involvement in their communities as well.

Ray serves as a consultant to some of the United States' foremost distillers and importers. He is also responsible for naming and inventing new drinks for the liquor industry.

Ray has the largest collection of cocktail recipe books in the world, dating back to the 1800s, and is one of the foremost collectors of cocktail shakers, with 368 shakers in his collection.

He is the author of *The Ultimate Cocktail Book, The Ultimate Little Shooter Book,* and *Advice from Anonymous.*

Ray resides in New Jersey with his wife and partner of 13 years, Jaclyn, and their son, Ryan.

For more information about *BARTENDER* Magazine, please contact Jackie Foley at P.O. Box 158, Liberty Corner, NJ 07938; phone: 908-766-6006; fax 908-766-6607; e-mail: barmag@aol.com; Web site: http://www.bartender.com.

Dedication

I dedicate this book to all who serve the public with long hours, tired bodies, and great patience (and still know how to have fun): bartenders.

And, of course, to Jaclyn Marie and Ryan Peter, who have made my cup overflow.

Author's Acknowledgments

I would like to pour out my gratitude to Sarah Kennedy and the overflowing enthusiasm at IDG Books in Chicago.

For mixing all the ingredients properly and adding just the right amount of garnish, Mr. Tim Gallan, the Project Editor of *Bartending For Dummies*.

I humbly acknowledge those at *BARTENDER* Magazine for serving this up in record speed, especially my best friend, Loretta Natiello.

And, for supplying all the ingredients in this mixture, Mr. & Mrs. Bill Samuels, Jr., and the gang at Makers Mark. Ansley J. Coale, Jr., Alambic, Inc.; Laura Baddish, The Alden Group; Crystal Harvey, Allied Domecq; Tyler B. Phillips and William N. Chango, Angostura International Ltd.; Diane Burnell, Michael McNeal, Myron Holtzman, and the crew at Anheuser-Busch; Austin, Nichols & Co., Inc.; Eduardo Sardina and Jose Aragon, Bacardi-Martini U.S.A.; John V.O. Kennard, John Overfield, Mary Ann Warren, Susan Gosselin, John Vidal, Brown-Forman Beverages Worldwide; Jean-Louis Carbonnier, Tiffany Sysum, Champagne Wines Information Bureau; Michel Roux, Jerry C. Ciraulo, Ernest Capria, Cary Schwartz, Carillon Importers; John Sapata, Carneros Alambic; Lance Brooks and Jeanne McIntyre, Cohn & Wolfe; Martin Jones, Gary Clayton, and Lori Tieszen, Domecq Importers, Inc.; Chester Brandes, Finnish National Distillers, Inc.; Tracy Nuelle, Fleishman Hillard, Inc.; Belinda Horton, Food and Wines from France; Michael Luftglass, Leah J. Karliner, Sally Wonsik, William Grant & Sons, Inc.; Susan Overton, Heaven Hill Distilleries, Inc.; Dan Tearno, Heineken U.S.A.; George DiBenedetto, Bob Shea, Bob Suffredini, Bill Donan, Jim Mingarelli, Doc Sullivan, Mark Mekenas, Hiram Walker & Sons, Inc.; Norton Cooper, Kevin O'Brien, and Patricia Bornman, Charles Jacquin et cie., Inc.; Michael Donohoe and Kathleen DiBenedetto, Jim Beam Brands Worldwide, Inc.; Korbel Champagne Cellars; Andrew Friedman and Caitlin Connelly, Kratz & Company; Laird & Co.;

Kate McManus, Margaret Stern Communications; Michael L. Avitable, Marie Brizard Wines and Spirits, USA; Keith Klein, Milton Samuels Advertising Agency, Inc.; Peter Nelson and Michelle Krause, Niche Marketing Corp.; Gail Finn-Cavell, Charles Phillips, Anthony Foglio, and the gang at IDV North America; Jose Suarez and Jake Jacobsen, Coco Lopez, Inc; Remy Amerique; Mary E. Waite, Rogers & Associates; Harrison Jones, Sazerac Company, Inc.; Special thanks to Jeff Pogash, Schieffelin & Somerset; Joseph E. Seagram & Sons, Inc.; Kristen McDonough, Seagram Chateau & Estate Wines; Chris Morris, Rene Cooper, Peter Angus, United Distillers North America; Debbie Sklar, VSM Public Relations; Eleanor Ruckman, Wine Institute; Maria Colon, Rums of Puerto Rico; Bob Bernstein, Seagram Americas.

Special thanks to Harry and Doris Knowles of The Manor Restaurant, West Orange, New Jersey, for the opportunity, knowledge and encouragement they gave me, and all the great "Terrace Lounge" crew, especially Millie Rinaldi (and of course Anthony), John Cowan, Mike Cammarano, Ann and John Guidice, Egon Gronau, Matt Wojack, and Hymie Lipshitz.

And a special tip to LeRoy Neiman and Lynn Quayle, The Wilsons, Jimmy Zazzali, Joe and Maryanne McClure, Ed DiMuro, Gary and Mardee Haidin Regan ("my bourbon buddies"), the famous Stephen & Arlene Visakay, Foster Tennant, Bruce Kalfus, Skip Hutchinson, Howard Jacobs, Marvin Solomon, Brian Rae, Bill Kull, Charles Chop, Rene Bardel, Dr. William Toth, and all those on the other side of the bar who tolerate me and, of course, the bartenders all over the world who take the chance and serve me!

Finally, I'd like to thank Karl Gericke; Louis Rubinacci; Lorraine Hale; Kobrand Corp.; John Jessey of Marti, Flores, Priesto & Wachtel; and Biff and Ralph Amato.

Publisher's Acknowledgments

We're proud of this book; please register your comments through our IDG Books Worldwide Online Registration Form located at http://my2cents.dummies.com.

Some of the people who helped bring this book to market include the following:

Acquisitions, Development,
and Editorial

Project Editor: Tim Gallan

Acquisitions Editor: Sarah Kennedy,
Executive Editor

Editorial Manager: Leah P. Cameron

Editorial Coordinator: Ann Miller

Editorial Assistant: Donna Love

Production

Project Coordinator: Valery Bourke

Layout and Graphics: Angela Bush-Sisson,
Maridee V. Ennis, Todd Klemme,
Anna Rohrer, Brent Savage,
M. Anne Sipahimalani, Deirdre Smith

Proofreaders: Chris Collins,
Christine Berman, Kelli Botta,
Michelle Croninger, Rachel Garvey,
Nancy Price, Janet Withers

Indexer: Steve Rath

Special Help: Jamie Klobuchar,
Shannon Ross, Nancy DelFavero,
Nickole Harris

General and Administrative

IDG Books Worldwide, Inc.: John Kilcullen, CEO; Steven Berkowitz, President and
Publisher

IDG Books Technology Publishing: Brenda McLaughlin, Senior Vice President and
Group Publisher

Dummies Technology Press and Dummies Editorial: Diane Graves Steele, V
ice President and Associate Publisher; Mary Bednarek, Director of Acquisitions
and Product Development; Kristin A. Cocks, Editorial Director

Dummies Trade Press: Kathleen A. Welton, Vice President and Publisher;
Kevin Thornton, Acquisitions Manager

IDG Books Production for Dummies Press: Michael R. Britton, Vice President of
Production and Creative Services; Cindy L. Phipps, Manager of Project Coordination, Production Proofreading, and Indexing; Kathie S. Schutte, Supervisor of Page
Layout; Shelley Lea, Supervisor of Graphics and Design; Debbie J. Gates, Production Systems Specialist; Robert Springer, Supervisor of Proofreading; Debbie
Stailey, Special Projects Coordinator; Tony Augsburger, Supervisor of Reprints
and Bluelines

Dummies Packaging and Book Design: Patty Page, Manager, Promotions Marketing

◆

The publisher would like to give special thanks to Patrick J. McGovern,
without whom this book would not have been possible.

◆

ABOUT IDG BOOKS WORLDWIDE

Welcome to the world of IDG Books Worldwide.

IDG Books Worldwide, Inc., is a subsidiary of International Data Group, the world's largest publisher of computer-related information and the leading global provider of information services on information technology. IDG was founded more than 30 years ago by Patrick J. McGovern and now employs more than 9,000 people worldwide. IDG publishes more than 290 computer publications in over 75 countries. More than 90 million people read one or more IDG publications each month.

Launched in 1990, IDG Books Worldwide is today the #1 publisher of best-selling computer books in the United States. We are proud to have received eight awards from the Computer Press Association in recognition of editorial excellence and three from Computer Currents' First Annual Readers' Choice Awards. Our best-selling ...For Dummies® series has more than 50 million copies in print with translations in 31 languages. IDG Books Worldwide, through a joint venture with IDG's Hi-Tech Beijing, became the first U.S. publisher to publish a computer book in the People's Republic of China. In record time, IDG Books Worldwide has become the first choice for millions of readers around the world who want to learn how to better manage their businesses.

Our mission is simple: Every one of our books is designed to bring extra value and skill-building instructions to the reader. Our books are written by experts who understand and care about our readers. The knowledge base of our editorial staff comes from years of experience in publishing, education, and journalism — experience we use to produce books to carry us into the new millennium. In short, we care about books, so we attract the best people. We devote special attention to details such as audience, interior design, use of icons, and illustrations. And because we use an efficient process of authoring, editing, and desktop publishing our books electronically, we can spend more time ensuring superior content and less time on the technicalities of making books.

You can count on our commitment to deliver high-quality books at competitive prices on topics you want to read about. At IDG Books Worldwide, we continue in the IDG tradition of delivering quality for more than 30 years. You'll find no better book on a subject than one from IDG Books Worldwide.

John Kilcullen
Chairman and CEO
IDG Books Worldwide, Inc.

Steven Berkowitz
President and Publisher
IDG Books Worldwide, Inc.

VIII
WINNER

Eighth Annual Computer Press Awards ≥1992

IX
WINNER

Ninth Annual Computer Press Awards ≥1993

X
WINNER

Tenth Annual Computer Press Awards ≥1994

XI
WINNER

Eleventh Annual Computer Press Awards ≥1995

Contents at a Glance

Table of Contents

Introduction

*W*hen you hear the words "Set 'em up, Joe," you better
have at least a basic knowledge of over 200 of the
most called-for cocktails in your head. I say cocktails
because a cocktail is, according to Webster, "any of various
alcoholic drinks made of a distilled liquor mixed with a wine,
fruit juice, etc., and usually iced."

In this book, I show you how to prepare and serve cocktails.
You'll find all the recipes you need to mix cocktails for your
guests. I show you the correct equipment to use and help
you set up for parties. What's more, I also provide an
excellent background on liquors, wine, and beer.

A bartender cannot be made overnight, though, and a head
full of recipes and facts will only get you so far. You need
experience, and you must respect and like people. If you
aren't a people person, all of the great information in this
book will not make you a bartender.

As a bartender for over 20 years, I always enjoyed the
atmosphere and people in bars and restaurants. They are
there to relax and have fun. My job was to serve and be a
part of the entertainment, to make the guests feel at home
and relaxed, never to be overbearing or intruding. So a good
attitude and a lot of experience are key. From here on in, I'm
going to assume that you have the former and are working
on the latter. You're a good person, especially because you
bought this book.

How to Use This Book

This book is a reference that you can read now and refer to
many years from now. Don't feel at all compelled to read the
thing from cover to cover. I would guess that you'll mostly
use this book for recipes, and the best place to find them is
the A to Z recipe section (Chapter 18), which is by far the
largest section of the book. Drinks are also listed by their
ingredients in the index.

This book has a complete table of contents and another index of topics. Feel free to use both to find whatever information you need.

How This Book Is Organized

Like all ...*For Dummies* books, this book is organized into parts and chapters. Each chapter is self-contained so that you don't have to read them in order. Here's what's in each of the book's four parts:

Part I: The Basics

In this part, I describe the bartending tools and glasses you need. I also cover some simple bartending techniques that will help you look like a pro. I tell you what you need to buy to prepare for a party, and I conclude this part with all kinds of interesting alcohol- and bartending-related tables and charts.

Part II: Short Shots from American Whiskey to Wine

I devote a chapter to each of the major kinds of liquor. I tell you where they come from, how they're made, and how to store and serve them. If you wonder what gin is made of, see Chapter 11. Why does Scotch Whisky have that smoky flavor? Check out Chapter 14.

Part III: The Recipes

The first chapter in this part, Chapter 18, contains almost a thousand cocktail recipes listed in alphabetical order by name. This section contains classic cocktails from years past plus the hot cocktails of today and the future. If that weren't enough, the remaining chapters in this part show you how to make pousse-cafés (layered drinks), punches, and non-alcoholic drinks.

Part IV: The Part of Tens

Every ...*For Dummies* book ends with lists of ten items, and this book is no exception. Chapter 22 contains roughly ten cures for hiccups and hangovers. Chapter 23 lists more than ten bartending-related Web sites and other resources.

The Indexes

This book has two indexes: an index of cocktails by their main ingredient and an index of topics. The cocktail index is simply another way of finding a drink in this book if you don't know its name. The topics index can help you find information in chapters other than the ones in Part III.

Icons Used in This Book

Scattered throughout the book are little pictures, which my publisher calls icons, in the margins next to certain blocks of text. Here's what they mean:

This icon lets you know that I'm presenting a neat hint or trick that can make your life easier.

This icon flags information that will keep you out of trouble.

This icon indicates that I'm about to tell a story or provide a little interesting background information.

Where to Go from Here

Look up some recipes. Read about Irish whiskey. Check out one of my hangover cures. This book was designed so that you can jump around.

When it comes to the recipes, I do have this bit of advice: I recommend that you use only the best ingredients when making cocktails. They represent your opinion of your guests, and you want them to have the best. In some drinks, you can get by with the cheap stuff, but in this day and age, people are drinking less and demanding higher quality. You can't go wrong when you serve the good stuff, so why serve anything else?

That said, get reading and start pouring.

The 5th Wave   By Rich Tennant

"I'M PRETTY SURE YOU'RE SUPPOSED TO JUST <u>SMELL</u> THE CORK."

Part I
The Basics

In this part . . .

First, I show you what tools and glassware you need to be a successful bartender. I then cover some basic bartending techniques. Next, I tell you what you need to buy to prepare for a party, and I conclude this part with all kinds of interesting alcohol- and bartending-related tables and charts.

Chapter 1

Just for Openers, the Right Tools and Glasses

*T*he most important assets for any profession are the right tools. The tools for bartending are the correct equipment, a knowledge of the products you pour, cocktail recipes, and the ability to handle people. This chapter covers equipment. (Part II can help you with product knowledge, and Part III gives you the recipes. As for people skills, you're on your own.)

The Basic Tools

You need basic bar tools to mix, serve, and store your food and drink. Whether you're stocking a home bar or working as a professional, the following are your basic tools:

Wine and bottle openers

The best wine opener is called a *waiter's* wine opener, and it's shown in Figure 1-1. It has a sharp blade, a corkscrew or worm, and a bottle opener. This wine opener can be found in most liquor stores or bar supply houses.

Cocktail shaker and measuring glass

There are two types of shakers, and both are shown in Figure 1-2. The Boston shaker is the one that most professional bartenders use. It consists of a mixing glass and stainless steel core that overlaps the glass. The Standard shaker usually consists of two or more stainless steel or glass parts and can be found in department stores or antique stores. Many of these shakers come in different shapes and designs.

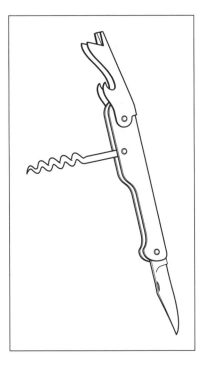

Figure 1-1: A waiter's wine opener.

Strainer

A couple of different types of strainers are available, but the most popular is the Hawthorn, shown in Figure 1-3. The Hawthorn is a flat, spoon-shaped utensil with a spring coil around its head. You can use it on top of a steel shaker or a bar glass to strain cocktails.

Other tools

There's not as much to say about the following tools. Many are shown in Figure 1-4.

- ✔ **Bar spoon (1):** A long spoon for stirring cocktails.
- ✔ **Blender (2):** There are many types of commercial or home blenders with various speeds. Always put liquid in first when making a drink. This will save your blade. Some blenders (but not all) can be used to make crushed ice. Check with the manufacturer or buy an ice crusher.

Boston   Standard

Figure 1-2: A Boston shaker and a Standard shaker.

- ✔ **Coasters or bar napkins:** These prevent rings from developing on your bar and other tables. Napkins also help your guests hold their drinks.

- ✔ **Ice bucket (3):** Pick one that's large enough to hold at least three trays of ice.

- ✔ **Ice scoop or tongs (4):** A must for every bar. Never use your hands to scoop ice.

- ✔ **Jigger or measuring glass (5):** A small glass or metal measuring container with usually a $1/2$ oz. measurer on one side and a 2 oz. measurer on the other.

- ✔ **Knife and cutting board (6):** You need a small, sharp paring knife to cut fruit.

- ✔ **Large water pitcher:** Someone always wants water.

- ✔ **Muddler (7):** A small wooden bat or pestle used to crush fruit or herbs.

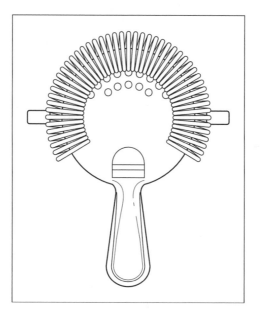

Figure 1-3: The Hawthorn strainer.

✔ **Pourer (8):** This device gives greater control to your pouring. A variety of different types is available, including some with a lidded spout, which prevents insects and undesirables from entering the pourer.

✔ **Stirrers and straws:** Used for stirring and sipping drinks.

✔ **Large cups or bowls:** Used to hold garnishes such as cherries, olives, onions, and so on.

Glassware

People generally expect certain drinks to be served in certain kinds of glasses. Problem is, there are more standard bar glasses than most people (and many bars) care to purchase. In any event, Figure 1-5 shows most of the glasses you're ever likely to use to serve drinks.

I have a few things to say about some of the glasses shown in Figure 1-5. Here goes:

Figure 1-4: A collection of bar tools.

✔ **Shot glass:** Can also be used as a measuring tool and is a must for every bar.

✔ **Cocktail or martini glass:** Available in 3 to 6 oz. sizes. Perfect for martinis, manhattans, stingers, and other classic drinks.

✔ **White wine glass:** Available in 5 to 10 oz. sizes. Stay with a smaller wine glass.

✔ **Red wine glass:** Available in 5 to 10 oz. sizes. The bowl is wider to permit the wine to breathe.

✔ **Champagne glass:** The bowl is tapered to prevent bubbles from escaping.

Figure 1-5: Glasses, glasses, glasses.

- ✔ **Rocks glass:** Also known as an old-fashioned glass. Sizes vary from 5 to 10 oz. Use the ,5 or 6 oz. variety and add plenty of ice.

- ✔ **Highball and collins glasses:** The most versatile glasses. Sizes range from 8 to 12 oz.

- ✔ **Cordial glass:** In addition to cordials, you can also use this glass for straight-up drinks.

- ✔ **Brandy or cognac snifter:** Available in a wide range of sizes, the short stemmed, large bowl should be cupped in hand to warm the brandy or cognac.

If you are planning a home bar or party, keep your glass selection small. You can simplify by using two types of glasses: a white wine glass and a red wine glass. Both are shown in Figure 1-5. These two glasses can be used for every type of cocktail (including shots, even though I said that a shot glass is essential for every bar) plus beer and wine, and using them makes cleaning and storing your glasses less complicated.

Chapter 2

Methods to the Madness

*M*aking good cocktails takes more effort than just pouring ingredients into a glass. This chapter shows you how to do some of the little things that make both you and your drinks look better, which ultimately results in your guests being happier.

Cutting Fruit

Many drinks require fruit garnishes. Your guests expect garnishes, so you can't forgo them, and you have to do them well. Presentation counts big time. You may mix the best drinks on the planet, but if they don't look good when you serve them, no one's going to want to drink them.

I've stepped away from the pulpit now. The next few diagrams and steps show you how to cut the most common garnishes.

Lemon twists

Figure 2-1 illustrates the procedure for cutting lemon twists.

1. **Cut off both ends of the lemon.**

2. **Insert a sharp knife or spoon between the rind and meat of the lemon and carefully separate them.**

3. **Cut the rind into strips.**

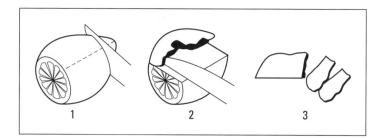

Figure 2-1: Cutting lemon twists.

Orange slices

The following steps for cutting orange slices are shown in Figure 2-2.

1. **With the ends of the orange removed, cut the orange in half.**

2. **Cut each half in half again (lengthwise).**

3. **Cut the orange quarters into wedges.**

Lime slices

The next few steps and Figure 2-3 show you how to cut lime slices.

1. **Cut off the ends of the lime.**

2. **Slice the lime in half.**

3. **Lay each half down and cut it into half-moon slices.**

Lemon and lime wedges

Figure 2-4 illustrates the following steps for cutting wedges.

1. **Slice the lemon or lime in half the long way.**

2. **Lay the cut halves down and halve them again.**

3. **Cut wedges from the lemon or lime quarters.**

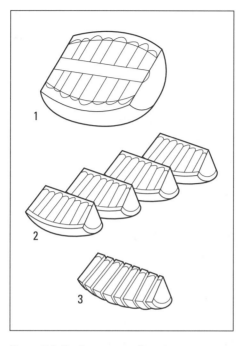

Figure 2-2: Cutting orange slices.

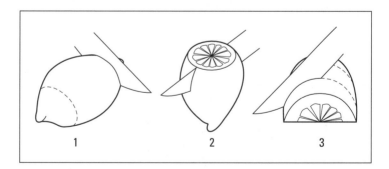

Figure 2-3: Cutting lime slices.

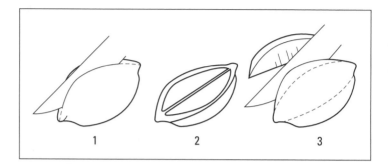

Figure 2-4: Cutting lemon or lime wedges.

Pineapple wedges

Figure 2-5 and the following steps show you how to cut pineapple wedges.

1. **Cut off the top and bottom of the pineapple.**

2. **From top to bottom, cut the pineapple in half.**

3. **Lay the half pineapple down and cut it in half again.**

4. **Remove the core section of the pineapple quarters.**

5. **Cut wedges.**

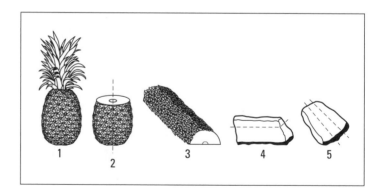

Figure 2-5: Cutting pineapple wedges.

Shaking a Drink

The main reason for shaking is to make a cocktail cold, mix ingredients, or put a head on some cocktails.

As a general rule, all cloudy drinks (including cream drinks and sours) should be shaken, and all clear drinks should be stirred. Never shake a cocktail that has carbonated water or soda. For some drinks, such as the stinger or martini, your guests will tell you whether they prefer them shaken or stirred.

To shake a cocktail in a Boston shaker, put some ice cubes (if called for in the recipe) in the glass container and add the cocktail ingredients. Now place the metal container over the glass container. Hold the metal and glass containers together with both hands and shake with an up and down motion. Make sure that you point the shaker away from your guests to avoid spilling anything on them if the shaker isn't properly sealed.

The two pieces of the shaker may stick together after you shake a drink. Never bang the shaker against the bar or any other object; instead, gently tap it three or four times at the point where the glass and metal containers come in contact.

When pouring or straining the cocktail, always pour from the glass container.

Opening Wine and Champagne Bottles

Opening bottles doesn't take much skill, just a little practice. It's a no-brainer task, so if you don't get it right, you'll look like a fool.

Wine bottles

Here's how you open a wine bottle with a waiter's opener, which is shown back in Chapter 1.

1. Using the blade on the opener, cut the lead foil or capsule by the middle of the bulge near the bottle neck.

2. Remove foil and wipe bottle tops with cloth to remove any mold or foreign particles.

3. Line up the screw or worm directly over the bottle, and with gentle downward pressure, screw the worm clockwise into the cork.

   Do not break the end of the cork, and screw in just enough to extract the cork.

4. Attach the lever of the opener to the lip on top of the bottle, and while holding the bottle firmly, slowly lift the cork straight up.

5. Wipe the neck of the bottle.

6. Present the cork to your guest and pour one ounce of wine into his or her glass.

If the wine is to your guest's satisfaction, pour more. Keep your towel handy to wipe the neck of the bottle as you pour the wine to other guests.

Champagne and sparkling wine bottles

You don't use a corkscrew when opening sparkling wine bottles.

1. Remove the wine hood and foil capsule.

2. Hold the bottle at an angle and point it away from you and anyone else (or anything valuable).

3. While holding the cork in one hand, twist the bottle with the other hand and gently remove the cork. Remember, twist the bottle, not the cork.

Keep a towel handy in case the bottle bubbles over after you remove the cork. To avoid the bubbling, don't shake the bottle before opening.

Making Simple Syrup

Several cocktail recipes call for simple syrup. To make it, dissolve some sugar in boiling water and reduce the mixture, stirring frequently, until it thickens. It shouldn't take more than a couple minutes.

Setting Up Your Home Bar

*W*hen doing any sort of entertaining, one of the biggest hassles is trying to figure how to set up your bar and how much liquor you need to buy. If you throw parties all the time, or if you're trying to plan just one big party, this chapter can help.

Some Logistical Advice

Before I get into what to buy and how much to buy, I'd like to provide some tips on how to set up a bar. Here goes:

Set up a traffic flow for your party

Keep the bar as far as possible from your food and snacks. This prevents large groups of people from staying in one area. If possible, base a wine and beer bar in one area and a cocktail bar in another.

Keep your bar in or near the kitchen

Cleaning up spills is a lot easier in your kitchen. What's more, you'll do a lot less running around if you are close to the sink and refrigerator. If you have to set up your bar in another location, put a small rug or cloth under and behind the bar to protect the floor or carpet. And no matter where your bar is, use a strong, steady table to avoid tipping or collapsing.

Serve smartly

Your party will run smoothly and your guests will be happy if you take the following suggestions to heart:

- ✔ Use nothing larger than a shot glass for shots, and do not serve doubles to your guests. You aren't doing anyone any favors by overserving. If a recipe calls for 1$\frac{1}{2}$ oz. of vodka, use just that amount. All mixed drinks should not exceed 2 oz. of liquor.
- ✔ Use lower proof products if they're available.
- ✔ Have fruit punch available for those "light" drinkers.
- ✔ Have alcohol-free drinks available plus coffee and tea.
- ✔ Use only clean, fresh ice and fruit.
- ✔ If possible, chill glasses and do not put them out until five minutes before the party begins.
- ✔ When serving hot drinks, make sure that the cups or glasses have handles.
- ✔ Use a scoop, tongs, or a large spoon to serve ice. Never use your hands.

- ✔ If you do not have bottle pourers, rub wax paper over the tip of liquor bottles to prevent dripping.
- ✔ Close the bar one to one and a half hours before the end of the party.
- ✔ If possible, hire a professional bartender.

What You Need to Buy for Your Home Bar

When setting up your home bar, always use popular name brands. These brands are not always the most expensive, but they tend to be the most recognizable.

The basic setup

A basic bar setup for your home and for spur-of-the-moment entertaining should consist of the following:

- ✔ One 750-ml bottle of the apéritif of your choice (Campari, Dubonnet, Lillet, and so on)

✔ One 750-ml bottle of sparkling wine or champagne

✔ Four 750-ml bottles of white domestic wine

✔ Two 750-ml bottles of red domestic wine

✔ One 750-ml bottle of dry vermouth

✔ One 750-ml bottle of sweet vermouth

✔ One 750-ml bottle of vodka (domestic or imported)

✔ One 750-ml bottle of gin (domestic or imported)

✔ One 750-ml bottle of rum

✔ One 750-ml bottle of scotch

✔ One 750-ml bottle of whiskey (domestic or imported)

✔ One 750-ml bottle of bourbon

✔ One 750-ml bottle of tequila

✔ One 750-ml bottle of brandy or cognac

✔ Twelve 12-oz.bottles of beer (domestic or imported)

✔ Three 750-ml bottles of the cordials of your choice (such as Irish cream, coffee liqueur or Kahlua, Grand Marnier, Sambucca, white or green crème de menthe, Galliano, B&B, Frangelico, amaretto, peach schnapps, and so on)

The approximate cost to set up this bar is between 175 and 250 U.S. dollars using domestic and local brands. If you are going to use premium brands, add 20 to 30 percent.

I recommend that you use mostly premium brands. You don't want your guests thinking that you'd serve them anything but the best.

A more complete bar

If you plan to serve more than the basics at your bar, add the following items to the basic bar outlined in the previous section:

✔ One 750-ml bottle of Russian or imported vodka

✔ One 750-ml bottle of flavored vodka

✔ One 750-ml bottle of imported gin

✔ One 750-ml or 1.5-liter bottle of 12-year-old scotch

✔ One 750-ml or 1.5-liter bottle of single-malt scotch

- ✔ One 750-ml bottle of Irish whiskey
- ✔ One 750-ml bottle of Canadian whisky
- ✔ One 750-ml bottle of Tennessee whiskey
- ✔ One 750-ml bottle of gold tequila
- ✔ One 750-ml or 1.5-liter bottle of V.S. or V.S.O.P. cognac
- ✔ One 750-ml bottle of port (imported)
- ✔ One 750-ml bottle of cream sherry
- ✔ One 750-ml bottle of Italian red wine
- ✔ One 750-ml bottle of French bordeaux
- ✔ One 750-ml bottle of French burgundy
- ✔ One 750-ml bottle of California white
- ✔ One 750-ml bottle of French champagne (non-vintage)
- ✔ Two 750-ml bottles of additional cordials
- ✔ Twelve 12-oz. bottles of imported beer
- ✔ Six 12-oz. bottles of ale

The added cost of these items is about 250 to 300 U.S. dollars.

The ultimate bar

If money is no object and you want the most complete home bar, add the following items:

- ✔ One 750-ml bottle of flavored vodka
- ✔ One 750-ml bottle of imported or super-premium domestic vodka
- ✔ One 750-ml bottle of 15-year-old single-malt scotch
- ✔ One 750-ml bottle of V.S.O.P. cognac
- ✔ One 750-ml bottle of armagnac
- ✔ One 750-ml or 1.5-liter bottle of imported brandy (from Germany, Spain, or Portugal)
- ✔ One 750-ml bottle of dark rum
- ✔ One 750-ml or 1.5-liter bottle of flavored rum
- ✔ One 750-ml or 1.5-liter bottle of gold tequila
- ✔ Two 750-ml bottles of additional cordials
- ✔ Two 750-ml bottles of vintage imported champagne

✔ Two 750-ml bottles of domestic champagne

✔ Two 750-ml bottles of French bordeaux

✔ Two 750-ml bottles of French burgundy

✔ Two 750-ml bottles of robust Italian red wine (Barolo)

✔ Two 750-ml bottles of California white wine

✔ Two 750-ml bottles of California red wine

✔ One 750-ml bottle of German white wine

✔ Six 12-oz. bottles of assorted microbrews

The added cost of the ultimate bar is roughly 250 to 350 U.S. dollars.

Other supplies for your bar

You need one bottle of the following mixers for every five guests.

✔ Ginger ale

✔ Lemon-Lime soda

✔ Cola or diet cola

✔ Tonic water

✔ Seltzer water or club soda

✔ Tomato juice

✔ Orange juice

✔ Pineapple juice

✔ Cranberry juice

✔ Grapefruit juice

✔ Lime juice

✔ Lemon juice or lemon mix

You also need the following fruits and garnishes:

✔ Orange slices

✔ Olives

✔ Maraschino cherries

✔ Lemon twists

✔ Lime and lemon wedges

Finally, don't forget these items:

- ✔ Angostura bitters
- ✔ Worcestershire sauce
- ✔ Tabasco sauce
- ✔ Superfine sugar
- ✔ Salt and pepper

The Party Charts

I saved the best part of the chapter for last. Say you're throwing a party. How much liquor and supplies should you buy for the number of guests you've invited? The next couple of tables have all the answers.

How much liquor should you buy?

Table 3-1 shows the amount of liquor you should buy for the number of guests at your party. The left column lists the products, and the remaining columns list the number of bottles of that product you should purchase. The last row of the table lists the total costs.

Table 3-1   How Much Liquor to Purchase for a Party

Product (750-ml Bottles)	10-30 Guests	30-40 Guests	40-60 Guests	60-100 Guests
White wine, domestic	4	4	6	8
White wine, imported	2	2	2	3
Red wine, domestic	1	2	3	3
Red wine, imported	1	1	2	2
Blush wine	1	2	2	2
Champagne, domestic	2	3	4	4
Champagne, imported	2	2	2	2
Vermouth, extra dry	1	1	2	2
Vermouth, red	1	1	1	1
Vodka	2	3	3	4
Rum	1	2	2	2

Product (750-ml Bottles)	10-30 Guests	30-40 Guests	40-60 Guests	60-100 Guests
Gin	1	2	2	3
Scotch	1	2	2	3
Whiskey, American or Canadian	1	1	2	2
Bourbon	1	1	1	1
Irish whiskey	1	1	1	2
Tequila	2	2	2	3
Brandy/cognac	1	2	2	3
Apéritifs (your choice)	1	1	2	2
Cordials (your choice)	3	3	3	3
Beer (12 oz. bottles)	48	72	72	96
Total cost	**$300–$400**	**$400–$550**	**$550–$700**	**$550–$700**

With the exception of beer, the preceding table is based on $1^{3}/_{4}$ oz. of liquor per drink. Cost totals are in U.S. dollars.

The number of products you purchase will vary depending on the age of the crowd. If a crowd is dominated by people aged 21 to 35, increase by one-half the amount of vodka, rum, tequila, and beer.

The time of the year should also be a consideration. In the fall and winter, serve less beer. In the spring and summer, serve more beer, vodka, gin, and tequila.

Geographical location is also important in selecting your liquor stock for your guests. Consult a local bartender or liquor clerk to find out what are the most popular products in your area.

How many supplies should you buy?

Your bar needs more than just liquor. Table 3-2 lists the other supplies that you'll have to purchase. Again, the total costs (in U.S. dollars) are listed in the bottom row.

Table 3-2	Other Bar Supplies			
Product	**10-30 Guests**	**30-40 Guests**	**40-60 Guests**	**60-100 Guests**
Soda (2-liter bottles)				
Club soda/seltzer water	3	3	4	5
Ginger ale	2	2	2	3
Cola	3	3	3	4
Diet cola	3	3	3	4
Lemon-lime soda	2	3	3	4
Tonic water	2	2	3	3
Juices (quarts)				
Tomato	2	2	3	3
Grapefruit	2	2	3	3
Orange	2	2	3	3
Cranberry	2	2	3	3
Miscellaneous Items				
Ice (trays)	10	15	20	30
Napkins (dozen)	4	4	6	8
Stirrers (1,000/box)	1	1	1	1
Angostura bitters (bottles)	1	1	1	2
Cream of coconut (cans)	1	2	2	2
Grenadine (bottles)	1	1	1	2
Horseradish (small jars)	1	1	1	2
Lime juice (bottles)	1	1	1	2
Lemons	3	4	5	6
Limes	2	3	3	4
Maraschino cherries (jars)	1	1	1	1
Olives (jars)	1	1	1	1
Oranges	1	2	2	3
Milk (quarts)	1	1	1	2

Product	10-30 Guests	30-40 Guests	40-60 Guests	60-100 Guests
Mineral water (1-liter bottle)	2	3	4	5
Superfine sugar (boxes)	1	1	1	1
Tabasco sauce	1	1	1	1
Worcestershire sauce (bottles)	1	1	1	1
Total cost	**$30–$40**	**$40–$45**	**$45–$50**	**$50–$55**

Chapter 4

Charts and Measures

· ·

In This Chapter

▶ Miscellaneous lists of measurements

· ·

*S*o how many ounces are in a jigger? How many glasses of beer can you pour from a keg? How many calories are in a shot of bourbon? These and many other questions are answered by the tables in this chapter.

Bottle-Related Measurements

Table 4-1 has some handy information about the capacities of standard distilled spirit bottles.

Table 4-1		Standard Bottles		
Bottle Size	*Fluid Ounces*	*Bottles/Case*	*Liters/Case*	*Gallons/Case*
1.75 liters	59.2	6	10.50	2.773806
1 liter	33.8	12	12.00	3.170064
750 ml	25.4	12	9.00	2.377548
500 ml	16.9	24	12.00	3.170064
200 ml	6.8	48	9.60	2.536051
50 ml	1.7	120	6.00	1.585032

Wine bottles come in different sizes than distilled spirit bottles. Table 4-2 lists the capacities of standard wine bottles.

Table 4-2	Standard Bottles			
Bottle Size	**Fluid Ounces**	**Bottles/Case**	**Liters/Case**	**Gallons/Case**
4 liters	135.0	na	na	na
3 liters	101.0	4	12.00	3.17004
1.5 liters	50.7	6	9.00	2.37753
1 liter	33.8	12	12.00	3.17004
750 ml	25.4	12	9.00	2.37763
375 ml	12.7	24	9.00	2.37753
187 ml	6.3	48	8.976	2.37119
100 ml	3.4	60	6.00	1.58502

Bar Measurements and Their Equivalents

You're likely to run across many of the measurements listed in Table 4-3.

Table 4-3	Standard Bar Measurements	
Measurement	**Metric Equivalent**	**Standard Equivalent**
1 dash	0.9 ml	$1/32$ oz.
1 teaspoon	3.7 ml	$1/8$ oz.
1 tablespoon	11.1 ml	$3/8$ oz.
1 pony	29.5 ml	1 oz.
1 jigger	44.5 ml	$1^1/2$ oz.
1 miniature (nip)	59.2 ml	2 oz.
1 wine glass	119.0 ml	4 oz.
1 split	177.0 ml	6 oz.
1 half pint	257.0 ml	8 oz.
1 tenth	378.88 ml	12.8 oz.
1 "pint" ($1/2$ bottle of wine)	375.2 ml	12 oz.
1 pint	472.0 ml	16 oz.

Measurement	Metric Equivalent	Standard Equivalent
1 "quart" (1 bottle wine)	739.0 ml	25 oz.
1 fifth	755.2 ml	25.6 oz.
1 quart	944.0 ml	32 oz.
1 imperial quart	1.137 liters	38.4 oz.
magnum	1.534 liters	52 oz.
1 half gallon	1.894 liters	64 oz.
jeroboam (4 bottles of wine)	3.078 liters	104 oz.
tappit-hen	3.788 liters	128 oz.
1 gallon	3.789 liters	128 oz.
rehoboam (6 bottles of wine)	4.434 liters	150 oz.
methuselah (8 bottles of wine)	5.912 liters	200 oz.
salmanazar (12 bottles of wine)	8.868 liters	300 oz.
balthazar (16 bottles of wine)	11.829 liters	400 oz.
nebuchadnezzar (20 bottles of wine)	14.780 liters	500 oz.

Beer Measurements

Ever wonder how much beer is in a keg? Table 4-4 tells you that and a whole lot more.

Table 4-4   Some Handy Beer Measurements

Barrel Size	Gallons	Equivalent Measurement
1 barrel of beer	31.0 gallons	13.8 cases of 12-oz. cans or bottles
1/2 barrel of beer	15.5 gallons	1 keg
1/4 barrel of beer	7.75 gallons	1/2 keg
1/8 barrel of beer	3.88 gallons	1/4 keg

Drinks Per Bottle

How many glasses can you get out of a standard spirit or wine bottle? Check out Table 4-5.

Table 4-5	The Number of Servings from Standard-Size Bottles		
Serving Size	*750-ml Bottle*	*1-Liter Bottle*	*1.75-Liter Bottle*
1 oz.	25	33	59
1¹/₄ oz.	20	27	47
1¹/₂ oz.	17	22	39

Serving Temperatures for Wine

There's no sense serving good wine if you're not going to do so at the right temperature. Table 4-6 can help.

Table 4-6	Wine Serving Temperatures
Wine Type	*Temperature Range*
Full-bodied red wines	65°–68° F
Light-bodied red wines	60°–65° F
Dry white wines	50°–55° F
Sweet red and sweet white wines	42°–46° F
Sparkling wines and champagnes	42°–46° F

Calories and Carbohydrates

Most of us are watching what we eat, but many of us sometimes forget to watch what we drink. Alcohol is a form of sugar, so it's high in calories. If you're counting calories or trying to keep tabs on your carbohydrate consumption, Table 4-7 can help.

Table 4-7   The Number of Calories and Carbohydrates in Many Drinks

Drink	Calories	Carbohydrates (Grams)
Beer (12 oz.)		
Light beer	110	6.9
Typical beer	144	11.7
Bourbon (1 oz.)		
80 proof	65	trace
86 proof	70	trace
90 proof	74	trace
94 proof	77	trace
100 proof	83	trace
Brandy (1 oz.)		
80 proof	65	trace
86 proof	70	trace
90 proof	74	trace
94 proof	77	trace
100 proof	83	trace
Champagne (4 oz.)		
Brut	92	2.1
Extra Dry	97	2.1
Pink	98	3.7
Coffee Liqueur (1 oz.)		
53 proof	117	16.3
63 proof	107	11.2
Gin (1 oz.)		
80 proof	65	0.0
86 proof	70	0.0
90 proof	74	0.0
94 proof	77	0.0
100 proof	83	0.0

(continued)

Table 4-7 *(continued)*

Drink	Calories	Carbohydrates (Grams)
Rum (1 oz.)		
80 proof	65	0.0
86 proof	70	0.0
90 proof	74	0.0
94 proof	77	0.0
100 proof	83	0.0
Scotch (1 oz.)		
80 proof	65	trace
86 proof	70	trace
90 proof	74	trace
94 proof	77	trace
100 proof	83	trace
Tequila (1 oz.)		
80 proof	64	0.0
86 proof	69	0.0
90 proof	73	0.0
94 proof	76	0.0
100 proof	82	0.0
Vodka (1 oz.)		
80 proof	65	0.0
86 proof	70	0.0
90 proof	74	0.0
94 proof	77	0.0
100 proof	83	0.0
Whiskey (1 oz.)		
80 proof	65	0.0
86 proof	70	0.0
90 proof	74	0.0

Drink	Calories	Carbohydrates (Grams)
Whiskey (1 oz.)		
94 proof	77	0.0
100 proof	83	0.0
Wine (1 oz.)		
Apéritif	41	2.3
Port	41	2.3
Sherry	41	2.3
White or red table	29	1.2

Part II

Short Shots from American Whiskey to Wine

In this part...

1 give you some background for just about every kind of liquor, including beer and wine. Each chapter tells you where a specific product comes from, how it's made, and how to store and serve it.

Chapter 5

American and Canadian Whisk(e)y

*T*his chapter deals with five kinds of whiskey: bourbon, Tennessee whiskey, rye whiskey, blended whiskey, and Canadian whisky.

How Whiskey Is Made

Whiskey is distilled from grain. The type of grain or grains used determines the type of whiskey. After grain is harvested, it is inspected and stored. It is then ground into a meal and cooked to solubilize the starch; malt is added, changing the starch to sugar. This mash is cooled and pumped into fermenters. Yeast is added to the mash and allowed to ferment, resulting in a mixture of grain residue, water, yeast cells, and alcohol. This mixture is pumped into a still where heat vaporizes the alcohol. The alcohol vapors are caught, cooled, condensed and drawn off. This new high-proof whiskey is stored in a cistern room. Water is added to lower the proof, and the whiskey is drawn into barrels. The barrels of whiskey are stored in a rack house for aging. After aging, the barrels of whiskey are drained into the tanks that feed the bottling line. In the case of blended whiskey (including Canadian), different whiskeys are mixed together, and grain spirits or other whiskeys are added.

Bourbon

Bourbon is the most well known and probably the most popular whiskey produced in the United States. It has an amber color and a slightly sweet flavor. By law, straight bourbon must be made from at least 51-percent corn, and it must be aged in brand new charred oak barrels for at least four years. Although Tennessee whiskey doesn't have to be made in this way, both Tennessee distilleries — George Dickel and Jack Daniel's — also follow these guidelines.

A little history

Settlers on the east coast of North America began making rye whiskey in the 1700s. They were mostly immigrants from Germany and Northern Ireland who weren't familiar with corn. In the 1790s, when the U.S. government imposed a tax on distilled spirits, the whiskey makers of Pennsylvania revolted, culminating in the Whiskey Rebellion of 1794. President Washington called out federal troops to put down the rebellion, and many distillers fled west to Kentucky where the law was not imposed quite so strictly.

In Kentucky, early settlers had already begun making whiskey from corn, and the newcomers quickly learned how to use this indigenous American grain to make what would be known as bourbon. Bourbon gained its name from being shipped from Bourbon County in Kentucky, down to places such as St. Louis and New Orleans where it soon became known as "whiskey from Bourbon," and eventually, bourbon whiskey.

Popular brands

When applicable, I've listed the varieties within each brand.

- **Blanton's Single Barrel Bourbon:** Produced in a variety of proofs and ages.
- **Booker's Bourbon:** Produced in a variety of proofs and ages.
- **Elijah Craig Bourbon:** 12 years old and 94 proof.
- **I.W. Harper Kentucky Straight Bourbon Whiskey:** 86 proof and 101 proof. I.W. Harper Gold Medal: 15 years old and 86 proof.

- ✔ **Jim Beam:** 4 years old and 80 proof. Beam Choice: 5 years old and 80 proof. Beam Black Label: 8 years old and 90 proof.

- ✔ **Maker's Mark:** 90 proof. Limited Edition: 101 proof.

- ✔ **Old Charter Kentucky Straight Bourbon Whiskey:** 8 years old and 80 proof; 10 years old and 86 proof. The Classic 90: 12 years old and 90 proof. Proprietor's Reserve: 13 years old and 90 proof.

- ✔ **Old Crow Bourbon:** 8 years old and 80 proof; 10 years old and 86 proof. The Classic: 12 years old and 90 proof.

- ✔ **Old Fitzgerald Kentucky Straight Bourbon Whiskey:** 86 and 90 proof. Very Special Old Fitzgerald (Bourbon Heritage Collection): 8 years old and 100 proof.

- ✔ **Old Grand Dad**: 86 proof. Bottled in Bond: 100 proof. 114 Barrel Proof.

- ✔ **Wild Turkey:** 80 proof. Wild Turkey Rare Breed: a blend of 6-, 8- and 12-year-old stocks and usually 109.5 and 112 proof. Wild Turkey Old Number 8 Brand: 101 proof.

- ✔ **Woodford Reserve:** 7 years old and 90.4 proof.

Note: A limited number of distilleries produce a whiskey bottled at *Barrel Proof,* which sometimes exceeds the 125-proof legal limit. This happens when the whiskey enters the barrel at 125 proof and gains strength during aging.

Tennessee Whiskey

Tennessee whiskey differs from bourbon in that it is filtered through sugar-maple charcoal before it is aged, and although both whiskeys are usually filtered before bottling, it's the sugar-maple charcoal that adds a different flavor to Tennessee whiskeys.

Popular brands

Actually, the following are the only two producers of Tennessee whiskey:

- ✔ **George Dickel Tennessee Whiskey:** Old No 8. Brand: 80 proof. Old No. 12 Superior Brand: 90 proof. Barrel Reserve: 10 years old and 86 proof.

 ✔ **Jack Daniel's Tennessee Sour Mash Whiskey:** Black Label: 86 proof. Green Label: 80 proof, available only in the U.S. Gentleman Jack: 80 proof.

Rye Whiskey

Rye whiskey is a fermented grain containing at least 51 percent rye and distilled at not more than 160 proof. It is matured in new charred oak barrels for a minimum of two years. Rye has a very strong, distinctive flavor.

Popular brands

 ✔ **Old Overholt**: 4 years old and 80 proof.

 ✔ **Bellows & Co.:** 80 proof.

 ✔ **Mount Vernon:** 80 proof.

Canadian Whisky

Canadian whisky (no "e" in whisky) is blended from cereal grains and aged in oak casks for a minimum of three years. There are no limitations as to the grain, distilling proof, formula, or type of barrels used. Each distiller is allowed to make its own type of whisky. Most Canadian whisky is aged in white oak barrels. Canadian whiskies sold to the U.S. are blends bottled at a minimum of 80 proof and are generally four years old or older.

Popular brands

 ✔ **Black Velvet:** 80 proof and 6 years old.

 ✔ **Canadian Club:** 80 proof and 6 years old.

 ✔ **Canadian Mist:** 80 proof and 6 years old.

 ✔ **Crown Royal:** 80 proof and 6 years old.

 ✔ **Seagram's V.O.:** 86 proof; aged 6 years (the V.O. means "Very Own" or "Very Old").

Blended Whiskey

American blended whiskey is a mixture of at least 20-percent straight 100-proof whiskey with neutral spirits or grain whiskey. Sometimes additional coloring and enhancers are added. Blends are bottled at not less than 80 proof.

Those whiskeys blended with neutral spirits are labeled on the back of the bottle stating percentages of straight and neutral spirits. The most famous and biggest seller of blended whiskey is Seagram 7 Crown. It, of course, is part of that famous drink, the "14" — a seven and seven.

Other brands of blended whiskey include the following:

- ✓ **Barton Reserve**
- ✓ **Carstairs**
- ✓ **Imperial**
- ✓ **Fleishmann's**
- ✓ **Mattingly & Moore**

Storing and Serving Suggestions

American whiskey and Canadian whisky can be served straight, on ice, with water or seltzer, or mixed as a cocktail. Store an unopened bottle in a cool, dry place. After opening, a typical bottle should have a shelf life of at least two years.

Chapter 6
Apéritifs

In This Chapter

▶ A list of popular apéritifs

A péritif comes from the Latin word *aperire,* meaning to open. An apéritif is usually any type of drink you would have before a meal. Most apéritifs are usually low in alcohol and mild tasting.

Many of the cordials and liqueurs listed in Chapter 10 can also be drunk as apéritifs. Other than that, there's not much more to say about apéritifs other than to talk about the individual products that are available. Here goes:

Amer Picon (French): A blend of African oranges, gentian root, quinine bark, and some alcohol. Usually served with club soda or seltzer water with lemon.

Campari (Italian): A unique combination of fruits, spices, herbs, and roots.

Cynar (Italian): A bittersweet apéritif that is made from artichokes. Best when served over ice with a twist of lemon or orange.

Dubonnet (American): Produced in California and available in blanc and rouge. Serve chilled.

Fernet Branca (Italian): A bitter, aromatic blend of approximately 40 herbs and spices (including myrrh, rhubarb, chamomile, cardamom, and saffron) in a base of grape alcohol.

Jagermeister (German): Composed of 56 botanicals, including citrus peel, aniseed, licorice, poppy seeds, saffron, ginger, juniper berries, and ginseng.

Lillet (French): Made in Bordeaux from a blend of 85-percent fine Bordeaux wines and 15-percent fruit liqueurs. Lillet Blanc is made from Sauvignon Blanc and Semillion and has a golden color. Lillet Rouge is made from Merlot and Cabernet Sauvignon and has a ruby-red color.

Pernod (French): Comes from the essence of Badiane (*anis star*) and from a spirit made from natural herbs such as mint and balm.

Punt e Mes (Italian): Vermouth with bitters and other botanicals added.

Ricard (French): Made from anise, fennel (green anise), licorice, and other Provencal herbs.

Suze (French): French bitters distilled from gentian root. Gentian is grown in the Auvergne and the Jura regions and is a large, originally wild flower with golden petals.

What is Angostura?

Angostura aromatic bitters is a blend of rare tropical herbs and spices that is used to flavor and season a great variety of food dishes and certain alcoholic and non-alcoholic drinks.

The formula was first compounded in 1824 by Dr. Johann Siegert, Surgeon-General in the army of the great liberator of South America, Simon Bolivar. Dr. Siegert's headquarters were in the port of Angostura, Venezuela, a city now known as Ciudad Bolivar. The doctor experimented for four years before finding the exact formula he was after to improve the appetites and well-being of his troops. Sailors pulling into the port discovered the bitters and bought bottles to carry away with them. Soon the fame of "Angostura" bitters spread around the world. Angostura bitters is used in many cocktails, including the Manhattan, Old Fashioned, and Rob Roy.

Chapter 7
Beer

*B*asically, beer is an alcoholic beverage that is fermented and brewed from rice, barley, corn, hops, water, and yeast. Beer has been brewed for thousands of years, beginning with the Egyptians. Today there are thousands of different varieties of beer throughout the world. The United States has over 900 microbrews alone. Germany brags of having over 1,200 breweries.

Beer enjoys the distinction of coming to the Americas on the Mayflower and, in fact, seems to have played a part in the Pilgrims' decision to land at Plymouth Rock instead of farther south, as intended. A journal kept by one of the passengers — and now in the U.S. Library of Congress — states in an entry from 1620 that the Mayflower landed at Plymouth because "we could not now take time for further search or consideration, our victuals being much spent, especially our beer. . . ."

The first commercial brewery in America was founded in New Amsterdam (New York) in 1613. Many patriots owned their own breweries, among them General Israel Putnam and William Penn. Thomas Jefferson was also interested in brewing and made beer at Monticello. George Washington even had his own brew house on the grounds of Mount Vernon, and his handwritten recipe for beer — dated 1757 and taken from his diary — is still preserved.

How Beer Is Made

The beer brewing process begins with pure water, corn grits, and malted barley. Malted barley is the basic ingredient in brewing and is often referred to as the "soul of beer." It contributes to the color and characteristic flavor of beer. What does *malted* mean? It means that the barley has been steeped or soaked in water and allowed to germinate or grow.

The corn grits and malt are cooked and blended to create mash. A sugary liquid, called *wort,* is extracted from the mash. (The remaining solid portion of the mash, the brewer's grain, is sold as feed.) The wort is transferred to the brew kettles, where it is boiled and hops are added. Hops are responsible for the rich aroma and the delicate bitterness in beer. The wort then moves to the wort cooler. Yeast, which converts sugar into alcohol and carbon dioxide, and sterile air are added next, and the wort moves to fermentation tanks for a carefully controlled time period. Two different types of yeast can be used: *bottom* and *top.* Bottom yeast settles to the bottom of the tank after converting all of the sugar, and the resulting beer is a lager. Top yeast rises to the top of the tank when it's done with the sugar, and the beer it produces is an ale.

Types of Beer

You've probably seen some of the following terms on beer labels, or maybe you've heard them in beer commercials.

- ✔ **Ale** is top-fermented beer. It is a little bitter, usually tastes hoppy, and has a higher alcohol content.
- ✔ **Bitter** beer is a strong ale, usually English, with higher than normal alcohol and, as the name implies, a bittersweet taste.
- ✔ **Bock** beer is a dark, strong, slightly sweet lager beer brewed from caramelized malt.
- ✔ **Ice** beer is brewed at colder than normal temperatures and then chilled to below freezing, forming crystals. The crystals are filtered out, leaving a smoother tasting beer with a slightly higher alcohol content.
- ✔ **Lager** is a bottom-fermented beer stored at very low (cold) temperatures for a long period of time (several months). Lager is German for *to store.*
- ✔ **Lambic** beer is brewed in Belgium. Ingredients such as peaches, raspberries, cherries, and wheat are added during the brewing process.

✔ **Light** beer has fewer calories and less alcohol.

✔ **Malt liquor** is fermented at a higher temperature than other beers, which results in a higher alcohol content.

✔ **Pilsner** is a light, hoppy, dry lager.

✔ **Sake** is beer brewed and processed from rice. (Some consider sake a wine.) Sake is served warm or at room temperature.

✔ **Stout** is an ale produced from heavily roasted barley. It is darker in color and has a slightly bitter flavor.

✔ **Trappist** beer is brewed in Belgium or The Netherlands by Trappist monks. It contains high levels of alcohol and is usually dark in color.

✔ **Wheat** beer is made with wheat. It is usually garnished with a lemon and sometimes raspberry syrup.

Storing and Serving Suggestions

In the United States, beer is served cold (40 degrees Fahrenheit). Lower temperatures tend to dull the taste, so consider 40 degrees the lower limit. Store beer away from sunlight, or you'll have *skunked beer,* which is never pleasant. Most beers now have labels that say when they were brewed or when to remove them from the shelf.

Chapter 8
Brandy

*B*randy is derived from the Dutch term *brandewijn,* meaning burnt wine. The term was known as *branntwein* or *weinbrand* in Germany, *brandevin* in France, and *brandywine* in England. Today, we have shortened the word to simply brandy. Brandy is distilled in most countries that produce wine.

What Is It?

Brandy is made by distilling wine or fruit and then aging in oak barrels. The difference in brandy varies from country to country. Soil, climate, grapes, production methods and blending give each brandy its own unique flavor and style.

When brandy is produced, it undergoes four basic processes: fermentation of the grape, distillation to brandy, aging in oak barrels, and blending by the master blender.

American Brandy

Brandy was introduced to California over 200 years ago by the Spanish missionaries. Much of the production of American brandy is in the San Joaquin Valley to take advantage of the soil, climate, and water. California produces the largest percentage of American brandy, and all California brandy has to be aged a minimum of two years.

Popular brands

- ✔ **Carneros Alambic:** The first *alambic* (cognac-style) brandy in California.
- ✔ **Christian Brothers:** This brandy is processed and aged in Napa Valley.
- ✔ **E&J Gallo:** They produce E&J Brandy (Gold), E&J V.S.O.P. Brandy, and E&J White Brandy.
- ✔ **Germain-Robin:** Another excellent alambic brandy from California.
- ✔ **Korbel:** A California brandy from the Korbel Distillery.

What the heck does *alambic* mean?

Alambic, the French word for *still,* is the word approved for label use by the U.S. Bureau of Alcohol, Tobacco, and Firearms (ATF). It denotes brandy distilled on a batch-process "pot" still rather than on a continued-column still. Cognac, armagnac, and high-quality fruit brandies are distilled on various types of pot stills. The major American "alambic" brandy producers, Germain-Robin and Carneros Alambic, use cognac stills, which entails two distillations, but small quantities have been made on single-distillation alsatian fruit stills by distillers of American fruit brandies such as St. George Spirits.

Brandies from Around the World

Brandy is distilled in most countries that produce wine.

- ✔ **Asbach Uralt (Germany):** The top-selling brandy in Germany.
- ✔ **Aztec DeOro (Mexico):** A 12-year-old brandy made using the solera method. (See the following sidebar.)
- ✔ **Carlos I (Spain):** Ranked among the finest in the world.
- ✔ **Don Pedro (Mexico):** Pot stilled and solera aged.
- ✔ **Fellipe II (Spain):** The number-one selling Spanish brandy in the United States.
- ✔ **Metaxa (Greece):** The most famous Greek brandy.

⮭ **Presidente (Mexico):** The largest selling brandy in the world and in Mexico.

⮭ **Stock 84 (Italy):** Produced by Stock Distillery of Trieste, Italy.

The solera method

The *solera* method of making brandy is comprised of three aging stages:

⮭ The wine spirits are blended and placed for some months in barrels.

⮭ Half of the brandy in each barrel is then blended in another barrel containing older brandy.

⮭ Finally, half of that barrel is placed in yet another barrel containing even older brandy.

Fruit Brandy

Fruit brandies are produced from all kinds of (guess what?) fruits. The fruit is washed and ground into a mash. Water and yeast is added and allowed to ferment. After the sugar has been metabolized, the mash is pressed and the liquid is then distilled. Some fruit brandies are aged in oak barrels. Here are some of the major types:

⮭ **Applejack:** An apple brandy produced in the United States.

⮭ **Calvados:** An apple brandy made from a variety of apples from northwestern France.

⮭ **Framboise:** Made from raspberries.

⮭ **Kirsch:** Made from cherries.

⮭ **Poire:** Made from pears, usually from Switzerland and France. (Poire William is a pear brandy that contains a fully mature pear. While each pear is still on the branch, it is placed in the bottle. When the pear is mature, it is washed in the bottle and the bottle is then filled with pear brandy.)

⮭ **Slivovitz:** Made from plums, usually from Germany or Hungary.

Fruit-Flavored Brandies

In the United States, fruit-flavored brandies are classified as cordials and are bottled usually over 70 proof. Sugar, natural coloring, fruit, and other flavorings are added. You can find brandies flavored with such diverse ingredients as apricots, bananas, coffee, and peaches.

Storing and Serving Suggestions

Brandy is traditionally served straight up in a snifter after dinner, but it is also mixed with water or soda and can be found in some famous cocktails. Store an unopened bottle out of sunlight. After opening, a bottle of brandy can last up to three years. Brandy does not age in the bottle, so a bottle will taste no better if you let it sit for ten years in your basement.

Chapter 9
Cognac and Armagnac

- -

- -

*F*rance produces two kinds of brandy: cognac and armagnac. Both are named after the region in which they are made.

Cognac

Cognac can only be produced in the legally-defined region of Cognac, France, located between the Atlantic and Massif Central, specifically at the junction between oceanic and continental climate zones. The region also straddles the dividing line between northern and southern climates. These four influences create a multitude of micro-climates. This, plus local soil characteristics, create a range of wine and, consequently, the cognac of each region. In 1909, the French government passed a law that only brandy produced in the "delimited area" surrounding the town of Cognac can be called cognac.

How it's made

The arduous, time-honored distilling and aging process is what makes cognac so special. The cognac you drink today was produced using methods dating back to the seventeenth century.

The distillation of cognac is a two-stage process:

✓ A first distillate, known as *brouillis,* is obtained, with an alcoholic strength of between 28 to 32 percent.

✔ The brouillis is returned to the boiler for a second heating, which produces a liquid known as *la bonne chauffe*. In this second distillation, the beginning and the end of distillation (the head and tail) are discarded, leaving only the *heart* of the spirit which becomes cognac.

The cognac is then sent to rest in oak casks made from wood from the Limousin and Troncais forests.

Maturing slowly over long years in cellars, the cognac acquires a smoothness and flavor beyond compare. The wood and the dark, saturated atmosphere of the cellars work together to develop the aroma of the cognac to its full potential. All cognac is aged a minimum of 30 months.

The angels' share

Aging cognac and armagnac is very expensive, not only because it ties up capital, but because millions of bottles per year disappear into the air through evaporation as the spirit sits in its oak casks. To make fine cognac and armagnac, you can't avoid this loss, and producers refer to it as the *angels' share.*

What are all those letters on the label?

When you shop for cognac, you'll see all kinds of designations on the labels of various brands — for example, Courvoisier V.S., Martell V.S.O.P., and Remy Martin X.O. The letters and phrases after the brand name are a general indication of the age (and, in turn, expensiveness) of the cognac.

Every major brand produces cognacs of different ages. When one of the following designations is used, it indicates the age of the youngest cognac used in the blend that makes up what's in the bottle.

✔ **V.S. (Very Superior) or Three Stars:** The cognac is aged less than 4 and a half years.

✔ **V.S.O.P. (Very Superior Old Pale):** The cognac has aged between 4 and a half and 6 and a half years. Sometimes called V.O. (Very Old) or Reserve.

> ✔ **X.O. (Extremely Old), Napoleon, Hors d'age, V.S.S.O.P., Cordon Bleu, Grand Reserve, and Royal:** The cognac has aged at least 5 and a half years and up to 40 years.

Generally speaking, each cognac producer uses blends that are much older than the minimum required. In the most prestigious cognacs, some of the blends may have matured over several decades.

You're also going to see some of these names on the labels:

> ✔ **Grand Fine Champagne or Grande Champagne:** These identify cognacs made exclusively from grapes grown in the Grande Champagne region of Cognac.
>
> ✔ **Petite Fine Champagne or Petite Champagne:** These names mean that the cognac is a blend made from grapes grown in the Grande Champagne and Petite Champagne sections of Cognac. At least 50 percent of the blend must be from grapes grown in the Grande Champagne Region.

The terms *fine cognac* and *grande fine,* which may also appear on cognac labels, have no legally defined meaning. The designations *extra old* (EO) and *very old pale* (VOP) are not officially recognized by the Bureau du Cognac, which makes up all the names and rules.

You won't see vintage dates on cognac labels because in 1963, the French passed a law prohibiting the placement of vintage labels on cognac bottles. Go figure.

Popular brands

Even though all cognacs are produced in the same region, and even though every brand seems to have the same jumble of age designations on their labels, you might be surprised at the degree of distinctiveness among the brands. Some brands have a strong, room-filling aroma; some have a mild grape flavor; others have hints of caramel and vanilla. If you're a fan of cognac, my advice is that you not only try several different brands, but that you also try some of the variations within each brand.

If you're curious to find out what an older cognac (X.O. or better) tastes like, visit a decent bar and order a glass (and be prepared to pay 10 to 20 U.S. dollars) before you decide to invest in an expensive bottle of cognac.

In the following list, the available styles for each brand are listed from least expensive to most expensive. All cognacs are 80 proof.

- **Courvoisier** produces V.S., V.S.O.P., Napoléon, Initiale Extra X.O., X.O. Imperial, and Succession J.L., a very old and very rare Grande Champagne Cognac.

- **Delamain** produces Vesper Grande Champagne Cognac, Pail & Dry Très Belle Grande Champagne Cognac, Très Vénérable Grande Champagne Cognac, and Réserve de la Famille Grande Champagne Cognac. All are at least 25 years or older.

- **Hennessy** produces V.S., V.S.O.P., Privilège, X.O., and Paradis.

- **Hine Cognac** produces V.S.O.P., Antique, Triomphe, and Family Reserve.

- **Martell** produces V.S., Médaillon V.S.O.P., Cordon Bleu, X.O. Suprême, Martell Extra, and L'Or de J&F Martell.

- **Remy Martin** produces V.S., V.S.O.P., X.O. Special, and Louis XIII.

Armagnac

Armagnac, though less well known than cognac, is France's oldest brandy and has been produced continuously since the 15th century (as early as 1422). It is distilled from premium white wine grown in the Armagnac region of southwest France.

How it's made

Armagnac is a distillate produced from the *continuous,* or single, distillation process. Neutral white wine registering about 9- to 10-percent alcohol is heated in a traditional copper alambic pot still at a relatively low temperature. The vapors pass through the swan neck coils and produce a spirit of no more than 63-percent alcohol. This combination of low temperature and lower alcohol produce a spirit that retains more flavor and aroma elements in the brandy. The clear brandy is then put into casks traditional to the region, hand crafted 400 liter-barrels made from Armagnac or Limousin oak. The aging process begins and can last from one year to fifty years. The spirit takes on flavors of the wood and other special nuances as it matures, creating a brandy of complexity and distinction. It is then up to the cellarmaster to blend the separate barrels into a harmonious whole to create the full range of armagnacs.

How to read the label

The French government regulates armagnac labeling. The following designations are used:

- ✔ **V.S. or Three Stars** means that the youngest brandy in the blend is at least three years old.
- ✔ **V.O. (Very Old), V.S.O.P. (Very Special Old Pale), and Reserve** mean that the youngest brandy in the blend is at least 4 and a half years old.
- ✔ **Extra, Napoleon, X.O., Vieille Reserve** and other similar labels indicate that the youngest brandy is at least 5 and a half years old.

Unlike cognac, armagnac products may carry a vintage date. All non-vintage armagnacs contain much older brandies than indicated on the labels. Vintage armagnacs are the unblended product of a single year's production.

Popular brands

- ✔ **Sempe** produces 6-year-old and 15-year-old varieties. Its Xtra Grand Reserve is a blend of brandies aged from 35 to 50 years.
- ✔ **Janneau** produces V.S.O.P., Selection (aged 8–10 years), and Reserve de la Maison. A 1966 vintage is also sold.
- ✔ **Armagnac Lapostolle X.O.** is matured for over 30 years.

Storing and Serving Suggestions

Cognac and armagnac are after-dinner drinks. Cognac is very seldom mixed, but people have been known to drink it with soda or water. Both cognac and armagnac are excellent companions to coffee, tea, and today's big fad — cigars. They should be served at room temperature and in clear, crystal brandy snifters. Like all fine brandies, cognac and armagnac should be gently swirled in the glass and then sipped and savored. If stored in a cool, dry place, an opened bottle of either brandy should last for two years.

Chapter 10

Cordials and Liqueurs

- -

In This Chapter

▶ What cordials and liqueurs are

▶ A list of varieties

▶ Storing and serving suggestions

- -

*C*ordial comes from the Latin word *cor,* meaning heart. Liqueur is derived from the Latin word meaning melt or dissolve. Both words are interchangeable, although liqueur is used more in Europe and cordials in the United States. From this point on, I'll use the word cordial to describe both.

Cordials are made by infusing the flavor of fruits, herbs, spices, and other plants with a spirit such as brandy or whiskey. As you'll discover from the list later in this chapter, there are many different varieties of cordials. Most are sweet. In fact, cordials sold in the United States contain up to 35 percent sugar and must contain a minimum of 2.5 percent sugar by weight.

Within the cordial category are crèmes and fruit-flavored brandies. Crèmes have a high sugar content, which makes them, well, creamy. Usually, the name of such a cordial indicates what it tastes like. Crème de banana tastes like bananas, and apricot brandy tastes like apricots.

A Whole Lotta Cordials

There are more cordials in the world than any one person can list. What I've tried to do is describe the ones that you're likely to see in the recipes in this book. Someone somewhere probably makes a soy-sauce-and-aloe-flavored cordial, and maybe it tastes great, but nobody you or I know is ever going to ask for it, so I'm not going to list it.

Advocaat (Advokaat) is a Dutch invention, combining brandy, egg yolks, sugar and other ingredients.

Akvavit is a barley and potato distillate that is clear, color-less and very potent. It is a Scandinavian drink originally made in Aalborg, Denmark.

Alizé is a blend of passion fruit juices and cognac.

Amaretto is an almond-flavored cordial.

Anisette gets its name from the anise seed, which imparts its rich licorice-like flavor to this cordial. Practically every Mediterranean country has a variation of the anise liqueur (sambuca in Italy; ouzo in Greece, and so on).

Applejack is distilled from the mash of apples and is the best known and most typical fruit brandy in the U.S.

Baileys Irish Cream is made from fresh dairy cream, Irish whiskey, and natural flavorings. The Irish whiskey acts as a preservative for the cream, which is why Baileys does not need to be refrigerated.

Benedictine contains over 27 herbs and spices, including cardamom, nutmeg, cloves, myrrh, and vanilla. B&B, which stands for Bendictine and Brandy, is a blend of Benedictine and cognac.

Black Haus is made from blackberries.

Blue Curacao is essentially the same as orange curacao except that a deep blue color has been added and it is slightly lower in proof.

Bunratty Meade is a blend of honey, selected herbs, and wine.

Calvados is an applejack made in Normandy and aged about four years.

Celtic Crossing is created by combining Irish malt whiskies and cognac.

Chambord is made with framboises (small black raspberries) and other fruits and herbs combined with honey. It has a dark purple color.

Chartreuse comes in green and yellow varieties and is made with more than 130 herbs and spices. It is normally sold at four years of age (aged in the bottle), but 12 year old labels are also produced.

CocoRibe is a liqueur of wild island coconuts laced with Virgin Island rum.

Cointreau is a clear cordial made from a blend of sweet and bitter oranges.

Crème de Cacao is made from vanilla and cacao beans. It comes in white and brown varieties.

Crème de Cassis is made from black currants imported from France and other selected fruits and berries.

Crème de Menthe is made from mint and spearmint. It comes in green and white (clear) varieties.

Crème de Noyaux is made from the combination of sweet and bitter almonds.

Cuarenta Y Tres (Licor 43) is made from a secret formula containing vanilla beans, citrus, and other fruits found in the Mediterranean, as well as carefully selected aromatic plants.

Der Lachs Goldwasser is a mysterious blend of 25 herbs, spices, and real 22-karat gold flakes.

Drambuie is made with the finest highland malt whiskies, not less than 15 years old, heather honey, and special herbs that are prepared in secret.

Echte Kroatzbeere is made with blackberries.

Frangelico is made from wild hazelnuts blended with berries and flowers.

Galliano is a golden-colored liqueur made with lavender, anise, yarrow musk, and juniper and blended with exotic flavors such as vanilla and fragrant balm. In all, it contains over 30 ingredients.

Godet Belgian White Chocolate Liqueur is a blend of Belgian white chocolate and aged cognac.

Godiva Liqueur is flavored with the same chocolate used in Godiva chocolate.

Goldschlager is an 87-proof cinnamon schnapps liqueur imported from Switzerland. It features real flakes of 24-karat gold.

Grand Marnier is made from wild oranges and cognac.

Irish Mist is a derivation of a heather wine.

Kahlua is made from coffee and the alcohol distilled from cane sugar. People also discern a chocolate flavor, but the recipe contains no chocolate. Its origin is a mystery. Some say Arabia; others say Turkey or Morocco. Today, as indicated by the sombrero on the label, it is made in Mexico using Mexican coffee beans.

Kirsch is distilled from cherries.

Kirschwasser is a true fruit brandy, or *eau de vie,* distilled from fermented cherries and cherry pits. It is clear and dry.

Kummel is made from caraway seeds, cumin, and aniseed. It is most esteemed as a digestive.

Lilé Supreme combines tropical rum with an assortment of fruits, including orange, lychee, mango, lime, and goyavier.

Lochan Ora is a Scotch whisky liqueur flavored with honey.

Malibu is a clear blend of coconut and Caribbean rum.

Midori is a green honeydew melon spirit.

Moringue Pistachio Cream Liqueur is a blend of rum with freshly pressed pistachio nuts and crushed sugared almonds.

Mozart Chocolate Liqueur is made from praline-nougat and milk chocolate blended with kirsch.

Nassau Royale is predominantly citrus-flavored with undertones of coffee.

Opal Nera is black sambuca with an added lemon twist.

Orange Curacao is made from the peel of the bittersweet Curacao orange, which grows on the Dutch island of Curacao in the West Indies.

Ouzo is an anise-based liqueur from Greece.

Passoa Passion Fruit Liqueur is a blend of Brazilian maracuja, or yellow passion fruit, with red berries and citrus and tropical fruits.

Rock & Rye is an old-time American favorite made with a special blend of aged rye whiskies and fresh fruit juices.

Rumple Minze is a peppermint schnapps imported from Germany.

Sabra is an Israeli chocolate orange liqueur originally made in the 1960s from the sabra cactus that grows in Israel and around the south and eastern Mediterranean. There is also a coffee version.

Sambuca is made from two main ingredients, witch elderbush (*sambucus nigra,* hence the name of the drink) and licorice, which gives this liqueur its dominant taste. It is related to the licorice-flavored anis and pastis drinks of France, ouzo of Greece, mastika of the Balkans, and the raki of Turkey.

Sloe Gin has a confusing name. It's not a gin (although small amounts of gin are used in its making). *Sloe* comes from sloeberry, a small, deep-purple wild plum that grows principally in France.

Southern Comfort is made from a secret recipe that contains bourbon, brandy, peaches and herbs.

Strega, the Italian word for witch, is made from more than 70 botanicals.

The Original Canton Delicate Ginger Liqueur is made from six varieties of ginger and mixed with other herbs, including ginseng, brandy, and honey.

Tia Maria is a Jamaican rum liqueur based on Blue Mountain coffee extracts and local spices.

Triple Sec is made principally from imported orange peel, the wild Curacao orange and the sweet, aromatic Spanish Valencia. Triple sec means *triple dry,* or three distillations.

Tuaca is an aged brandy flavored with orange and other fruits and botanicals indigenous to the Tuscan region of Italy.

Vandermint is a Dutch minted chocolate liqueur.

Wild Spirit is a special recipe of strong spirits, natural wild herbs, and a touch of fire-brewed cocoa.

Yukon Jack is a Canadian whisky-based liqueur with citrus and herbs.

Storing and Serving Suggestions

Most cordials are served after dinner or mixed as cocktails and served over crushed ice as *frappés*. Store an unopened bottle in a cool, dry area always out of direct light. After a bottle is opened, it should have a shelf life of three years.

Chapter 11

Gin

· ·

In This Chapter

▶ Where it came from

▶ Gin types

▶ Popular brands

▶ Storing and serving suggestions

· ·

*G*in is basically a distilled grain spirit flavored with extracts from different plants, mainly the juniper berry. The Dutch were the first to make gin and have been doing so since the late 1500s.

A Little History

Gin was invented by Franciscus de la Boe (Dr. Sylvius). Dr. Sylvius was a professor of medicine and physician at Holland's University of Leyden. Dr. Sylvius used a juniper berry elixir known as *genievere* — French for juniper. He thought that juniper berries could assist in the treatment of kidney and bladder ailments.

British soldiers sampled his elixir when returning from the wars in The Netherlands and nicknamed it "Dutch courage." When they brought the recipe back to England, they changed the name to gen and later to gin. Gin soon became the national drink of England, and at one time there were over 7,000 gin places in London alone.

Types of Gin

Though gin has been produced and consumed for centuries, the methods for making the quality gin that we drink today have only been around since the turn on the century. There are many types of gin, and the most popular include the following:

✔ **London dry gin (English)** is distilled from a grain mixture that contains more barley than corn. It is distilled at a high proof and then redistilled with juniper berries.

✔ **Dutch gin or Holland gin** contains barley, malt, corn, and rye. It is distilled at a lower proof and then redistilled with juniper berries in another still at low proof. Dutch gins are usually slightly sweet.

✔ **Flavored gin** is a new product. It is basically gin to which natural flavorings have been added (lime, lemon, orange, and so on). The flavoring always appears on the bottle.

Popular Brands

All of the following are London dry gins. Each brand has its own distinctive flavor that comes from a carefully guarded recipe.

✔ **Beefeater:** The only premium dry gin distillery in London.

✔ **Bombay:** Made from a well guarded recipe that dates back to 1761.

✔ **Bombay Sapphire:** Conceived by Michel Roux, President of Carillon Importers, Sapphire has more natural botanical ingredients than any other gin.

✔ **Gordon's:** First distilled over 225 years ago in London by Alexander Gordon, who pioneered and perfected the making of an unsweetened gin with a smooth character and aromatic flavors known as London Dry.

✔ **Plymouth:** Legend has it that a surgeon in the Royal Navy invented this gin to help the sailors make their angostura bitters more palatable (pink gin).

✔ **Seagram's Extra Dry:** A citrus-tasting golden gin.

✔ **Tanqueray:** Its unique green bottle is said to be inspired by an English fire hydrant.

Famous gin-related lines

From one of the most romantic movies of all time, after Ingrid Bergman comes into Rick's bar in Casablanca, what does Humphrey Bogart say? "Of all the gin joints in all the towns in all the world, she walks into mine."

Eliza Doolittle makes this remark of someone's drinking to Professor Henry Higgins at a fashionable horse race: "Gin was mother's milk to her."

Finally, a little poem:

I'm tired of gin
I'm tired of sin
And after last night
Oh boy, am I tired.
— Anonymous

Storing and Serving Suggestions

As you peruse the recipe section of this book (Chapter 18), you'll probably notice that gin appears in many cocktails, so choosing the right gin (that is, your favorite) can really affect your enjoyment of a given drink. Never, ever use cheap non-premium gin when making a drink. The results will be a disaster. Cheap gin tastes like disinfectant. Good gin has an herby, spicy, organic flavor, so stick to the premium brands like the ones listed in this chapter.

When you're at a bar, don't order a "gin 'n' tonic" because you'll end up with some awful bar gin. Order a "Tanq 'n' tonic" or a "Sapphire 'n' tonic" and you'll get a decent drink. The same goes for martinis: Always specify what gin you want or you'll be sorry.

Store an unopened bottle of gin in a cool, dry place out of direct light. After opening a bottle, it should last about two years.

Chapter 12
Irish Whiskey

. . . .

In This Chapter

▶ How it's made

▶ Popular brands

▶ Storing and serving suggestions

. . . .

The Irish have been distilling whiskey for at least 600 years, if not longer. While it's safe to say that Irish whiskey has a distinct character, it's also equally true to say that each brand of Irish whiskey is a unique product.

What Makes Irish Whiskey Taste So Yummy

Irish whiskey is triple distilled from barley and other grains in pot stills and aged between five and ten years. One major difference between Scotch and Irish whiskey is that when drying the barley malt from which the whiskey is to be distilled, the Irish use coal instead of peat, which prevents the smoky flavor found in Scotch whiskey.

What's more, Irish whiskey also gains a great deal of flavor from the casks in which it is aged. Depending on the brand, Irish whiskey is aged in casks that once held sherry, rum, or bourbon.

The Irish have for centuries produced an illegal distilled spirit called potcheen (po-cheen), a high in alcohol, colorless, and unaged spirit similar to the southern United States "white lightning." But as of March 17, 1997, it is now legal and will be produced and sold in Ireland and the rest of the world.

Popular Brands

- **Bushmills** produces Bushmills Premium, Black Bush Special, Bushmills Single Malt (10 years old), and Bushmills Rare Single Irish Malt (16 years old).

- **Connemara** makes Pot Still Peated Single Malt Irish Whiskey, a unique product, being the only peated single malt on the market.

- **John Jameson** is the world's largest selling Irish whiskey. It produces Jameson 1780 12-year-old Irish whiskey.

- **Kilbeggan** is gaelic for *little church.* What is now an idyllic village in the center of Ireland was for many years an active religious community built around a monastery. The first licensed whiskey distillery in the world was established in Kilbeggan in 1757.

- **Midleton** produces its Very Rare Irish Whiskey, which is aged for 10 and 15 years.

- **Paddy** is named for Paddy Flaherty, a salesman for the Cork Distilleries Company in the 1920s.

- **Powers** was the first to introduce bottling in Ireland.

- **Tullamore Dew** is famous for the slogan, "Give every man his Dew."

- **The Tyrconnell** Single Malt Irish Whiskey is made from a mash of pure malted barley produced at a single distillery. (In contrast, other whiskeys blend a variety of malt and grain products from several distilleries.)

Storing and Serving Suggestions

The storage of Irish whiskey is very simple. An unopened bottle will last indefinitely because Irish whiskey does not mature once it is bottled. After a bottle is opened, it has a shelf life of about two years.

Chapter 13
Rum

. . . .

In This Chapter

▶ A little history

▶ How rum is made

▶ Popular brands

▶ Storing and serving suggestions

. . . .

*R*um is a spirit distilled from sugar cane. It comes in light and dark varieties and is an ingredient in hundreds of cocktail recipes.

Rum History

Caribbean rum has been an exported product for hundreds of years, linked to the tropical and subtropical climates where sugar cane thrives. It was Christopher Columbus himself who first brought sugar cane to the Caribbean from the Azores. But the origins of rum are far more ancient, dating back, most experts say, more than 2,000 years.

Sugar cane grew like a weed in parts of southern China and India, and Alexander the Great, after conquering India, brought with him to Egypt "the weed that gives honey without the help of bees. . . ." The Saracens, or Islamic people from the Middle Ages, passed on their knowledge of distilling sugar cane to the Moors who made arak, a cane-based proto-rum and planted sugar cane in Europe some-time after 636 A.D.

Columbus brought sugar cane to Puerto Rico on his second voyage in 1493. Later, Ponce de Leon, the first Spanish governor of the island, planted the first cane fields in Puerto Rico, which were soon to become vital to the local economy and to the world's palate for fine spirits. Some historians speculate that Ponce de Leon's legendary search for a mythical "fountain of youth" was in fact a much more practical search for a source of pure water to use in his distillation of rum.

The first sugar mill, a precursor to the Puerto Rican rum industry, was built in 1524, when the product of cane distillation was called *brebaje,* the word rum being a later addition brought by crusading English seamen.

The popularity of rum continued to spread during the early 19th century. Distilleries prospered and grew in Puerto Rico. In 1893, the first modern column still was introduced to Puerto Rico. With this innovation, the foundation was laid for the island to produce a more refined, smoother-tasting rum at a dramatically increased pace. Distilleries relocated from vast, outlying sugar plantations to more accessible sites and soon became centrally organized and managed. The first Puerto Rican rum for export to the continental U.S. was shipped in 1897 — some 18,000 gallons.

During the prohibition period of the U.S., most Puerto Rican rum distillers stayed in business. Not by being "rumrunners," but by producing industrial alcohol. When prohibition ended in 1934, Puerto Rico refocused on the potential of the American liquor market and slowly began to rebuild its shipments to U.S. ports. It soon took steps to upgrade its rum production, and through special government funding and research, catapulted the island's rum to the forefront of the world's rum production.

With the onset of World War II, manufacturers of U.S. distilled spirits were ordered to limit their production and manufacture more quantities of industrial alcohol for the war effort. However, since the territorial mandate did not apply to Puerto Rico, demand for Puerto Rican rum increased. Sales were phenomenal throughout the war years, with rum and Coke being the "national drink" during World War II. In 1952, there were about 100 different brands of Puerto Rican Rum. Today there are just twelve.

Rums from Puerto Rico are the leaders in rum sales in the continental U.S. A staggering 77 percent of all rum sold on the mainland comes from Puerto Rico.

Rum folklore

Legend has it that Paul Revere ordered a mug of rum before his famous ride from Boston to Lexington. And a Benjamin Franklin invention, the "Rum Flip," made with rum and beer, was raised in 1773 in celebration after the Boston Tea Party.

Rum may have been the first of all shaken cocktails in the world: At Increase Arnold's Tavern in Providence, Rhode Island, thirsty patrons called for "rum, milk, sugar, cracked ice, shaken in a silver coffee pot until the frost is on the pot," topped with nutmeg and ginger.

How Rum Is Made

Rum is distilled from molasses, a sticky syrup that results when sugar cane is boiled down. When first distilled, the crude rum is between 130 and 180 proof. This rum is then aged for two to ten years to mellow it out. This aging process determines whether the rum is light or dark. Rum aged in charred oak casks becomes dark (caramel and other agents are added to affect its color). Rum aged in stainless steel tanks remains colorless.

Most light rum comes from Puerto Rico. Most dark rum comes from Jamaica, Haiti, and Martinique.

Popular Brands

Rum is produced throughout the Carribean.

- ✔ **Appleton Estate** (Jamaica)
- ✔ **Bacardi** (Puerto Rico): The best-selling liquor in the world
- ✔ **Captain Morgan Original Spiced Rum** (Puerto Rico)
- ✔ **Don Q Rums** (Puerto Rico)
- ✔ **Fernandes "19" Rum** (Trinidad)
- ✔ **Gosling's Black Seal Rum** (Bermuda)
- ✔ **Mount Gay Rum** (Barbados)

- ✓ **Myers's Original Dark Rum** (Jamaica)
- ✓ **Ocumare** (Venezuela)
- ✓ **Pampero** (Venezuela)
- ✓ **Pusser's** (Tortola)
- ✓ **Ron Del Barrilito** (Puerto Rico)
- ✓ **Royal Oak** (Trinidad)

Chapter 14

Scotch Whisky

Scotch whisky (spelled without the "e" in whisky) has a distinctive smoky flavor that is the result of both the choice of ingredients and the method of distillation.

Scotch whisky must be distilled in Scotland — but not necessarily bottled. Some Scotch whiskies are bottled in other countries but distilled in Scotland.

Types of Scotch Whisky

Two kinds of Scotch whisky are distilled: malt whisky (from barley) and grain whisky (from cereals). Malt whiskies are divided into four groups according to the geographical location of the distilleries in which they are made. Figure 14-1 shows the four main areas of Scotch production.

- ✔ **Lowland malt whiskies:** Made south of an imaginary line drawn from Dundee in the east to Greenock in the west.

- ✔ **Highland malt whiskies:** Made north of the aforementioned line.

- ✔ **Speyside malt whiskies:** Made in the valley of the River Spey. Although these whiskies come from within the area designated as Highland malt whiskies, the concentration of distilleries and the specific climatic conditions there produce whiskies of an identifiable character which enjoy a separate classification.

- ✔ **Islay malt whiskies:** Made on the island of Islay.

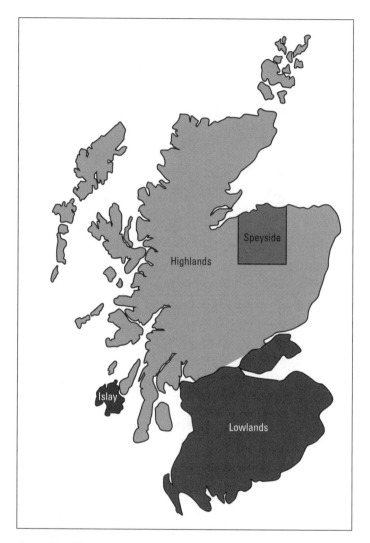

Figure 14-1: The four main scotch-producing regions.

Each group has its own clearly defined characteristics, ranging from the lighter-flavored gentle Lowland whiskies to those distilled on Islay, which are generally regarded as the heaviest malt whiskies.

Grain distilleries are mostly found in the central belt of Scotland near Glasgow and Edinburgh. Single grain whiskies display individual characteristics in the same way as malts, although there is not the same geographical influence.

Married together, malt whiskies and grain whiskies create *blended* Scotch whisky which accounts for ninety-five percent of world sales. As you might expect from the name, a *single-malt* Scotch whisky is made from one type of malt, and it is not blended with other malts or grain whiskies.

How Scotch Is Made

Scotch whisky made from malts can be dated back to 1494 to Friar John Cor and his fellow friars. Until the mid 1800s, nearly all scotches were single malt. Then Andrew Usher came up with the idea of mixing malt whisky and grain whisky to create blended Scotch whisky. There can be many (up to 50) different types of malt whiskies blended with grain whisky (from cereals) to make a blended whisky.

The first stage of making Scotch whisky is the malting of barley. The barley is soaked and dried for germination. During this period, the starch in the barley converts to fermentable sugar.

The germination is stopped by smoking the malted barley, usually over peat fires in open malt kilns, giving Scotch whisky its smoky taste. The barley is then mixed with water and yeast. Fermentation takes place, and alcohol is the result. This liquid is then usually pumped into stills and double distilled until the correct proof is attained.

After distillation, the whisky is then placed in used American oak wine or bourbon barrels and then aged by law for a minimum of three years. Most Scotch whiskies usually age from five to ten years, sometimes much longer. It is said the longer a whisky ages, the smoother it becomes. Whisky only ages in the barrel, never in the bottle.

Whisky does not improve or age after it is bottled.

After aging in the barrel, each distiller then completes its own blending, filtering, and bottling. There are over 100 distilleries and over 2,000 different Scotch whiskies.

Remember, whisky can only be called Scotch whisky if it is distilled and matured for at least three years in Scotland.

Popular Blended Scotch Whiskies

- ✓ Ballantine
- ✓ Chivas Regal
- ✓ Cutty Sark
- ✓ Dewar's
- ✓ Grant's
- ✓ Johnny Walker
- ✓ Justerini & Brooks (J&B)
- ✓ Teacher's
- ✓ The Famous Grouse
- ✓ Vat 69

Single-Malt Scotch

Single-malt Scotch whisky is unblended malt whisky from a single distillery. The water and malted barley, the raw materials of Scotch whisky, differ from distillery to distillery and region to region. In addition, the shape and size of the pot stills, production methods, and variations in topography and climate contribute to the uniqueness of each distillery's single-malt.

There are over 100 single-malt distilleries, so if you're a fan of single-malt Scotch whisky, it's unlikely that you'll run out of whiskies to sample and enjoy.

Storing and Serving Suggestions

Scotch can be served over ice, straight up, with water or club soda, or in a variety of mixed drinks. Single malts and aged Scotch whisky (over 12 years) can be served straight or on the rocks with a splash of water. After opening, store a bottle of Scotch whisky in a cool, dry place out of direct light, and it should have a shelf life of approximately two years.

Chapter 15
Tequila and Mezcal

*T*equila can be traced back to 1,000 A.D. and the Aztecs. It was a milky drink from the agave plants still known as *pulque*.

Since the seventeenth century and now by Mexican law, all tequila comes from a certain area known as Tequila, within the state of Jalisco. In this dry, volcanic soil of the foothills of the Sierra Madre, you can find the home of Tequila's largest producers.

How Tequila Is Made

Tequila is produced from the heart of one species of agave, the *Agave tequilana Weber,* of the blue variety. This heart is known as the pina or head, usually weighing between 80 and 150 pounds. The pina is steamed and shredded until the juice or aguamiel runs off. This juice is then mixed with cane sugar and yeast and fermented for two to three days. The fermented juice is double-distilled in traditional copper pot stills to 90 proof or higher. Tequila must contain a minimum of 51 percent distillate from the the blue agave plant.

Tequila is sold in four categories:

  ✔ **Tequila Blanco** (white or silver tequila): This tequila comes fresh from the still and may be brought to commercial proof with the addition of demineralized water.

  ✔ **Tequila Joven Abocado** (gold tequila): This is silver tequila with the addition of colorings and flavorings to mellow the flavor.

✔ **Tequila Reposado** (reposed or rested tequila): This tequila is aged for two months to one year in oak tanks or barrels. Flavorings and coloring agents may be added, as well as demineralized water to bring the tequila to commercial proof.

✔ **Añejo** (aged tequila): This tequila is aged for at least one year in government sealed oak barrels. Flavorings and coloring agents may be added, as well as demineralized water to bring it to commercial proof. When tequilas of different ages are blended, the youngest age is designated.

Reading a tequila label

The Mexican Government established NORMA (Norma Oficial Mexicana de Calidad) on March 31, 1978 to set standards of quality in the production of tequila. On every bottle, the following must appear: the letters NOM followed by four numbers designating the distillery from which the tequila was produced. Prior to 1978, you'll find the letters DGN. Besides the brand name and NOM, the label must say if the tequila is 100-percent agave tequila, the proof, and the category of tequila.

Popular Tequila Brands

✔ **Herradura:** The name is Spanish for "horseshoe." It's available in Añejo, Reposado Gold, and Silver varieties.

✔ **Jose Cuervo:** The world's oldest and largest tequila maker and the oldest spirit company in North America. Available in these versions: Blanco, Especial, Centenario, and 1800.

✔ **Patron:** Available in Silver and Añejo versions, both containing 100-percent blue agave.

✔ **Pepe Lopez:** Available in de Oro (Gold) and Superior Silver (White) labels.

✔ **Sauza:** The first tequila exported to the United States. It's available in these versions: Silver, Extra Gold, Hornitos, Conmemorativo, and Tres Generaciones.

✔ **Two Fingers:** Available in Gold, Limitado, and White. Named after a rogue entrepreneur, tequila producer, and occasional bandit from the Guadalajara area of Mexico who had only two fingers, the index and thumb, on his right hand.

Storing and Serving Suggestions

The traditional way to drink straight tequila requires a little coordination and a steady hand. Place salt on the web of the hand between your thumb and forefinger. Hold a wedge of lime or lemon with the same two fingers and have a 1 ounce shot glass filled with tequila in the other hand. In one quick continuous motion, lick the salt, drink the tequila, and bite the lime or lemon wedge.

An opened bottle of tequila has a shelf life of many years if kept in a cool, dry place.

Mezcal

The process of making mezcal has not changed much since the Spanish arrived in Mexico in the early 1800s and brought with them distillation technologies. The Aztecs near the mountain top settlement of Monte Alban in Oaxaca had cultivated a certain species of agave plant for juice which they would ferment into what they called pulque. The Spaniards, wanting something much more potent, began to experiment with agave.

Mezcal, like tequila, is made from the agave plant, but the process is different. What's more, while tequila is made exclusively in the northwestern state of Jalisco, mezcal is exclusive to Oaxaca.

Mezcal has a high potency and strong smoky flavor. Distillers insist that the drink has medicinal and tonic qualities. In Mexico, tribal women drink mezcal to withstand the pain of childbirth, and laborers drink it for added strength.

The famous worm

Worms live in the agave plant and are hand-harvested during the rainy summer season. They are stored in mezcal, drained and sorted, and placed in bottles near the end of the process. The worm is what makes mezcal unique; it is added as a reminder that it comes from the plant from which the alcohol is made.

Apocryphal legends note that the worm gives strength to anyone brave enough to gulp it down. Some even believe it acts as an aphrodisiac. Like the drink itself, the worm is something of an acquired taste.

A few brands

There aren't as many mezcal brands as tequila brands. Here are a few:

- ✔ Gusano Rojo Mezcal
- ✔ Miguel de la Mezcal
- ✔ Monte Alban

Chapter 16

Vodka

. . . .

In This Chapter

▶ Some background on vodka

▶ A list of Vodka brands

▶ Flavored vodkas

▶ Storing and serving suggestions

. . . .

*V*odka, a clear, almost flavorless spirit, is usually thought of as the national spirit of Russia and other Slavic countries, for both Russia and Poland claim the invention of vodka and explain that the name is a diminutive of the word "voda," meaning "little water." Slavic countries have been producing vodka for more than 600 years.

Vodka was originally distilled only from potatoes, but today, it is also made from grain, mostly wheat, rye, and corn. But distillers don't seem at all hindered by tradition — in Turkey they use beets! Vodkas are distilled at a very high proof (190 or higher) and most are filtered through activated charcoal. Certain charcoals are so important to the making of vodka that they are patented by distillers. High-end vodkas are triple- and even quadruple-distilled, and some are filtered through fine quartz sand.

Popular Brands

Vodka is now produced in almost every country in the world, and each location tends to put its spin on the classic. You might sample some of the following brands to see if you can find differences:

✔ **Absolut:** From Sweden, Absolut Vodka is the number one imported vodka in the United States.

✔ **Finlandia:** Classic Finlandia is imported from Finland. It is made from spring water and barley.

✔ **Fris:** Produced in Scandinavia.

- **Gilbey's:** An American vodka.
- **Glacier:** Distilled in Rigby, Idaho, using Idaho potatoes and water from the Rocky Mountains.
- **Gordon's:** Has been distilled in the U.S. since 1957.
- **Ketel One:** From Holland, Ketel One is handmade in small batches according to the techniques and secret family recipe developed by the Nolet family over 300 years ago.
- **Kremlyovskaya:** "Kremly" is made in the Vladimir Region of Russia.
- **Luksusowa:** An original potato vodka (unlike most vodkas, which are grain based) made in Poland.
- **Skyy:** An American vodka.
- **Smirnoff:** From the U.S., the largest selling vodka in the world.
- **Stolichnaya:** A Russian vodka also known as "Stoli."
- **Tanqueray Sterling:** An English vodka from the makers of Tanqueray gin.

How that Red drink got big in the U.S.A.

FABLES & LORE

American John Martin of Heublein & Co. is largely credited with encouraging Americans to drink vodka. He and his friend Jack Morgan, the owner of the Cock 'n' Bull Restaurant in Los Angeles, were discussing his Smirnoff Vodka when Jack remembered that he had an overstock of ginger beer. Jack and John mixed the two, added a dash of lime juice, and thus created the Moscow Mule. The Moscow Mule spread rapidly, smartly promoted by Heublein ("It leaves you breathless!"), who had it served in a copper mug. Smirnoff vodka became in high demand and is still the number-one-selling vodka in the United States.

Flavored Vodkas

Flavored vodkas are made with the addition of natural flavoring materials. There are more than 30 different flavored vodkas from cranberry to zubowka. Zubowka is a vodka that was once sold with a single blade of grass in each bottle. It is no longer available with grass in the United States (as some believed the grass contained a toxic compound), but you can still get it *sans flora*. Here are some of the most popular flavored vodkas:

- ✔ **Absolut Citron:** A lemon theme with subtle hints of lime, mandarin orange, and grapefruit.
- ✔ **Absolut Kurant:** A blend of the tart taste of black currant berries.
- ✔ **Absolut Peppar:** A jalapeño pepper and paprika flavored vodka.
- ✔ **Finlandia Pineapple:** A rich pineapple scent and delicate pineapple tang.
- ✔ **Finlandia Cranberry:** Features the ruby-red color and distinctive flavor of cranberry.
- ✔ **Gordon's Citrus:** Has a tangy lemon and lime flavor enhanced with oil of orange from the West Indies.
- ✔ **Gordon's Wildberry:** A blend of berries and natural flavorings.
- ✔ **Okhotnichya:** Made from honey and herbs.
- ✔ **Smirnoff Citrus Twist:** A vodka with a lemon-lime flavor.
- ✔ **Stoli Kafya:** Made with a blend of coffee beans from Guatemala, Costa Rica, Mexico, Indonesia, and Colombia.
- ✔ **Stoli Limonnaya:** Made from the zest of lemon peel.
- ✔ **Stoli Ohranj:** Flavored with orange zest, juice, and pulp.
- ✔ **Stoli Persik:** Made with the aromatic essence and oils of white peaches.
- ✔ **Stoli Pertsovka:** Infused with white, black, cubeb and red chile peppers.
- ✔ **Stoli Razberi:** Features the flavor of raspberries.

✓ **Stoli Strasberi:** Made with the juice and oil of strawberries.

✓ **Stoli Vanil:** Flavored by the essence of Madagascan and Indonesian vanilla beans.

✓ **Stoli Zinamon:** Created from oils of Sri Lankan cinnamon bark and Chinese cassis for a "red hot" taste.

Storing and Serving Vodka

Store at least one bottle in the freezer or refrigerator. It will not freeze because of the high alcohol content. Vodka should be served neat or straight up in a small cordial glass, especially with caviar, smoked fish, salmon, sardines, steak tartare, and spicy foods.

Vodka is one of the most mixable and versatile of spirits and is used in hundreds of cocktail recipes. When an opened bottle is refrigerated or stored in a cool, dry place, it should last up to three years.

Chapter 17

Wine

. . . .

In This Chapter

▶ Wines from around the world

▶ A little info on sparkling wines

▶ A few words about port, sherry, and vermouth

. . . .

*W*ine, as most of you know, is made from fermented grapes. It comes in red, white, or rosé (pink or blush) varieties. Wine making dates back to roughly 3000 B.C., and it's here to stay.

Wines from Around the World

Climate is a big factor in making good wine. To grow wine-worthy grapes, summers can't be too hot and autumns need to be cool. Light rainfall is necessary in the winter and spring, and the rain needs to taper off in the summer and fall. Harsh, cold winters with hail, frost, and heavy winds are very bad for growing grapes.

The type of grape determines the type of wine, and only certain types of grapes grow in certain climates. To make things even more complicated, the soil of a particular region plays a big role in how its grapes will turn out. So while the climate in certain regions of California and France may be perfect for, say, chardonnay grapes, the soil in those regions affects the grapes to the point that the resulting wines from each region are very different.

Many wines receive their names from the grape from which they are produced. Here's a list of some popular wines named after grapes:

▸ Barbera (red): Italy

▸ Cabernet Sauvignon (red): France, United States

▸ Chardonnay (white): France, United States, Argentina, Australia, South America

- Chenin Blanc (white): France, United States
- Camay (red): France, United States
- Gewurztraminer (white): Germany
- Grenache (rose): France, United States
- Merlot (red): France, United States, South America
- Pinot Noir (red): France, United States
- Reisling (white): Germany, United States, France
- Sauvignon Blanc (white): France, United States
- Semillon (white): France, United States, Australia
- Zinfandel (red and white): United States

Here are some popular French wines. They're named after the region of France from which they originate.

- Alsace (white)
- Beaujolais (red) from Burgundy
- Bordeaux (red and white)
- Burgundy (red and white)
- Rhône (red)
- Sauternes (white) from Bordeaux

Here are some German wines worth noting (all are white):

- Gewurztraminer
- Johannisberg Riesling
- Spalleseen

Italy produces all kinds of regional wines.

- Barbaresco (red) from Piedmont
- Bardolino (red) from Veneto
- Barolo (red) from Piedmont
- Chianti (red) from Tuscany
- Orvieto (white) from Umbria
- Pinot Grigio (white) from Trentino
- Riserva (red) from Tuscany
- Soave (white) from Veneto
- Valpolicella (red) from Veneto

In the United States, California produces 90 percent of all wine. Most California wine comes from Napa or Sonoma Valley, and they produce both red and white wines in varieties too numerous to list here.

Port

Port is a sweet fortified wine to which brandy has been added. It is named for the city of Oporto in northern Portugal and is made from grapes grown from some 72,000 acres of vineyard in a designated area along the Douro River, known as the Alto Douro.

Although many wines are sold as port throughout the world, authentic port wine is the unique product of Portugal. By law, it must be made only from approved grape varieties native to the Alto Douro district and grown no where else in the country.

Fortification with brandy gives port extra strength and, more importantly, preserves the fresh flavor of grapes that makes port so delicious.

There are three varieties of port:

- ✔ **Ruby:** Dark in color and fairly sweet.
- ✔ **Tawny:** Lighter in color and drier because it is aged in casks longer.
- ✔ **Vintage port:** Released only in certain exceptional years; the fullest and sweetest of all ports.

The following are some popular brands:

- ✔ **Royal Oporto**
- ✔ **Sandeman**
- ✔ **Cockburn's**
- ✔ **Croft**

Port is a great after-dinner drink. It also goes well with cheese and (excuse me for being trendy) cigars. An opened bottle of port has a shelf life of 4 to 6 months.

Sherry

The wines of Jerez, Spain, were discovered by the English. They called them *Jerries,* and the word later became sherry. Sherry is a fortified wine to which grape brandy has been added. It is no longer limited to production in Spain and is now produced all over the world.

There are five basic styles of sherry:

- **Fino:** Light and very dry, usually served chilled as an apéritif.
- **Manzanilla:** Pale, dry, and light-bodied; also served chilled as an apéritif.
- **Amotillanda:** Medium dry and full-bodied; perfect between meals or with soup and cheese.
- **Oloroso:** Gold in color with a strong bouquet; more hardy than Amotillanda.
- **Cream:** A smooth, sweet wine. Cream sherry is the result when Oloroso is blended with a sweetening wine such as Moscatel. Cream is the largest selling sherry. It can be served at any time, chilled or over ice.

The following are popular sherry brands:

- **Dry Sack**
- **Harvey's Bristol Cream**
- **Gonzalez Byass**
- **Savory and James**

Sparkling Wines

The first sparkling wine was developed in the 1600s in the Champagne region of France by a monk whose name is now familiar: Dom Perignon. Without going into the details, he developed a method of bottling wine so that carbon dioxide, a product of fermentation, remains in the bottle with the wine, and the result is the presence of bubbles.

Sparkling wine made in the Champagne region of France is called, of course, champagne. It is made with a mix of different grapes (including pinot noir, pinot meunier, and chardonnay) through a process called *méthod champenoise,* which is quite costly and time consuming. Sparkling wines from other places in the world are made in different ways with different grapes. But you can find sparkling wines from places such as California that were made using the méthod champenoise.

Champagne and other sparkling wines should be stored in a cool, dark place away from heat, light, vibrations, and severe temperature variations. Unlike the best wines from Bordeaux or California, sparkling wines are ready for consumption when they are shipped to the market. However, some wine lovers also enjoy cellaring their champagnes for a few extra years.

 Before serving, chill the wine well, but do not freeze it. Champagne is best chilled by placing the bottle in a bucket filled with ice and water for 30 to 40 minutes. You can also chill a bottle by refrigerating it for several hours.

Champagne is best served in tall flute or tulip glasses at a temperature of 42 to 47 degrees Fahrenheit. Tiny bubbles will rise in a continuous stream. When serving, pour a small quantity of wine into each glass and allow it to settle. Then fill each glass two-thirds full.

Vermouth

Vermouth originated in the 18th century when wine growers in the foothills of the French and Italian Alps developed a method of enhancing the taste of sour or uncompromising wines with the infusion of a variety of sweeteners, spices, herbs, roots, seeds, flowers, and peels. Just a few of the herbs and spices used to flavor and aromatize the wine include cloves, bitter orange peel, nutmeg, gentian, chamomile, and wormwood, which in German is *wermut,* from which vermouth got its name. Once flavored, the wine is clarified, pasteurized, and finally fortified to an alcoholic content of about 18 percent, close to that of sherry.

The standard classification of vermouth is white/dry and red/sweet, but exceptions do exist, including a half-sweet variety know as rosé. And while most dry vermouths are considered French and sweet vermouths considered Italian, both types are produced in France and Italy as well as throughout the world, including the United States.

Vermouth is an ingredient in many cocktails, and just as carefully as you select other liquor to pour at the bar, so you should take care and time in selecting a good vermouth. Choose the brand of vermouth that tastes best to you — crisp and light, not too heavy or burnt. Here are some popular brands:

✔ Boissiere

✔ Cinzano

✔ Martini and Rossi

✔ Noilly Prat

✔ Stock

You need to refrigerate a bottle of vermouth after opening. The shelf life of an opened bottle, when refrigerated, is approximately one year.

One Final Word on Wines

I haven't said nearly enough about wine as I would like. Fact is, people have written whole books on single types of wine, so it's sort of foolish for me to even pretend to give a comprehensive overview in a single chapter. The focus of this book, after all, is cocktail recipes.

A great introduction to buying, serving, and drinking wine is *Wine For Dummies* (published by IDG Books Worldwide, Inc.). It's full of very useful and interesting information, and it makes a great companion to this book.

Part III
The Recipes

In this part...

Chapter 18 contains almost a thousand great cocktail recipes listed in alphabetical order by name. Chapter 19 shows you how to make pousse-cafés (layered drinks). Chapter 20 deals with punches. Chapter 21 presents some tasty non-alcoholic drinks.

Chapter 18
Recipes from A to Z

· ·

In This Chapter

▶ Many, many cocktail recipes

· ·

*Y*ou probably bought this book just for this section. I've listed here the recipes for almost a thousand drinks. Some are classic drinks that you've probably heard of; others are new and trendy. Most are quite good; some are strange concoctions that few people like.

 Classic drinks are indicated by a cute little icon to the right of the drink name. The appropriate glass for each drink is shown to the left of its list of ingredients. I put little stories and anecdotes in *sidebars* — text set apart in gray boxes.

If you're looking for non-alcoholic drinks, see Chapter 21. You won't find punches in this chapter either. They're in Chapter 20.

One final note: Just in case you don't know, the term *straight up* means *without ice*.

A Tinker Tall

1¹/₄ oz.	Irish Mist	Combine ingredients with lots
3 oz.	Ginger Ale	of ice in a tall glass.
3 oz.	Club Soda	

A-Bomb #1

¹/₂ oz.	Vodka	Shake with ice, strain, and
¹/₂ oz.	Coffee Liqueur	serve in a highball glass.
¹/₂ oz.	Irish Cream	
¹/₂ oz.	Orange Liqueur	

A-Bomb #2

¹/₂ oz.	Baileys Irish Cream	Shake with ice and strain.
¹/₂ oz.	Kahlua	
¹/₂ oz.	Stolichnaya	
¹/₄ oz.	Tia Maria	

You can also serve this one in a rocks glass.

Absohot

1¹/₂ shot	Absolut Peppar Vodka	Combine ingredients in a shot
1 dash	Hot Sauce	glass with a beer chaser.

This one really is hot.

Absolut Citron Rickey

1¹/₄ oz.	Absolut Citron Vodka	In a glass filled with ice, add
	Club Soda	Vodka. Fill with Club Soda and
		garnish with a Lemon.

A classic cocktail with a summer twist.

Absolution

1 part	Absolut Vodka	In a fluted champagne glass,
5 parts	Champagne	add ingredients. Cut a lemon
		peel in the form of a ring to
		represent a halo. The lemon
		peel can be either wrapped
		around the top of the glass
		or floated on top of the
		champagne.

Created by Jimmy Caulfield at the River Café, New York, New York.

Absolut Quaalude

1 oz.	Baileys Irish Cream	Shake ingredients with ice and
1 oz.	Frangelico	strain into a glass filled with ice.
1 oz.	Absolut Vodka	

Acapulco Gold

1¹/₄ oz.	Jose Cuervo Especial Tequila	Blend with ice.
⁵/₈ oz.	Grand Marnier	
1 oz.	Sweet & Sour Mix	

Adios Mother

¹/₂ oz.	Vodka	Build over ice in 12 oz. snifter
¹/₂ oz.	Blue Curacao	glass and fill with soda water.
¹/₂ oz.	Gin	
¹/₂ oz.	Rum	
2 oz.	Sweet & Sour Mix	

See you at the border. By the way, we've abbreviated the name of this drink.

After 5

| 1 part | Irish Cream | Pour the ingredients in a shot |
| 1 part | Rumple Minze | glass. |

After 8

¹/₂ oz.	Irish Cream	Shake with ice. Strain into a
¹/₂ oz.	Coffee Brandy	shot glass.
¹/₂ oz.	Green Crème de Menthe	

Afterburner

| 1 part | Rumple Minze | Pour the ingredients in a shot |
| 1 part | Tia Maria | glass. |

Put this one on the back burner.

Alabama Slammer

1 part	Amaretto	Shake ingredients and serve in
1 part	Sloe Gin	a shot glass.
1 part	Southern Comfort	
splash	Lemon Juice	

One of the first popular shots. Cover with napkins or a coaster. You can also serve this one over ice in a highball glass.

The Alamo Splash

1½ oz.	Jose Cuervo Gold Tequila	Mix well with cracked ice,
1 oz.	Orange Juice	strain and serve right from a
½ oz.	Pineapple Juice	glass in a thin, well-aimed
splash	7-Up	stream directly into the
		recipient's mouth.

Alaska

1¾ oz.	Cork Dry Gin	Shake with ice and strain into
¼ oz.	Yellow Chartreuse	a shot glass.

Albuquerque Reál

1½ oz.	Jose Cuervo Especial Tequila	Stir all but Grand Marnier
½ oz.	Triple Sec	in the glass. Float the Grand
½ oz.	Sweet & Sour Mix	Marnier on top.
¼ oz.	Cranberry Juice	
splash	Grand Marnier	

You can also serve this one in a cocktail glass.

Algonquin

1½ oz.	Blended Whiskey	Combine all ingredients in a
1 oz.	Dry Vermouth	shaker and shake. Strain into
1 oz.	Pineapple Juice	chilled cocktail glass.
3	Ice Cubes	

Could be named for the famous round table.

Alice in Wonderland

1 part	Herradura Tequila	Shake with ice and strain into
1 part	Tia Maria	a shot glass.
1 part	Grand Marnier	

This one will get the cast smiling.

Alice-Be-Bananaless

¾ oz.	Vodka	Shake with ice and strain into
¾ oz.	Amaretto	a rocks glass with ice.
¾ oz.	Midori	
1 oz.	Cream	

Alliance

A

1 oz.	Gin	Shake with ice and strain into
1 oz.	Dry Vermouth	a rocks glass over ice.
2 dashes	Akvavit	

Almond Lemonade

1¼ oz.	Vodka	Shake with ice and strain into
¼ oz.	Amaretto	a shot glass.
	Lemonade	

Summer in Italy.

Ambrosia

1 oz.	Apple Jack	Shake the first four ingredients
1 oz.	Brandy	over ice and strain into a
¼ oz.	Cointreau	champagne flute. Fill with
¼ oz.	Lemon Juice	Champagne.
	Champagne	

This drink was created at Arnaud's restaurant in New Orleans immediately following the end of Prohibition. The word ambrosia *comes from the Greek* mabrotos, *meaning "immortal."*

Ambush

1 oz.	Bushmills Irish Whiskey	Serve hot in mug. Top with
1 oz.	Amaretto	whipped cream if desired.
5 oz.	Coffee	

Americano

1 oz.	Martini & Rossi Rosso Vermouth	Build with ice in a highball glass. Top with Club Soda and
1 oz.	Campari	a twist.
	Club soda	

A classic from Italy.

A

Angel Martini

1¹/₂ oz.	Ketel One Vodka	Shake ingredients with ice and
¹/₂ oz.	Frangelico	strain into a chilled martini
		glass.

A little Italy and a littler Netherlands. (This one was invented at the Bowery Bar of New York, New York.)

Angel's Delight

1 part	Grenadine	Layer this drink in the order
1 part	Triple Sec	listed. Start with Grenadine on
1 part	Sloe Gin	the bottom and finish with
1 part	Heavy Cream	Cream on top.

See Chapter 19 for more on layered drinks.

Angostura Costa Del Sol

1¹/₂ oz.	Cream Sherry	Shake with ice and serve in a
2 oz.	Orange Juice	rocks or highball glass.
2 oz.	Cream	
2 dashes	Angostura	

Anti-Freeze

1¹/₂ oz.	Vodka	Shake with ice, strain, and
¹/₂ oz.	Midori	serve.

You can also serve this one in a rocks glass.

Apple Kir

1 oz.	Jose Cuervo Gold Tequila	Mix in a rocks glass over ice.
¹/₂ oz.	Crème de Cassis	Garnish with a Lemon Wedge.
1 oz.	Apple Juice	
1 tsp.	Fresh Lemon Juice	

Apple Pie

¹/₂ oz.	Apple Schnapps	Shake with ice and strain into
¹/₂ oz.	Vodka	a shot glass.
¹/₂ oz.	Pineapple Juice	
dash	Powdered Cinnamon	

B

Apricot Martini

1 part	Godiva Liqueur	Combine with ice; shake well.
1 part	Absolut Vodka	Serve chilled with a Cherry.
1 part	Apricot Brandy	

It's not the pits.

Apricot Sour

2 tbsp.	Lemon Juice	Combine all ingredients
1/2 tsp.	Superfine Sugar	in a shaker and shake
2 oz.	Apricot Brandy	vigorously. Strain into
3-4	Ice Cubes	a chilled cocktail glass.
		Garnish with Lemon.

The hot drink of the 60s.

Aunt Rose

1 1/4 oz.	Irish Mist	Shake. Serve in a tall glass
2 oz.	Cranberry Juice	with ice.
2 oz.	Orange Juice	

Yes, there is an Aunt Rose from Ireland.

B&B

1 oz.	Benedictine	Stir and serve in a snifter.
1 oz.	Brandy	

An easy one to remember.

B-52

1 part	Grand Marnier	Shake with ice. Strain or serve
1 part	Kahlua	over ice.
1 part	Baileys Irish Cream	

You can also serve this one as a shot.

B

B-52 with Bombay Doors

1 part	Kahlua	Shake with ice and strain into
1 part	Baileys Irish Cream	a shot glass.
1 part	Grand Marnier	
1 part	Bombay Gin	

Keep the door open.

Bacardi & Cola

1¹/₂ oz.	Bacardi Light or	Pour Rum into tall glass filled
	Dark Rum	with ice. Fill with your favorite
	Cola	Cola and garnish with a
		squeeze of a Lemon.

Bacardi & Tonic

1¹/₄ oz.	Bacardi Light Rum	Pour Rum into a tall glass
	Tonic	filled with ice. Fill with Tonic.

A change in mixer.

Bacardi Blossom

1¹/₄ oz.	Bacardi Light Rum	Blend with crushed ice and
1 oz.	Orange Juice	pour.
¹/₂ oz.	Lemon Juice	
¹/₂ tsp.	Sugar	

Sweet as a spring flower.

Bacardi Champagne Cocktail

1 oz.	Bacardi Silver Rum	In a tall glass, mix Rum, Sugar
	Champagne	and Bitters. Fill with
1 tsp.	Sugar	Champagne.
dash	Bitters	

Bacardi Cocktail

1¼ oz.	Bacardi Light Rum	Mix in a shaker with ice and
1 oz.	Rose's Lime Juice	strain into a chilled cocktail
½ tsp.	Sugar	glass.
½ oz.	Rose's grenadine	

The New York Supreme Court ruled in 1936 that a Bacardi Cocktail is not a Bacardi Cocktail unless it's made with Bacardi Rum. You can also serve this one over ice in a rocks glass.

Bacardi Collins

1½ to 2 oz.	Bacardi Light Rum	Combine first two ingredients
2 tsp.	Frozen Lemonade or Limeade Concentrate	in a tall glass with ice. Fill with Club Soda.
½ tsp.	Sugar	
	Club Soda	

A collins with rum, instead of gin, whisky, vodka, and so on.

Bacardi Daiquiri

1¼ oz.	Bacardi Light Rum	Mix in shaker with ice and
½ oz.	Lemon Juice	strain into a chilled cocktail
½ tsp.	Sugar	glass.

The original Daiquiri was made with Bacardi Rum in 1896. You can add bananas, orange juice, peaches, and any other fruit that you enjoy. You can also serve this one in a highball glass over ice.

Bacardi Dry Martini

2 oz.	Bacardi Light Rum	Shake with ice and strain.
½ oz.	Martini & Rossi Dry Vermouth	

A new Caribbean classic. You can also serve this one over ice in a highball glass.

Bacardi Fireside

1¼ oz.	Bacardi Light or Dark Rum	In a mug, add Sugar and Rum. Fill with very Hot Tea and one
1 tsp.	Sugar	Cinnamon Stick. Stir.
	Hot Tea	

B

B

Bacardi Fizz

1¼ oz.	Bacardi Light Rum	Pour Rum and Lemon Juice in
¼ oz.	Lemon Juice	a highball glass filled with ice.
¼ oz.	Rose's Grenadine	Add the Grenadine and fill
	Club Soda	with Club Soda.

Bacardi Hemingway

1½ oz.	Bacardi Light Rum	Mix with ice and serve.
	Juice of ½ Lime	
¼ oz.	Grapefruit Juice	
¼ oz.	Maraschino Liqueur	

Ernest would have written about this one.

Bacardi Limón Martini

2 oz.	Bacardi Limón	Stir in a cocktail glass. Garnish
dash	Martini & Rossi Extra	with Lemon.
	Dry Vermouth	
splash	Cranberry Juice	

It's a new twist on an old classic. First invented at the Heart and Soul in San Francisco, California.

Bacardi Pink Squeeze

1½ oz.	Bacardi Light Rum	Pour Rum into tall glass filled
	Pink lemonade	with ice. Fill with Pink
		Lemonade.

Bacardi Sunset

1¼ oz.	Bacardi Light Rum	Combine in a tall glass with
3 oz.	Orange Juice	crushed ice. Add a squeeze
	Squeeze of Lime	of Lime. Garnish with an
		Orange Wheel.

What a way to end the day.

Bacardi Sweet Martini

2 oz.	Bacardi Light Rum	Stir gently with ice in a
½ oz.	Martini & Rossi Sweet	cocktail glass.
	Vermouth	

Bagpiper

	1 1/2 oz.	100 Pipers Scotch	Stir in an Irish coffee glass
	3 oz.	Coffee	and top with whipped cream.

Bailey Shillelagh

	1 part	Baileys Irish Cream	Pour ingredients in a shot
	1 part	Romana Sambuca	glass.

Baileys & Coffee

	1 1/2 oz.	Baileys Irish Cream	Pour the Irish Cream into a cup
	5 oz.	Coffee	of steaming Coffee.

Easy enough.

Baileys Alexander

	1 1/2 oz.	Baileys Irish Cream	Shake well with ice and serve
	1/2 oz.	Cognac	over ice.

You can also strain this one into a cocktail glass.

Baileys Banana Blaster

	1 oz.	Baileys Irish Cream	Blend with ice until smooth.
	1 oz.	Malibu	
	1/2 oz.	Banana Liqueur	
		or 1/2 Banana	

You can also serve this one in a margarita glass.

Baileys Chocolate Covered Cherry

	1/2 oz.	Baileys Irish Cream	Layer Grenadine, Kahlua, and
	1/2 oz.	Grenadine	then Irish Cream in a shot
	1/2 oz.	Kahlua	glass.

You can also serve this one over ice in a rocks glass (without layering the ingredients, of course).

B

Baileys Coconut Frappe

2 parts	Baileys Irish Cream	Shake or blend until frothy;
1 part	Malibu Rum	pour over ice and garnish with
2 parts	Milk	Toasted Coconut.

You can also serve this one in a cocktail glass.

Baileys Cream Dream

2 oz.	Baileys Irish Cream	Blend for 30 seconds and serve.
2 oz.	Half & Half	
4 oz.	Ice Cubes	

Baileys Dublin Double

| 1 part | Baileys Irish Cream | Pour ingredients in a shot glass. |
| 1 part | Di Saronno Amaretto | |

Baileys Eggnog

1 oz.	Baileys Irish Cream	Mix with cracked ice in a
1/2 oz.	Irish Whiskey	shaker, strain, and serve in a
1	Medium Egg	tall glass. Sprinkle Nutmeg.
2 cups	Milk	
dash	Nutmeg	

Baileys Fizz

| 2 oz. | Baileys Irish Cream | Combine ingredients and pour |
| 3 oz. | Club Soda | over crushed ice. |

Baileys Float

2 oz.	Baileys Irish Cream	Blend ingredients until frothy.
2 scoops	Softened Ice Cream	Top with one more scoop of
		Ice Cream.

Baileys French Dream

1 1/2 oz.	Baileys Irish Cream	Blend for 30 seconds and serve.
1/2 oz.	Raspberry Liqueur	
2 oz.	Half & Half	
4 oz.	Ice Cubes	

Baileys Godet Truffle

| 1 part | Baileys Irish Cream | Combine over ice. |
| 1 part | Godet | |

B

Baileys Hot Milk Punch

1 oz.	Baileys Irish Cream	Combine Baileys, Cognac and
1/4 oz.	Cognac	Sugar. Add Hot Milk and stir.
1 1/2 tsp.	Sugar	Sprinkle with Nutmeg.
3 parts	Hot Milk	
dash	Freshly Ground Nutmeg	

Baileys Iced Cappuccino

1/2 cup	Ice	Brew a pot of double-strength
2 oz.	Baileys Irish Cream	Coffee and set aside to cool. In
5 oz.	Double-Strength Coffee	a blender, combine the other
1 oz.	Half & Half	ingredients. Blend for ten
2 tsp.	Sugar	seconds and pour into a 10 oz.
		glass filled with ice. Top with a
		dollop of Whipped Cream and
		sprinkle of Cinnamon, if
		desired.

Baileys Irish Coffee

1 part	Baileys Irish Cream	After brewing Coffee, combine
1/2 part	Irish Whiskey	with Irish Cream and Whiskey.
4 parts	Freshly Brewed Coffee	Top with whipped cream.
1 tbsp.	Whipped Sweetened Cream	

Baileys Irish Mudslide

1 part	Baileys Irish Cream	Mix ingredients and pour into
1 part	Coffee Liqueur	a rocks glass.
1 part	Vodka	

You can also blend the ingredients with ice and serve the drink as a frozen beverage in a margarita glass.

Baileys Malibu Slide

1 part	Baileys Irish Cream	Blend with ice and serve in a
1 part	Kahlua	rocks glass.
1 part	Malibu	

You can also serve this one in a margarita glass.

Baileys Mint Kiss

1 oz.	Baileys Irish Cream	Combine ingredients.
3 oz.	Coffee	Top with fresh Whipped Cream.
$^1/_2$ oz.	Rumple Minze	
$^1/_2$ oz.	Peppermint Schnapps	

You can also serve this drink in a margarita glass.

Baileys Mist

2 oz.	Baileys Irish Cream	Pour in a glass filled with crushed ice.

Simple and delicious.

Baileys O'

1 part	Baileys Irish Cream	Combine in a shot glass.
1 part	Stolichnaya Vodka	
1 part	Stoli Ohranj Vodka	

Baileys Roma

1 part	Baileys Irish Cream	Pour over ice and serve.
1 part	Romana Sambuca	

It's the Irish and Italian together again.

Baileys Sunset

1 part	Kahlua	Gently layer the Kahlua, then
1 part	Baileys Irish Cream	the Baileys, followed by the
1 part	Triple Sec	Triple Sec. Garnish with an Orange Slice.

B

Bald Head Martini

4 parts	Beefeater Gin	Stir gently with ice. Strain or
1 part	French Vermouth	serve on the rocks. Sprinkle
1 part	Italian Vermouth	the oil from a twist of
2 dashes	Pernod	Lemon Peel on top.

Ballsbridge Bracer

1¹/₂ oz.	Irish Whiskey	Mix all ingredients with
³/₄ oz.	Irish Mist	cracked ice in a shaker or
3 oz.	Orange Juice	blender. Shake or blend.
1	Egg White (for two drinks)	Strain into a chilled whiskey
		sour glass.

Bamboo Cocktail

1¹/₂ oz.	Sherry	Stir with ice and strain.
³/₄ oz.	Dry Vermouth	
dash	Angostura Bitters	

This drink was invented around 1910 by bartender Charlie Mahoney of the Hoffman House in New York, New York.

Banana Boat

³/₄ oz.	Malibu Rum	Combine in a shot glass.
³/₄ oz.	Hiram Walker Banana Liqueur	
¹/₄ oz.	Pineapple Juice	

Day-o – Day-o!

Banana Boomer

1 oz.	Puerto Rican Rum	Shake with ice and strain into
¹/₂ oz.	Hiram Walker Banana Liqueur	a shot glass.
¹/₂ oz.	Orange & Pineapple Juice	

B

Banana Daiquiri

1¼ oz.	Light Rum	Blend with ice and serve.
¼ oz.	Lemon Juice or Rose's Lime Juice	
½ tsp.	Sugar	
1	Banana	

Peel the banana, of course.

Banana Man

1 oz.	Bacardi Light Rum	Blend with ice and serve.
¼ oz.	Hiram Walker Banana Liqueur	
½ oz.	Lemon Juice or Rose's Lime Juice	

Banana Rum Cream

1½ oz.	Puerto Rican Dark Rum	Shake well. Serve straight up
½ oz.	Crème de Banana	or with ice.
1 oz.	Light Cream	

The Barbados Cocktail

2 oz.	Mount Gay Rum	Shake with ice and serve.
½ oz.	Cointreau	
½ oz.	Sweet & Sour	

Barnumenthe & Baileys

1½ oz.	Baileys Irish Cream	Combine in a rocks glass over
½ oz.	White Crème de Menthe	cracked ice.

Serve this one when the circus is in town.

Barracuda

1¼ oz.	Ronrico Dark Rum	Shake everything but the
1 oz.	Pineapple Juice	Champagne. Serve in a
½ oz.	Rose's Lime Juice	champagne glass and fill to
¼ tsp.	Sugar	the top with Champagne.
	Champagne	

Bat Bite

	1¼ oz.	Bacardi Silver Rum	Pour ingredients in a glass
	4 oz.	Cranberry Juice	filled with ice. Squeeze and
			drop in one Lime or Lemon
			Wedge. Stir and serve.

B

Bay Breeze

	1½ oz.	Absolut Vodka	Stir. Serve over ice.
	3 oz.	Pineapple Juice	
	1 oz.	Cranberry Juice	

Quite refreshing.

Beach Bum

	1 oz.	Vodka	Mix in a shaker with ice. Strain.
	1½ oz.	Midori	
	1 oz.	Cranberry Juice	

Beach Party

	1¼ oz.	Bacardi Light or Dark Rum	Blend with ice.
	1 oz.	Pineapple Juice	
	1 oz.	Orange Juice	
	1 oz.	Rose's Grenadine	

Keep the sand out of this one.

Beachcomber

	1½ oz.	Puerto Rican White Rum	Shake. Serve straight up or
	¾ oz.	Rose's Lime Juice	with ice.
	¼ oz.	Triple Sec	
	dash	Maraschino Liqueur	

Beam Me Up Scotty

	1 part	Kahlua	Shake with ice and strain into
	1 part	Baileys Irish Cream	a shot glass.
	1 part	Hiram Walker Crème de Banana	

It's bar wars.

B

Bee's Kiss

1 oz.	Puerto Rican White Rum	Shake. Serve over ice.
1/4 oz.	Myers's Dark Rum	
3/4 oz.	Cream	
2 barspoons	Honey	

Beefeater Lemoneater

2 oz.	Beefeater Gin	Add Gin to a glass filled with ice. Fill with Lemonade.
	Lemonade	

Beefeater Red Coat

1 1/2 oz.	Beefeater Gin	Serve in a tall glass over ice.
5 oz.	Cranberry Juice	

Bellini Easy

1 oz.	Peach Schnapps	Pour Schnapps in a champagne glass and add Champagne.
3 oz.	Champagne	

Bellini

1	Peach Half	Muddle the Peach in a champagne glass with a little Simple Syrup. Fill the glass with Champagne.
	Champagne	
	Simple Syrup	

Invented at Harry's Bar in Venice, Italy, by Giuseppi Cipriani on the occasion of an exhibition of the work of Venetian painter Bellini.

Bermuda Rose

1 oz.	Bombay Gin	Shake with ice and strain.
1/4 oz.	Apricot Flavored Brandy	
1/2 oz.	Rose's Lime Juice	
dash	Rose's Grenadine	

Berrypicker

1¹/₂ oz.	Hiram Walker Blackberry Brandy	Pour Blackberry Brandy and Lime Juice in a tall glass over ice. Fill with Club Soda.
	Juice of One Lime	
	Club Soda	

B

Between the Sheets

1 part	Remy Martin Cognac	Shake with ice. Strain into a sugar-rimmed glass.
1 part	Cointreau	
1 part	Bacardi Light Rum	
dash	Lemon Juice	

Bewitched

1 part	B&B	Stir over ice or shake with ice and pour.
1 part	Vodka	
1 part	Cream	

The Bigwood Girls

³/₄ oz.	Puerto Rican Light Rum	Shake with ice and serve.
¹/₂ oz.	Brandy	
¹/₂ oz.	Cointreau or Triple Sec	
¹/₂ oz.	Lemon Juice	

Bitch on Wheels

¹/₄ oz.	Martini & Rossi Extra Dry Vermouth	Shake ingredients with ice and strain into a chilled cocktail glass.
1 oz.	Bombay Gin	
¹/₄ oz.	Pernod	
¹/₄ oz.	White Crème de Menthe	

Invented at Stars in San Francisco, California.

B

Black and Tan

1¹/₂ oz.	Irish Whiskey	Combine Irish Whiskey, Rum,
1 oz.	Jamaican Dark Rum	Lime and Orange Juice, Sugar,
¹/₂ oz.	Lime Juice	and 3 to 4 ice cubes in shaker
¹/₂ oz.	Orange Juice	and shake vigorously. Put the
¹/₂ tsp.	Superfine Sugar	remaining ice in a glass. Strain
6-8	Ice Cubes	the mixture into the glass and
4 oz.	Chilled Ginger Ale	fill with Ginger Ale.

Black Buck

1¹/₄ oz.	Bacardi Black Rum	Pour Rum in a tall glass with
	Ginger Ale	ice. Fill with Ginger Ale and
		garnish with Lemon.

Black Currant Martini

1 oz.	Godiva Liqueur	Combine ingredients with ice,
1 oz.	Seagram's Gin	shake well, and strain into a
¹/₄ oz.	Crème de Cassis	cocktail glass. Garnish with a
¹/₆ oz.	Lemon Juice	Cherry.
¹/₆ oz.	Lime Juice	

Black Devil

1¹/₂ oz.	Puerto Rican Light Rum	Stir well with ice and strain.
¹/₂ oz.	Dry Vermouth	
1	Pitted Black Olive	

A hot drink.

Black Ice

1 oz.	Opal Nera Sambuca	Shake with ice and strain.
1 oz.	Vodka	
¹/₄ oz.	Crème de Menthe	

You can also serve this one over ice in a highball glass.

Black Magic

1¹/₂ oz.	Vodka	Mix the first two ingredients with cracked ice in a shaker.
³/₄ oz.	Coffee Liqueur	Add a dash of Lemon Juice.
dash	Lemon Juice	

B

Black Manhattan

1¹/₂ oz.	Bushmills Black Bush Irish Whiskey	Fill mixing glass with ice. Add Irish Whiskey and Sweet Vermouth. Stir and strain into a chilled cocktail glass filled with ice. Garnish with a Cherry.
¹/₄ oz.	Sweet Vermouth	

Black Maria

1 oz.	Myers's Dark Rum	Stir with ice and strain into a cocktail glass.
³/₄ oz.	Tia Maria	
1 barspoon	Sugar	
1 cup	Cold Coffee	
	Lemon Peel	

You can also serve this drink over ice in a highball glass.

Black Martini

1¹/₂ oz.	Absolut Kurant	Stir ingredients and serve straight up or over ice.
splash	Chambord	

Invented at the Continental Cafe in Philadelphia, Pennsylvania.

Black Orchid

1 oz.	Vodka	Build over ice in a 7 oz. rocks glass.
¹/₂ oz.	Blue Curacao	
1¹/₂ oz.	Cranberry Juice	

A flower very rare and a drink very sweet.

B

Black Russian

1¹/₂ oz.	Vodka	Add Vodka and then Coffee
³/₄ oz.	Coffee Liqueur	Liqueur to a glass filled with
		cubed ice. Stir briskly. Garnish
		with a Swizzle Stick. Add
		cream for a White Russian.

You should use Russian Vodka.

Black Tie Martini

1¹/₂ oz.	Skyy Vodka	Stir and serve straight up or
spritz	Campari	over ice.
spritz	Chivas	
2	Cocktail Onions	
1	Black Olive	

Invented at the Continental Cafe in Philadelphia, Pennsylvania.

Blackthorn #1

1¹/₂ oz.	Irish Whiskey	Shake or blend with ice. Pour
1¹/₂ oz.	Dry Vermouth	into a chilled rocks glass. Note:
3–4 dashes	Pernod	Sloe Gin can be used in place
3–4 dashes	Angostura Bitters	of Irish Whiskey.

Blackthorn #2

1¹/₂ oz.	Bushmills Irish Whiskey	Stir with ice. Serve in a cocktail
¹/₂ oz.	Noilly Prat Dry Vermouth	glass.
dash	Anisette	

Black Velvet (a.k.a. Bismarck or Champagne Velvet)

1 part	Guinness Stout	Layer the Champagne over the
1 part	Champagne	Guinness in a champagne
		flute.

B

Why combine champagne and stout?

The Black Velvet was created in 1861 at Brooks's Club in London, England. Prince Albert had died, and a steward decided the champagne should also be in mourning, so he mixed it with Guinness. This drink became very popular and was the favorite of Prince Otto Von Bismarck of Germany (1815-98).

Blarney Cocktail

1¹/₂ oz.	Irish Whiskey	Shake well with ice. Strain into
1 oz.	Italian Vermouth	a cocktail glass. Serve with a
splash	Green Crème de Menthe	Green Cherry.

Blarney Stone Cocktail

2 oz.	Irish Whiskey	Shake with ice and strain.
¹/₂ tsp.	Pernod	Serve with a twist of Orange
¹/₂ tsp.	Triple Sec	Peel and an Olive.
¹/₄ tsp.	Grenadine	
1 dash	Angostura Bitters	

Blighter Bob

1 oz.	Puerto Rican Light Rum	Stir and serve straight up or
¹/₂ oz.	Puerto Rican Dark Rum	with ice. Garnish with a Lemon
¹/₂ oz.	Crème de Cassis	Twist.
1 oz.	Orange Juice	
2 dashes	Orange Bitters	
2 oz.	Ginger Ale	

Blizzard

1 ¹/₄ oz.	Vodka	Add Vodka to a tall glass filled
	Fresca	with ice. Fill with Fresca.

Nice and cold.

Blood Ohranj Martini

	3 parts	Stoli Ohranj Vodka	Stir ingredients with ice.
	1 part	Campari	
	splash	Club Soda	

Bloody Bull

	1 1/4 oz.	Vodka	Combine with ice in a shaker.
	2 1/2 oz.	Tomato Juice	Strain into a coffee glass.
	1 1/2 oz.	Beef Bouillon	
	1–2 tsp.	Lemon Juice	
	dash	Worcestershire Sauce	
	dash	Tabasco Sauce	
	dash	Pepper	

Bloody Caesar

	1 1/4 oz.	Vodka	Pour Vodka into a glass with
	2 1/2 oz.	Clamato Juice	ice and fill with Clamato Juice.
	dash	Worcestershire Sauce	Add a dash of Tabasco,
	dash	Tabasco Sauce	Worcestershire, Pepper, and
	dash	Salt and Pepper	Salt. Garnish with a Celery
			Stalk or a Lime Wheel.

A popular drink in Canada.

Bloody Mary

	1 1/4 oz.	Vodka	Pour Vodka over ice in a
	2 1/2 oz.	Tomato Juice	glass. Fill with Tomato Juice.
	dash	Worcestershire Sauce	Add a dash or two of
	dash	Tabasco Sauce	Worcestershire Sauce and
	dash	Salt and Pepper	Tabasco Sauce. Stir and
			garnish with a Celery Stalk. For
			those who enjoy their Bloody
			Marys extremely spicy, add
			more Tabasco.

The most famous of the "Hair of the Dog" morning after cocktails.

Bloody Molly

1½ oz.	Jameson Irish Whiskey	Combine in a tall glass over
3 oz.	Tomato Juice (seasoned to taste) or prepared Bloody Mary Mix	ice and stir. Garnish with a Celery Heart.
dash	Lemon Juice	

Irish Whiskey and Tomato Juice? Hmmmm.

The Bloomin' Apple

1¼ oz.	Jameson Irish Whiskey	Combine in a mixing glass
2 oz.	Apple Juice	with ice and stir. Pour into a
dash	Cointreau	highball glass and garnish with a slice of Orange Peel.

Blue Blazer

2 parts	Irish Whiskey	Pour all ingredients into a pan
1 part	Clear Honey	and heat very gently until the
½ part	Lemon Juice	Honey has dissolved. Place a
1-3 measures	Water	teaspoon into a short tumbler and pour drink carefully into the glass (the spoon keeps the glass from cracking). Serve with Cinnamon Sticks.

C'mon baby, light my fire

The Blue Blazer drink was created in 1849 by 'Professor' Jerry Thomas at the El Dorado Saloon in San Francisco, California. Thomas made this drink famous by perfecting the technique of igniting the whiskey and tossing the flaming liquid between two silver tankards, thus mixing the ingredients while illuminating the bar with liquid fire.

B

Blue Blocker

| 1 oz. | Stoli Ohranj Vodka | Combine over ice and stir. |
| 1/2 oz. | Blue Curacao | |

You can also serve this drink in a shot glass (without ice).

Blue Kamakazi

1 oz.	Absolut Vodka	Shake with ice and strain into
1/4 oz.	Rose's Lime Juice	a shot glass.
1/4 oz.	Hiram Walker Blue Curacao	

Blue Lagoon

1 1/2 oz.	Vodka	Combine ingredients over ice
1/2 oz.	Blue Curacao	in a highball glass. Garnish
3 oz.	Lemonade	with a Cherry.

Created around 1960 at Harry's Bar in Paris, France, by Harry's son, Andy MacElhone.

Blue Shark

3/4 oz.	Tequila	Combine with ice and shake
3/4 oz.	Vodka	well. Strain over ice.
1–2 dashes	Blue Curacao	

Blue Skyy Martini

| 2 oz. | Skyy Vodka | Stir gently with ice and strain. |
| 1/4 oz. | Blue Curacao | |

Invented at the Continental Cafe in Philadelphia, Pennsylvania.

Blue Whale

1/4 oz.	Blue Curacao	Shake with ice and strain into
1 oz.	Puerto Rican Rum	a shot glass.
1/4 oz.	Pineapple Juice	

A big drink in a small glass.

B

Blues Martini

	¹/₂ oz.	Ketel One Vodka	Stir gently with ice. Serve
	¹/₂ oz.	Bombay Sapphire Gin	straight up or over ice.
	few drops	Blue Curacao	

Bobby Burns

	1 oz.	Scotch	Build in a cocktail glass over
	¹/₄ oz.	Rosso Vermouth	ice. Stir and serve.
	3 dashes	Benedictine	

A great Scotsman.

Bocci Ball #1

	¹/₂ oz.	Di Saronno Amaretto	Shake with ice. Serve straight
	¹/₂ oz.	Stolichnaya Vodka	up in a shot glass.
	¹/₂ oz.	Orange Juice	

You can also serve this one over ice in a rocks glass.

Bocci Ball #2

	1¹/₂ oz.	Di Saronno Amaretto	Shake with ice and serve.
	3 oz.	Orange Juice	

You can also top this drink with Club Soda.

Boilermaker

	1¹/₄ oz.	Irish Whiskey	Serve Whiskey in a shot glass
	10 oz.	Beer	with a glass of Beer on the
			side as a chaser.

Bolero

	1¹/₂ oz.	Rhum Barbancort	Stir. Serve straight up or
	¹/₂ oz.	Calvados	with ice.
	2 tsp.	Sweet Vermouth	
	dash	Bitters	

You can also serve this drink as a shot.

B

Bonbini

1 oz.	Bacardi Light or Dark Rum	Stir and serve with ice.
1/4 oz.	Orange Curacao	
dash	Bitters	

Bongo Drum

1 oz.	Bacardi Light Rum	Pour Rum into a tall glass
1/4 oz.	Blackberry Flavored	filled with ice. Fill with
	Brandy	Pineapple Juice. Float the
	Pineapple Juice	Brandy on top.

Bootlegger Martini

2 oz.	Bombay Gin	Stir gently with ice; serve
1/4 oz.	Southern Comfort	straight up or over ice. Garnish
		with a Lemon Twist.

Created at the Martini Bar at the Chianti Restaurant in Houston, Texas.

Boston Breeze

1 oz.	Coco Lopez Cream of	Blend and serve in a margarita
	Coconut	glass.
1 1/4 oz.	Rum	
3 oz.	Cranberry Juice	
1 cup	Ice	

Bourbon Sling

2 oz.	Bourbon	In a shaker half-filled with ice
1 tsp.	Superfine Sugar	cubes, combine the Sugar,
2 tsp.	Water	Water, Lemon Juice and
1 oz.	Lemon Juice	Bourbon. Shake well. Strain
		into a glass. Top with a Lemon
		Twist.

Bourbon Street

| 1 1/2 oz. | Bourbon | Shake with ice and strain into |
| 1/2 oz. | Di Saronno Amaretto | a shot glass. |

Bow Street Special

1¹/₂ oz.	Irish Whiskey	Mix with cracked ice in a
³/₄ oz.	Triple Sec	shaker or blender. Shake or
1 oz.	Lemon Juice	blend and strain into a chilled
		cocktail glass.

Brain

1 oz.	Baileys Irish Cream	Serve straight up in a shot
1 oz.	Peach or Strawberry	glass.
	Schnapps	

This will keep you thinking.

Brain Hemorrhage

3 parts	Irish Cream	Combine in a shot glass.
1 part	Peach Schnapps	
dash	Grenadine	

Brainstorm

1³/₄ oz.	Irish Whiskey	Stir all ingredients and strain
¹/₄ oz.	Dry Vermouth	into a cocktail glass. Decorate
dash	Benedictine	with a twist of Orange Peel.

Brandy Alexander

1¹/₂ oz.	Brandy or Cognac	Shake with ice. Strain.
¹/₂ oz.	Dark Crème de Cacao	
1 oz.	Sweet Cream or Ice Cream	

A sweet and tasty classic.

The Brandywine

2 parts	Bunratty Meade	Stir with ice.
1 part	Brandy	

Brass Knuckle

1 oz.	Bourbon	Shake with ice and serve in a
1/2 oz.	Triple Sec	highball glass with ice.
2 oz.	Sweetened Lemon Mix	

Brave Bull

| 1 1/2 oz. | Tequila | Stir and serve over ice. |
| 1/2 oz. | Coffee Liqueur | |

You can also serve this one as a shot.

Bronx

1 1/2 oz.	Gin	Shake with ice and strain.
1/2 oz.	Dry Vermouth	
1/2 oz.	Sweet Vermouth	
1/2 oz.	Fresh Orange Juice	

Brown Derby

1 1/4 oz.	Puerto Rican Dark Rum	Shake with ice. Serve straight
1/2 oz.	Lime Juice	up or over ice.
1/6 oz.	Maple Syrup	

Bubble Gum #1

1/2 oz.	Melon Liqueur	Serve in a shot glass.
1/2 oz.	Vodka	
1/2 oz.	Crème de Banana	
1/2 oz.	Orange Juice	
dash	Rose's Grenadine	

Bubble Gum #2

1 oz.	Finlandia Cranberry Vodka	Shake. Serve with ice.
1/4 oz.	Peach Schnapps	
1/4 oz.	Crème de Banana	
1 oz.	Orange Juice	

Buck-a-Roo

1¼ oz.	Bacardi Light or Dark Rum	Pour Rum into a collins glass
	Root Beer	filled with ice. Fill with Root Beer.

Bucking Irish

1¼ oz.	Irish Whiskey	Combine in an ice-filled collins
5 oz.	Ginger Ale	glass. Garnish with a Lemon Twist.

Buff Martini

5 parts	Finlandia Vodka	Stir gently with ice and strain.
1 part	Baileys Irish Cream	Add a sprinkle of freshly
1 part	Kahlua	Ground Coffee or Cinnamon.

Bullshot

1½ oz.	Vodka	Shake and serve in a glass.
1 tsp.	Lemon Juice	Garnish with a Lemon
dash	Worcestershire	Wedge.
dash	Tabasco	
4 oz.	Chilled Beef Bouillon	
dash	Salt and Pepper	

One of the "Hair of the Dog" hangover cures, along with the Bloody Mary.

Bungi Jumper

1¼ oz.	Irish Mist	Mix all but the Amaretto in a
4 oz.	Orange Juice	highball glass. Float the
½ oz.	Cream	Amaretto on top. Serve
splash	Amaretto	straight up or over ice.

Stretch this one for awhile.

Bunratty Peg

1½ oz.	Irish Whiskey	Stir with ice and strain into a
¾ oz.	Irish Mist	chilled cocktail glass.
¼ oz.	Amaretto or Drambuie	

You can also serve this drink with ice in a rocks glass.

Bushmills Fuzzy Valencia

1½ oz.	Bushmills Irish Whiskey	Serve in a tall glass over ice.
¾ oz.	Amaretto	
5 oz.	Orange Juice	

B

Bushmills Hot Irish Tea

| 1½ oz. | Bushmills Irish Whiskey | In a mug stir the ingredients |
| 4 oz. | Hot Tea | well. Add a Cinnamon Stick. |

Definitely not for the morning.

Bushmills O'thentic Irish Kiss

1½ oz.	Bushmills Irish Whiskey	Combine over ice in a highball
1 oz.	Peach Schnapps	glass and garnish with a
2 oz.	Orange Juice	wedge of Lime.
5 oz.	Ginger Ale	

Bushmills Summer Sour

1¼ oz.	Bushmills Irish Whiskey	Shake. Serve over ice in a
2 oz.	Orange Juice	collins glass.
2 oz.	Sweet & Sour Mix	

Bushmills Surprise

1 oz.	Bushmills Irish Whiskey	Shake well with ice and strain
½ oz.	Triple Sec	into a cocktail glass.
2 oz.	Lemon Juice	

Bushmills Tea

1½ oz.	Bushmills Irish Whiskey	Combine in a tall glass over
6 oz.	Iced Tea	ice. Garnish with a Lemon
		Twist.

Bushmills Triple Treat

1½ oz.	Bushmills Irish Whiskey	Combine in a tall glass
¾ oz.	Amaretto	over ice.
5 oz.	Orange Juice	

Bushranger

1 oz.	Dubonnet	Stir and serve over ice.
1 oz.	Puerto Rican White Rum	
2 dashes	Angostura Bitters	

Bushwacker

2 oz.	Coco Lopez Cream of Coconut	Blend and serve in a margarita glass.
2 oz.	Half & Half	
1 oz.	Kahlua	
$^1/_2$ oz.	Dark Crème de Cacao	
$^1/_2$ oz.	Rum	
1 cup	Ice	

Butterscotch Bomber

$^1/_2$ oz.	Vodka	Shake with ice and serve in a shot glass.
$^1/_2$ oz.	Baileys Irish Cream	
$^1/_2$ oz.	Butterscotch Schnapps	

You can also serve this one over ice in a highball glass.

Buttery Finger

$^1/_4$ oz.	Irish Cream	Combine in a shot glass.
$^1/_4$ oz.	Vodka	
$^1/_4$ oz.	Butterscotch Schnapps	
$^1/_4$ oz.	Coffee-Flavored Liqueur	

You can also serve this drink over ice in a highball glass.

Buttery Nipple

$^1/_3$ oz.	Irish Cream	Combine in a shot glass.
$^1/_3$ oz.	Vodka	
$^1/_3$ oz.	Butterscotch Schnapps	

Cafe Cooler

$^1/_2$ oz.	Romana Sambuca	Pour Coffee over ice. Add Sambuca and Half & Half. Add Brown Sugar to taste.
5 oz.	Coffee	
$^1/_2$ oz.	Half & Half	
dash	Brown Sugar	

Cajun Martini

| 2 oz. | Absolut Peppar Vodka | Serve chilled and straight up. |
| 1/4 oz. | Dry Vermouth | Garnish with a Habernero-Stuffed Olive. |

Created at the Continental Cafe in Philadelphia, Pennsylvania.

Cameron's Kick

3/4 oz.	Irish Whiskey	Shake well with cracked ice
3/4 oz.	Scotch Whisky	and strain into a cocktail glass.
	Juice of 1/4 Lemon	
2 dashes	Angostura Bitters	

Camino Reál

1 1/2 oz.	Gran Centenario Plata or Reposado Tequila	Shake or blend. Garnish with a Lime Slice.
1/2 oz.	Banana Liqueur	
1 oz.	Orange Juice	
dash	Lime Juice	
dash	Coconut Milk	

Campari & Soda

| 2 oz. | Campari | Top Campari with Club Soda in |
| | Club Soda | a collins glass. Add a Lemon Twist. |

Can-Can

1 jigger	Tequila	Shake together over ice and
1/2 jigger	French Vermouth	serve with a twist.
2 jiggers	Grapefruit Juice	
1 tsp.	Sugar	
	Orange Twist	

Candy Apple

1 part	Apple Schnapps	Shake with ice and strain into
1 part	Cinnamon Schnapps	a shot glass.
1 part	Apple Juice	

Candy Ass

	1 oz.	Chambord	Shake with ice and strain into
	1 oz.	Mozart	a shot glass.

Cannonball

	1½ oz.	Captain Morgan Spiced Rum	Pour the Rum and Pineapple Juice over ice. Float the Crème
	3 oz.	Pineapple Juice	de Menthe on top.
	¼ oz.	White Crème de Menthe	

Big noise in a rocks glass.

Canton Sunrise

	1½ oz.	Canton Delicate Ginger Liqueur	Combine over ice.
	1½ oz.	Orange Juice	
	splash	Grenadine	

Cape Codder #1

	1¼ oz.	Vodka	Combine in a chilled cocktail
	3 oz.	Cranberry Juice	glass over ice.
	dash	Lime Juice	

Cape Codder #2

	1½ oz.	Vodka	Combine Vodka and
	4 oz.	Cranberry Juice	Cranberry Juice over ice in a
		Club Soda	tall glass. Fill with Club Soda. Garnish with an Orange Slice.

Captain & Cola

	1½ oz.	Captain Morgan Spiced Rum	Stir in a tall glass with ice.
	3 oz.	Cola	

Captain & OJ

1¼ oz.	Captain Morgan Spiced Rum	Combine in a tall glass with ice.
5 oz.	Orange Juice	

Captain Morgan Sour

1¼ oz.	Captain Morgan Spiced Rum	Shake and serve over ice or straight up.
1 oz.	Lemon Juice	
1 tsp.	Sugar	

Captain's Berry Daiquiri

1¼ oz.	Captain Morgan Spiced Rum	Blend. Garnish with Berries.
½ cup	Strawberries or Raspberries	
1 tsp.	Lime Juice	
½ tsp.	Sugar	
½ cup	Crushed Ice	

Captain's Colada

1¼ oz.	Captain Morgan Spiced Rum	Blend. Garnish with a Pineapple Spear.
1 oz.	Cream of Coconut	
3 oz.	Pineapple Juice (unsweetened)	
½ cup	Crushed Ice	

Captain's Cream Soda

1¼ oz.	Captain Morgan Spiced Rum	Combine in a collins glass with ice. Garnish with a Lemon or Lime Twist.
5 oz.	Lemon-Lime Soda	

Captain's Daiquiri

1¼ oz.	Captain Morgan Spiced Rum	Shake or blend with ice. Garnish with a Lime Wedge.
2 tsp.	Lime Juice	
½ tsp.	Sugar	

Captain's Morgarita

1 oz.	Captain Morgan Spiced Rum	Blend until smooth.
$1/2$ oz.	Triple Sec	
16 oz.	Frozen Limeade	
1 cup	Ice Cubes	

Captain's Seabreeze

$1^1/_4$ oz.	Captain Morgan Spiced Rum	Serve over ice in a tall glass.
5 oz.	Cranberry Juice	

Captain's Spiced Ginger Ale

$1^1/_4$ oz.	Captain Morgan Spiced Rum	Serve over ice in a tall glass.
5 oz.	Seagram's Ginger Ale	

Captain's Tropical Spiced Tea

$1^1/_4$ oz.	Captain Morgan Spiced Rum	Serve over ice in a tall glass. Garnish with a Lemon Wedge.
5 oz.	Iced Tea	
$1/2$ tsp.	Lemon Juice	

Caribbean Cruise Shooter

1 part	Baileys Irish Cream	Shake with ice and strain into
1 part	Kahlua Coffee Liqueur	a shot glass.
1 part	Coco Ribe	

Caribbean Grasshopper

$1^1/_2$ oz.	Coco Lopez Cream of Coconut	Combine ingredients. Serve straight up or over ice.
1 oz.	White Crème de Cacao	
$1/2$ oz.	Green Crème de Menthe	

Caribbean Joy

1¼ oz.	Castillo Silver Rum	Shake and serve over ice.
1 oz.	Pineapple Juice	
³/₄ oz.	Lemon Juice	

Carnival Cooler

³/₄ oz.	Lime Juice	In a collins glass, mix first
2 oz.	Fernandes "19"	three ingredients with ice and
	White Rum	stir. Fill with Club Soda.
2 dashes	Angostura Bitters	
	Club Soda	

Carolaretto

1 part	Carolans Irish Cream	Shake or stir over ice.
1 part	Amaretto	

Cassis Cocktail

1 oz.	Bourbon	Shake with cracked ice. Strain
¹/₂ oz.	Dry Vermouth	into a chilled cocktail glass.
1 tsp.	Crème de Cassis	

The Catalina Margarita

1¼ oz.	Jose Cuervo Gold Tequila	Blend with crushed ice.
1 oz.	Peach Schnapps	
1 oz.	Blue Curacao	
4 oz.	Sweet & Sour Mix	

Cavalier

1¹/₂ oz.	Sauza Tequila	Blend with crushed ice and
¹/₂ oz.	Galliano	strain into a cocktail glass.
1 ¹/₂ oz.	Orange Juice	
¹/₂ oz.	Cream	

CC & Soda

1³/₄ oz.	Canadian Club Whisky	Serve in a collins glass
3 oz.	Club Soda	with ice.

A Canadian favorite.

Celtic Bull

1¹/₂ oz.	Irish Whiskey	Mix all ingredients with
2 oz.	Beef Consommé or	cracked ice in a shaker or
	Bouillon	blender. Pour into a chilled
2 oz.	Tomato Juice	highball glass.
1–2 dashes	Worcestershire Sauce	
dash	Tabasco Sauce	
dash	Freshly Ground Pepper	

A variation of the Bloody Bull, which is derived from the Bloody Mary.

Cement Mixer

³/₄ shot	Irish Cream	Pour ingredients directly into
¹/₄ shot	Lime Juice	the glass. Let the drink stand
		for 5 seconds and it will
		coagulate.

This drink will stick to your ribs.

Chambord Iceberg

¹/₂ oz.	Chambord	Combine in a champagne
¹/₂ oz.	Vodka	glass packed to the top
		with ice.

Chambord Kamikazi

1 oz.	Vodka	Shake with ice and strain into
¹/₂ oz.	Chambord	a shot glass.
¹/₄ oz.	Triple Sec	
¹/₄ oz.	Lime Juice	

Tastes sort of like a Purple Hooter.

Champagne Cocktail

3 oz.	Champagne, chilled	Stir ingredients slowly. Garnish
1 cube	Sugar	with a Lemon Twist.
dash	Angostura Bitters	

How can you do this to champagne?

Champerelle

1 part	Orange Curacao	Layer this drink in the order
1 part	Anisette	listed. Start with Orange
1 part	Green Chartreuse	Curacao on the bottom and
1 part	Cognac	finish with Cognac on top.

Champs Élyssés

1 part	Grenadine	Layer this drink in the order
1 part	Brown Crème de Cacao	listed. Start with Grenadine on
1 part	Orange Curacao	the bottom and finish with
1 part	Green Crème de Menthe	Cognac on top.
1 part	Cognac	

Chamu

1/2 oz.	Chambord	Combine ingredients in a tall
1 oz.	Malibu	glass with ice. Fill with
1/2 oz.	Vodka	Pineapple Juice.
3 oz.	Pineapple Juice	

Cherried Cream Rum

1 1/2 oz.	Rhum Barbancort	Shake with ice and strain.
1/2 oz.	Cherry Brandy	
1/2 oz.	Light Cream	

Cherry Blossom

1 oz.	Cherry Marnier	Moisten the rim of cocktail
1 tsp.	Superfine Sugar	glass with drop of Cherry
1 1/2 oz.	Brandy	Marnier and Sugar Frost.
3–4 dashes	Triple Sec or Curacao	Combine all ingredients in a
3–4 dashes	Grenadine	shaker and shake vigorously.
1/2 oz.	Lemon Juice	Strain drink into the prepared
3–4	Ice Cubes	cocktail glass.

Cherry Bomb

¹/₂ oz.	Cherry Brandy	Shake with ice and strain into
1 oz.	Rum	a shot glass.
¹/₂ oz.	Sour Mix	

Chi-Chi

1 oz.	Coco Lopez Cream of Coconut	Blend until smooth.
2 oz.	Pineapple Juice	
1¹/₂ oz.	Vodka	
1 cup	Ice	

Move over rum, vodka is in this one.

Chicago Style

³/₄ oz.	Bacardi Light Rum	Blend with ice.
¹/₄ oz.	Hiram Walker Triple Sec	
¹/₄ oz.	Hiram Walker Anisette	
¹/₄ oz.	Lemon or Lime Juice	

The windy one.

The Chimayo Cocktail

1¹/₄ oz.	Herradura Silver Tequila	Fill a glass with ice. Pour the
¹/₄ oz.	Crème de Cassis	ingredients over ice and stir.
1 oz.	Fresh Apple Cider or Apple Juice	Garnish with an Apple Wedge.
¹/₄ oz.	Lemon Juice	

China Beach

³/₄ oz.	Canton Delicate Ginger Liqueur	Shake with ice and serve over ice.
1 oz.	Cranberry Juice	
splash	Vodka	

Chinese Torture

1 part	Canton Delicate Ginger Liqueur	Shake with ice and strain into a shot glass.
1 part	Bacardi 151 Rum	

Chip Shot

³/₄ oz.	Devonshire Irish Cream	Combine in a glass and stir.
³/₄ oz.	Tuaca	
1¹/₂ oz.	Coffee	

Perfect after golf or cookies.

Chocolate Martini #1

1 oz.	Absolut Vodka	Shake over ice; strain into a
¹/₂ oz.	Godiva Chocolate Liqueur	chilled cocktail glass with a
		Lemon Twist garnish.

For your sweet tooth.

Chocolate Martini #2

1¹/₂ oz.	Absolut Kurant Vodka	Pour Kurant and Crème de
dash	White Crème de Cacao	Cacao over ice. Shake or stir
		well. Strain and serve in a
		chocolate-rimmed cocktail
		glass straight up or over ice.
		Garnish with an Orange Peel.

To rim the glass, first rub a piece of orange around the top of the glass and then gently place the glass upside down in a plate of unsweetened chocolate powder.

Cilver Citron

1¹/₄ oz.	Absolut Citron	Combine in a champagne
2 oz.	Chilled Champagne	glass.

Citron Cooler

1¹/₄ oz.	Absolut Citron	Pour Citron and Lime Juice
¹/₂ oz.	Fresh Lime Juice	over ice in a tall glass. Fill with
	Tonic	Tonic. Garnish with a Lime
		Wedge.

Citron Kamikaze

³/₄ oz.	Absolut Citron Vodka	Pour Citron, Triple Sec and
³/₄ oz.	Triple Sec	Lime Juice over ice in a shaker.
	Lime Juice	Shake well and strain into a
		glass. Serve straight up or over
		ice. Garnish with a Lime
		Wedge.

C

Citron Martini

1¹/₄ oz.	Absolut Citron Vodka	Pour Citron and Vermouth over
dash	Extra Dry Vermouth	ice. Shake or stir well. Strain
		and serve in a cocktail glass
		straight up or over ice. Garnish
		with a Twist or an Olive.

A real twist to the classic martini.

Clam Voyage

1 oz.	Bacardi Light or Dark Rum	Blend with ice and serve in a
¹/₄ oz.	Apple Flavored Brandy	margarita glass.
1 oz.	Orange Juice	
dash	Orange Bitters	

Claridge

¹/₂ oz.	Cork Dry Gin	Mix with ice. Serve over ice or
¹/₂ oz.	Dry Vermouth	straight up.
¹/₂ oz.	Cointreau	
¹/₂ oz.	Apricot Brandy	

Cocktail na Mara (Cocktail of the Sea)

2 oz.	Irish Whiskey	Stir all ingredients well in a
2 oz.	Clam Juice	mixing glass with cracked ice
4 oz.	Tomato Juice	and pour into a chilled
¹/₂ oz.	Lemon Juice	highball glass.
3–4 dashes	Worcestershire Sauce	
dash	Tabasco Sauce	
pinch	White Pepper	

Coco Loco (Crazy Coconut)

1½ oz.	Herradura Tequila	Blend. Garnish with a
3 oz.	Pineapple Juice	Pineapple Spear.
2 oz.	Coco Lopez	
	Cream of Coconut	

Coco Margarita

1¼ oz.	Jose Cuervo 1800 Tequila	Shake or blend ingredients.
1 oz.	Sweet & Sour Mix	Garnish with fresh Pineapple.
1½ oz.	Pineapple Juice	
½ oz.	Fresh Lime Juice	
½ oz.	Coco Lopez Cream	
	of Coconut	

Cocolou

1 part	Carolans Irish Cream	Stir well over ice.
1 part	Crème de Cacao	

And this has not a drop of coconut.

Cocomistico

½ oz.	Jose Cuervo Mistico	Shake ingredients and strain
½ oz.	Baileys Irish Cream	into a rocks glass.
½ oz.	Godiva Liqueur	
1 oz.	Half & Half	

Cocomotion

4 oz.	Coco Lopez	Blend and serve in a margarita
	Cream of Coconut	glass.
2 oz.	Lime Juice	
1½ oz.	Puerto Rican Dark Rum	
1½ cups	Ice	

Coconut Almond Margarita

1¼ oz.	Jose Cuervo 1800 Tequila	Shake and serve over ice.
2½ oz.	Sweet & Sour Mix	Garnish with a wedge of Lime.
½ oz.	Cream of Coconut	
¼ oz.	Amaretto Liqueur	
½ oz.	Fresh Lime Juice	

You can also blend the ingredients with ice.

C

Coconut Bellini

2 oz.	Coco Lopez	Blend until smooth.
	Cream of Coconut	
3 oz.	Champagne	
2 oz.	Peach Puree	
½ oz.	Peach Schnapps	
1 cup	Ice	

This famous Bellini made with Coco Lopez.

Coffee Cream Cooler

1¼ oz.	Bacardi Light or Dark Rum	Pour Rum into a tall glass half
	Cold Coffee	filled with ice. Fill with cold
	Cream	Coffee and Cream to desired
		proportions.

Cointreau Santa Fe Margarita

1½ oz.	Jose Cuervo Gold Tequila	Blend ingredients and serve in
¾ oz.	Cointreau	a margarita glass.
2 oz.	Sweet & Sour Mix	
2 oz.	Cranberry Juice	

Cointreau Strawberry Margarita

1¼ oz.	Jose Cuervo Gold Tequila	Blend ingredients and serve in
¾ oz.	Cointreau	a margarita glass.
2 oz.	Sweet & Sour Mix	
3 oz.	Frozen Strawberries	

Cold Irish

1½ oz.	Irish Whiskey	Pour the Irish Whiskey and the
½ oz.	Irish Mist	Irish Mist over ice. Fill with
2–3 drops	Crème de Cacao	Coffee Soda and stir. Touch up
	Whipped Cream	the Whipped Cream with the
	Coffee Soda	Crème de Cacao and use it to
		top the drink.

Colorado Bulldog

1½ oz.	Coffee Liqueur	Pour first two ingredients over
4 oz.	Cream	ice. Add a splash of Cola. Stir
splash	Cola	briefly.

There is another name for this drink. You've heard it but won't see it in print.

Colosseum Cooler

1 oz.	Romana Sambuca	Combine Sambuca and
3 oz.	Cranberry Juice	Cranberry Juice in a tall glass.
	Club Soda	Fill with Soda and garnish with
		a Lime Wedge.

Columbus Cocktail

1½ oz.	Puerto Rican Golden Rum	Mix or blend with crushed ice.
¾ oz.	Apricot Brandy	
	Juice of ½ Lime	

Commando Fix

2 oz.	Irish Whiskey	Fill a glass with ice. Add Irish
¼ oz.	Cointreau	Whiskey, Cointreau, and Lime
½ oz.	Lime Juice	Juice. Stir slowly. Dot the
1–2 dashes	Raspberry Liqueur	surface of the drink with
		Raspberry Liqueur.

Commodore

1 part	Bourbon	Shake with ice and serve over ice.
1 part	Crème de Cacao	
1 part	Sweetened Lemon Juice	
1 dash	Grenadine	

Conchita

1¼ oz.	Tequila	Combine first two ingredients
½ oz.	Lemon Juice	in a chilled highball glass. Fill
6 oz.	Grapefruit Juice	with Grapefruit Juice and stir.

Continental

1 oz.	Bacardi Light Rum	Blend with ice.
¼ oz.	Green Crème de Menthe	
¾ oz.	Rose's Lime Juice	
¼ tsp.	Sugar (optional)	

Cool Citron

| 1 oz. | Absolut Citron Vodka | Shake and serve over ice. |
| ½ oz. | White Crème de Menthe | |

Cool Mist

| 2 oz. | Irish Mist | Combine in a tall glass with |
| | Tonic Water | crushed ice. Add a Shamrock for a garnish. |

Copper Illusion Martini

1 oz.	Gin	Stir ingredients and garnish
½ oz.	Grand Marnier	with an Orange Slice.
½ oz.	Campari	

Invented at the Gallery Lounge at the Sheraton in Seattle, Washington.

Copperhead

| 1¼ oz. | Vodka | Combine in a tall glass filled |
| | Ginger Ale | with ice. Add a squeeze of Lime and garnish with a Lime Wedge. |

Cork Comfort

1½ oz.	Irish Whiskey
¾ oz.	Sweet Vermouth
3–4 dashes	Angostura Bitters
3–4 dashes	Southern Comfort

Shake with ice or blend. Pour into a chilled rocks glass.

Corkscrew

¾ oz.	Bacardi Light Rum
¼ oz.	Asbach Uralt
¼ oz.	Port Wine
½ oz.	Lemon or Rose's Lime Juice

Stir. Serve over ice.

Cosmo Kazi

4 parts	Vodka
1 part	Triple Sec
Dash	Lime Juice
Splash	Cranberry Juice

Combine ingredients and pour over ice.

A red, non-shot variation of the Kamikazi.

Cosmopolitan Martini

1 part	Cointreau
2 parts	Vodka
	Juice of ½ Lime
splash	Cranberry

Shake with ice and strain.

There are many variations of the martini. This one works.

Cossack Charge

1½ oz.	Vodka
½ oz.	Cognac
½ oz.	Cherry Brandy

Mix all ingredients with cracked ice in a shaker or blender and pour into a chilled cocktail glass.

County Clare Cooler

3 oz.	Bunratty Meade
	7-Up

Pour Bunratty Meade over ice in a tall glass. Fill with 7-Up and garnish with a Lemon Slice.

Cow Puncher

1 oz.	Bacardi Light or Dark Rum	Pour Rum and Crème de Cacao
1 oz.	White Crème de Cacao	into a tall glass half filled with
	Milk	ice. Fill with Milk.

Cowcatcher

C

1 part	O'Mara's Irish Country	Mix together. Pour over ice
	Cream	and serve.
1 part	Sambuca Sarti	

Cream Whiskey

1 part	Carolans Irish Cream	Stir well over ice.
2 parts	Rye Whiskey	

Cranberry Cocktail

2 oz.	Finlandia Cranberry Vodka	Serve alone over ice or with
		splash of Club Soda.

Cran Razz

2 oz.	Two Fingers Tequila	In a shaker, mix all ingredients.
2 oz.	Cranberry Juice	Serve over ice.
1 oz.	Raspberry Liqueur	

Cran-Rum Twister

2 oz.	Puerto Rican Light Rum	Combine the first two
3 oz.	Cranberry Juice	ingredients in a tall glass with
	Lemon-Lime Soda	ice. Fill with Lemon-Lime Soda
		and garnish with a Lemon
		Slice.

Cranberry Martini

1 part	Godiva Liqueur	Combine with ice and shake
1 part	Absolut Vodka	well. Garnish with a Lime Twist.
1 part	Cranberry Juice	

Cranberry Sauce Martini

1 oz.	Stoli Ohranj Vodka	Shake with ice and strain or serve over ice. Garnish with Cranberries that have been soaked in Simple Syrup.
¹/₄ oz.	Cranberry Juice	

Cranpeppar

1¹/₄ oz.	Absolut Peppar Vodka	Pour Peppar over ice in a tall glass. Fill with Cranberry Juice.
	Cranberry Juice	

Crantini

2 oz.	Bacardi Limón	Shake and serve straight up. Garnish with Cranberries and a Lemon Twist.
touch	Martini & Rossi Extra Dry Vermouth	
splash	Cranberry Juice	

Invented at Mr. Babbington's in New York, New York.

Creamed Sherry

2 parts	Carolans Irish Cream	Stir well over ice.
1 part	Duff Gordon Cream Sherry	

Creamsicle #1

1¹/₂ oz.	Stoli Ohranj Vodka	Combine over ice.
¹/₂ oz.	Irish Cream	

Creamsicle #2

1 oz.	Liquore Galliano	Combine over ice.
1 oz.	Half & Half or Heavy Cream Orange Juice	

Creature from the Black Lagoon

1 oz.	Jagermeister	Shake with ice and strain into a shot glass.
1 oz.	Romana Black	

Back to the water.

C

Creole

1³/₄ oz.	Puerto Rican White Rum	Combine over ice.
2 splashes	Lemon Juice	
3¹/₂ oz.	Beef Bouillon	
dash	Pepper	
dash	Salt	
dash	Tabasco Sauce	
dash	Worcestershire Sauce	

Crest of the Wave

1¹/₄ oz.	Bombay Gin	Combine in a tall glass over ice.
1¹/₂ oz.	Grapefruit Juice	
1¹/₂ oz.	Cranberry Juice	

Cricket

³/₄ oz.	Bacardi Light Rum	Blend ingredients with ice.
¹/₄ oz.	White Crème de Cacao	
¹/₄ oz.	Green Crème de Menthe	
1 oz.	Cream	

Cripple Creek

¹/₂ oz.	Herradura Tequila	Shake the first three ingredients
¹/₂ oz.	Benchmark Bourbon	and strain into a glass. Float the
1 oz.	Orange Juice	Galliano on top.
¹/₂ oz.	Galliano	

Crocodile Bite

1¹/₄ oz.	Jameson Irish Whiskey	Combine in a tall glass with
2 oz.	Orange Juice	ice. Garnish with a slice of
1 oz.	Grand Marnier	Orange or Lemon and serve
1 bottle	7-Up	with straws.

Are there crocodiles in Ireland?

Cuba Libre

1³/₄ oz.	Bacardi Rum	Add Rum to a glass filled with
	Cola	ice. Fill with Cola. Add Lime
	Juice of ¹/₄ Lime	Juice and stir.

A Rum and cola with a lime.

Cuba Libre Lore

This drink is a political statement as well as a cocktail. It translates to "Free Cuba," a status the country enjoyed in 1898 at the end of the Spanish-American War. Cuban-American relations were friendly around the turn of the century, when a U.S. Army lieutenant in Havana mixed some light native rum with a new-fangled American soft drink called Coca Cola and braced the libation with a lime.

Cuervo Alexander

1 oz.	Jose Cuervo Gold Tequila	Blend until smooth.
1 oz.	Coffee-Flavored Liqueur	
1 oz.	Wild Cherry Brandy	
2 scoops	Vanilla Ice Cream	

A little kick to the Brandy Alexander.

Cuervo Side-Out

1½ oz.	Jose Cuervo Gold Tequila	Blend.
1 oz.	Triple Sec	
2 oz.	Cranberry Juice	
1½ oz.	Lime Juice	

Cuervo Sunrise

1½ oz.	Jose Cuervo Gold Tequila	Shake and serve over ice.
3 oz.	Cranberry Juice	Garnish with a Lime.
½ oz.	Lime Juice	
½ oz.	Grenadine	

Cuervo Traditional Aztec Ruin

½ oz.	Jose Cuervo Traditional Tequila	Shake with ice and strain into a shot glass.
½ oz.	Rose's Lime Juice	

Cuervo Traditional Aztec Sky

³/₄ oz.	Jose Cuervo Traditional Tequila	Shake with ice and strain into a shot glass.
³/₄ oz.	Blue Curacao	

Cuervo Tropical

1¹/₂ oz.	Jose Cuervo Gold Tequila	Mix in highball glass filled with cracked ice. Garnish with half an Orange Slice and a Cherry.
3 oz.	Orange Juice	
1 tsp.	Lemon Juice	
¹/₂ oz.	Grenadine	

D

Cutthroat

1¹/₄ oz.	Finlandia Cranberry Vodka	Add Vodka to a tall glass with ice. Fill with Orange Juice.
	Orange Juice	

Sort of a cranberry screwdriver.

Daiquiri

1¹/₄ oz.	Light Rum	Shake or blend with ice.
¹/₂ oz.	Sweetened Lemon Juice	

Dancing Leprechaun

1¹/₂ oz.	Irish Whiskey	Combine the Whiskey and the Lemon Juice. Shake with ice. Strain and add ice. Fill the glass with equal parts Club Soda and Ginger Ale. Stir gently. Touch it up with a twist of Lemon.
1¹/₂ oz.	Lemon Juice	
	Club Soda	
	Ginger Ale	

Dean Martini

2 oz.	Ketel One Vodka, chilled	Pour the Vodka into a cocktail glass and garnish with an Olive. Place the Cigarette and Matches on the side.
	Olive	
	A Lucky (cigarette) and a book of matches.	

Invented at the Continental Cafe in Philadelphia, Pennsylvania.

Dempsey Rum Runner

1 shot	Gin	Fill with Pineapple Juice. Shake.
	Pineapple Juice	
1 tsp./pkt.	Sugar	
dash	bitters	

Derry Delight

2 oz.	O'Mara's Irish	Shake together well and
	Country Cream	pour over ice.
2 oz.	Half & Half	

Derry Delight with a Kick

1 1/2 oz.	O'Mara's Irish	Shake together well; pour
	Country Cream	over ice.
1/2 oz.	Copa De Oro Coffee	
	Liqueur	
1/2 oz.	Burnett's Vodka	
2 oz.	Half & Half	

Dewars Summer Splash

1 1/2 oz.	Dewars	Combine over ice. Garnish
3 parts	Ginger Ale	with a Lime Slice.
dash	Lime Juice	

Dewey Martini

1 1/2 oz.	Absolut Vodka	Shake and strain into a
dash	Martini & Rossi Extra	cocktail glass or serve over ice.
	Dry Vermouth	
dash	Orange Bitters	

Dillatini Martini

1 1/2 oz.	Absolut Vodka	Shake and strain into a
dash	Martini & Rossi Extra	cocktail glass or serve over ice.
	Dry Vermouth	
	Dilly Bean	

Try and find a Dilly Bean.

Dingle Dram

1¹/₂ oz.	Irish Whiskey	Pour Irish Whiskey and Irish
¹/₂ oz.	Irish Mist	Mist into a chilled highball
	Coffee Soda	glass along with several ice
dash	Crème de Cacao	cubes. Fill with Coffee Soda.
	Whipped Cream	Stir gently. Add a float of
		Crème de Cacao. Top with
		dollop of Whipped Cream.

Dirty Girl Scout Cookie

D

²/₃ shot	Irish Cream	Shake with ice and strain.
¹/₃ shot	Green Crème de Menthe	

Dirty Harry

1 oz.	Grand Marnier	Shake with ice and strain.
1 oz.	Tia Maria	

Do you feel lucky? This will make your day.

Disarita Margarita

1 oz.	Jose Cuervo 1800 Tequila	Blend. Garnish with Lime.
¹/₂ oz.	Di Saronno Amaretto	
3 oz.	Margarita Mix	
¹/₂ cup	Crushed Ice	

Her Italian sister.

Dixie Dew

1¹/₂ oz.	Bourbon	In a mixing glass half-filled
¹/₂ oz.	White Crème de Menthe	with ice cubes, combine all of
¹/₂ tsp.	Cointreau or Triple Sec	the ingredients. Stir well.
		Strain into a cocktail glass.

Dixie Stinger

3 oz.	Bourbon	In a shaker half-filled with ice
¹/₂ oz.	White Crème de Menthe	cubes, combine all of the
¹/₂ tsp.	Southern Comfort	ingredients. Shake well. Strain
		into a cocktail glass.

Dizzy Lizzy

1¹/₂ oz.	Bourbon	Combine first three ingredients
1¹/₂ oz.	Sherry	in a tall glass with ice. Fill with
dash	Lemon Juice	Club Soda.
	Club Soda	

Double Gold

| ¹/₂ oz. | Jose Cuervo Gold Tequila | Shake with ice and strain into |
| ¹/₂ oz. | Goldschlager | a shot glass. |

Dream Shake

| 1 part | Baileys Irish Cream | Shake with ice and strain into |
| 1 part | Tia Maria | a shot glass. |

Dublin Handshake

¹/₂ oz.	Baileys Irish Cream	Shake with crushed ice. Strain
¹/₂ oz.	Irish Whiskey	into a cocktail glass.
³/₄ oz.	Sloe Gin	

Dubonnet Cocktail

1¹/₂ oz.	Dubonnet	Combine over ice and garnish
¹/₂ oz.	Gin	with a Lemon Twist.
dash	Angostura Bitters	

Duck Pin

1 oz.	Chambord	Shake with ice and strain into
1 oz.	Southern Comfort	a shot glass.
¹/₂ oz.	Pineapple Juice	

Eclipse

1¹/₂ oz.	Bushmills Black Bush	Fill a highball glass with ice.
	Irish Whiskey	Add Irish Whiskey. Fill with
	Seltzer	Seltzer water and stir. Garnish
		with an Orange Slice.

Egg Nog

1¼ oz.	Bacardi Light or Dark Rum	Mix in a shaker and strain into a glass. Sprinkle with Nutmeg.
1	Egg	
1 tsp.	Sugar	
1 oz.	Milk	

1800 Bite the Berry

1¼ oz.	Jose Cuervo 1800 Tequila	Combine in a rocks glass.
½ oz.	Triple Sec	Garnish with an Orange Slice.
¼ oz.	Raspberry Liqueur	
2 ½ oz.	Sweet & Sour Mix	
2 oz.	Cranberry Juice	

E

1800 Lemon Drop

1¼ oz.	Jose Cuervo 1800 Tequila	Combine in a rocks glass and
½ oz.	Triple Sec	stir. Add a Lemon Juice float.
1 oz.	Sweet & Sour Mix	Garnish with Lemon.
1 oz.	Lemon-Lime Soda	
splash	Fresh Lemon Juice	

Electric Lemonade

1¼ oz.	Vodka	Blend. Pour over ice in a tall
½ oz.	Blue Curacao	glass and garnish with a
2 oz.	Sweet & Sour Mix	Lemon Slice.
splash	7-Up	

Electric Peach

1 oz.	Vodka	Blend. Pour over ice in a tall
¼ oz.	Peach Schnapps	glass and garnish with a
½ oz.	Cranberry Juice Cocktail	Lemon Slice.
¼ oz.	Orange Juice	

Elegant Martini (Gin)

1¾ oz.	Bombay Sapphire Gin	Stir the first three ingredients
½ oz.	Martini & Rossi Dry Vermouth	with ice. Strain or serve on ice. Float Grand Marnier on top.
¼ oz.	Grand Marnier	
dash	Grand Marnier (on top)	

Elegant Martini (Vodka)

1¹/₂ oz.	Absolut Vodka	Stir the first three ingredients
dash	Martini & Rossi Extra	with ice. Serve on ice or
	Dry Vermouth	straight up. Float Grand
¹/₄ oz.	Grand Marnier	Marnier on top.
dash	Grand Marnier	

Elephant's Ear Martini

1 oz.	Dry Gin	Stir with ice. Serve on ice or
³/₄ oz.	Martini & Rossi	straight up.
	Dry Vermouth	
³/₄ oz.	Dubonnet	

Did I hear this drink right?

E

Emerald City Martini

1³/₄ oz.	Fris Vodka	Stir with ice. Serve on ice or
¹/₄ oz.	Midori	straight up and garnish with a
		Lime Wheel.

Emerald Isle

³/₄ shot	Irish Whiskey	Blend the first three ingredients
³/₄ shot	Green Crème de Menthe	and then add Soda Water. Stir
2 scoops	Vanilla Ice Cream	after adding Soda Water.
	Soda Water	

It's green.

Emerald Martini

2 oz.	Bacardi Limón	Stir with ice. Serve on ice or
splash	Martini & Rossi	straight up.
	Extra Dry Vermouth	
splash	Midori	

Invented at the Heart and Soul in San Francisco, California.

Erie Tour

1 part	Irish Mist	Combine over ice.
1 part	Carolans Irish Cream	
1 part	Irish Whiskey	

Erin Go Burrr

3 oz.	Carolans Irish Cream	Serve chilled Irish Cream straight up in a chilled cocktail glass.

Extra Nutty Irishman

1 part	Irish Mist	Shake. Top with Whipped
1 part	Frangelico	Cream. Serve in a goblet-type
1 part	Carolans Irish Cream	glass.
	Whipped Cream	

Eye Drop

1 part	Rumple Minze	Shake with ice and strain into
1 part	Ouzo	a shot glass.
1 part	Stolichnaya Vodka	

F

Eyes R Smilin'

1 oz.	Baileys Irish Cream	Build over ice. Stir and serve.
1 oz.	Vodka	
$1/2$ oz.	Gin	
$1/2$ oz.	Triple Sec	

Fascinator Martini

$1^1/_2$ oz.	Absolut Vodka	Stir and serve straight up or
dash	Martini & Rossi	over ice. Garnish with a Mint
	Extra Dry Vermouth	Sprig.
dash	Pernod and Sprig Mint	

You can also serve this one over ice in a highball glass.

Fifth Avenue #1

1 part	Dark Crème de Cacao	Layer this drink in the order
1 part	Apricot Brandy	listed. Start with Crème de
1 part	Cream	Cacao on the bottom and finish with Cream on top.

See Chapter 19 for more on layered drinks.

Fifth Avenue #2

½ oz.	Baileys Irish Cream	Shake with ice. Strain into a
½ oz.	Apricot Brandy	cocktail glass.
½ oz.	White Crème de Cacao	

Great for Easter.

'57 T-Bird with Honolulu License Plates

1 part	Orange Liqueur	Shake with ice and strain into
1 part	Dark Rum	a shot glass.
1 part	Sloe Gin	
1 part	Orange Juice	

Get a designated driver.

'57 T-Bird with Texas License Plates

1 part	Orange Liqueur	Shake with ice and strain into
1 part	Dark Rum	a shot glass.
1 part	Sloe Gin	
1 part	Grapefruit Juice	

Fire

1 ¼ oz.	Stoli Ohranj Vodka	Combine over ice.
¼ oz.	Cinnamon Schnapps	

A hot one.

Fire Fly

1¼ oz.	Vodka	Combine Vodka, and Grape-
2 oz.	Grapefruit Juice	fruit Juice in a tall glass over
dash	Grenadine	ice. Add Grenadine.

Fireball

2 oz.	Cinnamon Schnapps	Combine in a shot glass.
dash	Tabasco	

Firebird

1¼ oz.	Absolut Peppar Vodka	Combine over ice.
4 oz.	Cranberry Juice	

Flamingo

1½ oz.	Rhum Barbancort	Shake and serve over ice.
dash	Grenadine	
1 oz.	Pineapple Juice	
	Juice of ¼ Lime	

Flirting with the Sandpiper

1½ oz.	Puerto Rican Light Rum	Stir well. Serve over ice.
½ oz.	Cherry Brandy	
3 oz.	Orange Juice	
2 dashes	Orange Bitter	

F

Flying Kangaroo

1 oz.	Vodka	Shake or blend with ice.
¼ oz.	Galliano	
1 oz.	Rhum Barbancort	
1½ oz.	Pineapple Juice	
¾ oz.	Orange Juice	
¾ oz.	Coconut Cream	
½ oz.	Cream	

Foggy Day Martini

1½ oz.	Dry Gin	Shake and pour over ice or
¼ oz.	Pernod	serve straight up. Garnish with
	Twist of Lemon Peel	a Lemon Peel Twist.

Fools Gold

1 part	Vodka	Shake with ice and strain into
1 part	Galliano	a shot glass.

43 Amigos

1¹/₂ oz.	Jose Cuervo Gold Tequila	Shake. Strain into a chilled
¹/₂ oz.	Licor 43	martini glass. Garnish with a
¹/₂ oz.	Triple Sec	Lime Wedge.
¹/₂ oz.	Lime Juice	

Four Leaf Clover

¹/₄ oz.	Bushmills Irish Whiskey	Shake first three ingredients
2 oz.	Orange Juice	and top with Crème de
2 oz.	Sweet & Sour	Menthe. Serve over ice or
splash	Green Crème de Menthe	straight up.

Don't overlook this one.

Fourth Degree Martini

³/₄ oz.	Dry Gin	Stir gently with ice; serve
³/₄ oz.	Dry Vermouth	straight up or over ice. Garnish
³/₄ oz.	Sweet Vermouth	with a Lemon Peel Twist.
¹/₄ oz.	Pernod	

Fourth of July

¹/₃ shot	Grenadine	Layer this drink in the order
¹/₃ shot	Vodka	listed. Start with Grenadine on
¹/₃ shot	Blue Curacao	the bottom and finish with
		Blue Curacao on top.

Freddie Fudpucker

1 oz.	Tequila	Shake and serve over ice.
4 oz.	Orange Juice	
¹/₂ oz.	Galliano	
¹/₂ oz.	Kahlua	

Yes, there was this guy named Freddie.

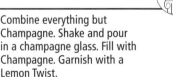

French 75

1¹/₂ oz.	Cognac	Combine everything but
¹/₂ tsp.	Lemon Juice	Champagne. Shake and pour
¹/₂ tsp.	Powdered Sugar	in a champagne glass. Fill with
	Champagne	Champagne. Garnish with a
		Lemon Twist.

The origins of the French 75

FABLES & LORE

If you request this drink, you might receive a mix of gin and champagne. In the French trenches of World War I, however, gin was scarce, but cognac and champagne were not. American soldiers soon discovered that a combination of the two produced an effect similar to getting zapped by an artillery piece known as French 75.

French Colada

F

1¹/₂ oz.	Puerto Rican White Rum	Blend with ice.
³/₄ oz.	Cognac	
1 scoop	Crushed Ice	
³/₄ oz.	Sweet Cream	
³/₄ oz.	Coco Lopez Cream of Coconut	
1¹/₂ oz.	Pineapple Juice	
splash	Crème de Cassis	

French Connection

¹/₂ oz.	Cognac	Serve straight up in a brandy snifter or shake with ice and strain.
¹/₂ oz.	Grand Marnier	

You can also serve this drink as a shot.

French Kiss

1 part	Martini & Rossi Rosso Vermouth	Combine over ice.
1 part	Martini & Rossi Dry Vermouth	

French Kiss Martini

2 oz.	Stolichnaya Ohranj Vodka	Stir gently with ice. Serve straight up or over ice.
¹/₄ oz.	Lillet	

French Tickler

	1 part	Goldschlager	Shake with ice and strain into
	1 part	Grand Marnier	a shot glass.

Frisco Cocktail

	1¹/₄ oz.	Whiskey	Stir with cracked ice and
	³/₄ oz.	Benedictine	strain. Serve with a twist of
			Lemon Peel.

Fru-Fru

	³/₄ oz.	Banana Liqueur	Shake with ice and strain into
	1 oz.	Peach Schnapps	a shot glass.
	dash	Rose's Lime Juice	
	1 oz.	Pineapple Juice	

Fruity Irishman

	2 parts	Baileys Irish Cream	Stir well over ice.
	1 part	Midori Melon Liqueur	

You can serve this one without ice in a shot glass.

Fudgesicle

	1 oz.	Vodka	Shake and serve over ice.
	¹/₄ oz.	Crème de Cacao	
	¹/₄ oz.	Chocolate Syrup	

Fuzzy Navel

	1¹/₄ oz.	Peach Schnapps	Pour Schnapps over ice in a
	3 oz.	Orange Juice	rocks glass. Fill with Orange
			Juice and stir well.

This famous drink was invented by National Distillers, which is now Jim Beam.

Fuzzy Rita

	1¹/₂ oz.	Jose Cuervo Gold Tequila	Combine over ice in a tall
	¹/₂ oz.	Peach Liqueur	glass.
	¹/₂ oz.	Cointreau	
	1¹/₂ oz.	Lime Juice	

Margarita's cousin.

G. & C.

	1 oz.	Galliano	Shake with ice and strain into
	1 oz.	Cognac	a shot glass.

Galliano Hot Shot

	1 oz.	Galliano	Combine in a shot glass.
	1 oz.	Hot Coffee	
	dash	Whipped Cream	

Hot and sweet.

G

Gator

	1 part	Vodka	Shake the ingredients with ice
	1 part	Gin	and strain into shot glasses.
	1 part	Rum	
	1 part	Scotch	
	1 part	Blackberry Brandy	
	1 part	Blue Curacao	
	1 part	Triple Sec	
	1 part	Sweet & Sour Mix	
	1¹/₂ parts	Orange Juice	
	1¹/₂ parts	7-Up	

This cocktail should be green when all is said and done. It's not practical to make just one, by the way. If each part is a ¹/₂ oz., then this recipe will make about 3 shots.

Gentle Bull

	1¹/₂ oz.	Two Fingers Tequila	Shake. Top with Whipped
	1 oz.	Heavy Cream	Cream and a Cherry.
	³/₄ oz.	Coffee Liqueur	
	1 scoop	Crushed Ice	
		Whipped Cream	

George Bush

	1½ oz.	Bushmills Irish Whiskey	Fill a glass with crushed ice to
	3–4 oz.	Ginger Ale	the ¾ level. Add Irish
	1 strip	Lemon Peel	Whiskey. Twist Lemon Peel
		Crushed Ice	over the drink to release its oil;
			then drop it in. Top with
			Ginger Ale.

Who's George Bush?

Gibson

	2 oz.	Dry Gin	Stir with ice. Add the Cocktail
	dash	Martini & Rossi	Onion. Serve straight up or on ice.
		Extra Dry Vermouth	
		Cocktail Onion	

G

Where'd the Gibson come from?

Some say this drink is named after New York artist Charles Dana Gibson by his bartender, Charles Connoly, of the Players Club in New York. Another story credits Billie Gibson, a fight promoter.

Gimlet

	1¼ oz.	Vodka	Mix Vodka and Lime Juice in a
	½ oz.	Fresh Lime Juice	glass with ice. Strain and serve
			in a cocktail glass. Garnish
			with a Lime Twist.

You can also serve this one on ice in a highball glass.

Gin & Tonic

	1¼ oz.	Gin	In a glass fllled with ice, add
		Tonic	Gin and fill with Tonic. Add a
			Lime Wedge.

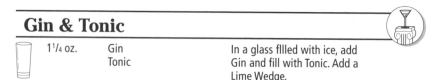

Gin Cocktail

| 1 part | Gin | Stir over ice. Add a Lemon |
| 2 parts | Dubonnet | Twist. |

Also know as the Dubonnet Cocktail.

Gin Fizz

2 oz.	Gin	Shake first three ingredients
1 tsp.	Sugar	with ice and strain. Fill with
	Juice of 1 Lemon	Club Soda.
	Club Soda	

Gin Rickey

1½ oz.	Gin	In a tall glass filled with ice,
	Club Soda	add Gin. Fill with Club Soda
		and stir. Garnish with a Lime
		Wedge.

Okay, it's just Gin and Club Soda.

Ginger Colada

1½ oz.	Coco Lopez	Blend with ice.
	Cream of Coconut	
1 oz.	Canton Delicate	
	Ginger Liqueur	
½ oz.	Rum	

Ginger Mist

| 1 part | Irish Mist | Combine in a tall glass and |
| 3 parts | Ginger Ale | serve with a Lime Wedge. |

Ginolans

| 2 parts | Carolans Irish Cream | Stir well and serve over ice. |
| 1 part | Gordon's Gin | |

Girl Scout Cookie #1

³/₄ oz.	Peppermint Schnapps	Shake with ice and serve over ice.
¹/₂ oz.	Coffee Liqueur	
3 oz.	Half & Half	

You can also serve this drink in a shot glass (but strain the ice).

Girl Scout Cookie #2

1 oz.	Green Crème de Menthe	Shake with ice and strain into
1 oz.	White or Dark	a shot glass.
	Crème de Cacao	
¹/₄ oz.	Cream	

You can also serve this drink over ice in a highball glass.

Glenbeigh Fizz

1¹/₂ oz.	Irish Whiskey	Pour all ingredients except
1 oz.	Medium Sherry	Club Soda in a chilled highball
¹/₂ oz.	Crème de Noyaux	glass with several ice cubes
¹/₂ oz.	Lemon Juice	and stir. Fill with Club Soda.
	Club Soda	

G

Godfather

1¹/₂ oz.	Scotch	Combine in a rocks glass over ice.
¹/₂ oz.	Amaretto	

A drink you can't refuse.

Godmother

1 oz.	Vodka	Combine in a rocks glass over ice.
¹/₄ oz.	Amaretto	

A woman you can't refuse.

Gold Digger Martini

1¹/₂ oz.	Finlandia Pineapple Vodka	Stir with ice; serve straight up
¹/₂ oz.	Cointreau	or over ice.

For millionaire-chasing maids.

Gold Furnace

| | 2 oz. | Goldschlager | Combine in a shot glass. |
| | 2 dashes | Tabasco | |

This is hot.

Gold Rush

| | 1 oz. | Goldschlager | Shake with ice and strain into |
| | 1 oz. | Cuervo Gold | a shot glass. |

This is not.

Golden Boy

	1¹/₂ oz.	Bourbon	Mix all ingredients, except the
	¹/₂ oz.	Rum	Grenadine, in a shaker. Strain
	2 oz.	Orange Juice	mixture into a chilled glass.
	1 tsp.	Lemon Juice	Top with a dash of Grenadine.
	1 tsp.	Sugar Syrup	
	1 scoop	Crushed Ice	
	dash	Grenadine	

G

Golden Cadillac

	¹/₄ oz.	Liquore Galliano	Mix in a blender with a little ice
	1 oz.	White Crème de Cacao	at a low speed for a short time.
	1 oz.	Cream	Strain into a champagne glass.
			A scoop of Vanilla Ice Cream
			can be substituted for Cream.

Golden Day

| | ³/₄ oz. | Vodka | Serve in a rocks glass over ice. |
| | ¹/₂ oz. | Liquore Galliano | |

Golden Dream

	1 oz.	Liquore Galliano	Shake with cracked ice. Strain
	¹/₄ oz.	Triple Sec	into a cocktail glass.
	¹/₂ oz.	Orange Juice	
	¹/₂ oz.	Cream	

You can also serve this one over ice in a highball glass.

Golden Girl Martini

1³/₄ oz.	Dry Gin	Stir gently with ice. Serve
³/₄ oz.	Dry Sherry	straight up or over ice.
1 dash	Angostura bitters	

Golden Martini

7 parts	Seagram's Extra Dry Gin	Stir gently with ice. Serve
1 part	French Vermouth	straight up or over ice. Garnish with a Lemon Peel Twist.

Good and Plenty

1 oz.	Anisette	Shake with ice and strain into
1 oz.	Blackberry Brandy	a shot glass.

Gorilla Sweat

1¹/₂ oz.	Tequila	Pour Tequila into a rocks glass
¹/₂ tsp.	Sugar	and fill with Hot Water. Add
1 pat	Butter	Sugar and stir in Butter.
	Hot Water	Garnish with a Cinnamon Stick and a sprinkle of Nutmeg.

A great name?

Grafton Street Sour

1¹/₂ oz.	Irish Whiskey	Mix all ingredients except the
¹/₂ oz.	Triple Sec	Raspberry Liqueur with
1 oz.	Lime Juice	cracked ice in a shaker or
¹/₄ oz.	Raspberry Liqueur	blender and strain into a chilled cocktail glass. Top with Raspberry Liqueur.

You can also serve this one on ice.

Grand Am

1 part	Grand Marnier	Shake with ice and strain into
1 part	Di Saronno Amaretto	a shot glass.

Grand Margarita

	1 oz.	Sauza Conmemorativo	Fill shaker with ice. Add
		Añejo Tequila	Sauza and Grand Marnier. Fill
	³/₄ oz.	Grand Marnier	with Lime Juice and add Sugar
		Fresh Lime Juice	to taste. Shake. Pour over ice
		Sugar	or strain. Garnish with a Lime
			Wedge.

Grand Ohranj

	1¹/₂ oz.	Stoli Ohranj Vodka	Stir gently with ice; serve
	dash	Extra Dry Vermouth	straight up or over ice. Garnish
	splash	Grand Marnier	with a slice of Orange Peel.

Grape Crush

	1 oz.	Vodka	Serve over ice in collins glass.
	1 oz.	Black Raspberry Liqueur	Garnish with an Orange Slice
	2 oz.	Sour Mix	or Cherry.
	1 oz.	7-Up	

G

Grape Punch

	1¹/₄ oz.	Bacardi Light Rum	Pour Rum into a tall glass
		Grape Juice	filled with ice. Fill with Grape
			Juice and add a squeeze of
			Lime or Lemon.

Grasshopper

	¹/₂ oz.	Green Crème de Menthe	Combine in a blender with ice
	¹/₂ oz.	White Crème de Cacao	and blend until smooth. Strain
	¹/₂ oz.	Cream	into a margarita glass.

*A grasshopper walks into a bar. Bartender says, "We have a drink named after you."
The grasshopper replies, "You have a drink named Bruce?"*

Gravure

	1 part	Grenadine	Layer this drink in the order
	1 part	Brown Crème de Cacao	listed. Start with Grenadine on
	1 part	Triple Sec	the bottom and finish with
			Triple Sec on top.

The Great White

1¼ oz.	Jameson Irish Whiskey	Combine over ice in a tall
2 oz.	Apple Juice	glass and garnish with a
1 oz.	White Curacao	Mint Sprig.

Green Chili

1 part	Hiram Walker Peach Schnapps	Shake with ice and strain into a shot glass.
1 part	Midori	
dash	Tabasco Sauce	

Green Devil #1

1 oz.	Gin	Shake with ice and strain into
½ oz.	Green Crème de Menthe	a shot glass.
½ oz.	Rose's Lime Juice	

Green Devil #2

G

2 oz.	Irish Whiskey	Combine with ice.
2 oz.	Clam Juice	

This is a devil of a drink.

Green Hornet

½ oz.	Vodka	Shake with ice; serve straight
¼ oz.	Midori	up or over ice.
½ oz.	Sweet & Sour Mix	

Green Lizard

1 part	Chartreuse (Green)	Layer this drink by pouring
1 part	Bacardi 151 Rum	Chartreuse first, then the Rum,
1 part	Rose's Lime Juice	and then the Lime Juice.

Green Parrot

1½ oz.	Appleton Estate Rum	Pour ingredients, one at a time in
4 oz.	Orange juice	the order listed into large
1 oz.	Blue Curacao	stemmed glass over ice. Do not
		mix. Garnish with an Orange Slice.

Green Sneaker

1 oz.	Vodka	Stir with ice, strain, and serve
¹/₂ oz.	Midori	straight up.
¹/₂ oz.	Triple Sec	
2 oz.	Orange Juice	

Gremlin

1¹/₂ oz.	Vodka	Shake with ice, strain, and
³/₄ oz.	Blue Curacao	serve straight up.
³/₄ oz.	Rum	
¹/₂ oz.	Orange Juice	

Greyhound

1¹/₂ oz.	Vodka	Pour Vodka over crushed ice in a
	Grapefruit Juice	tall glass. Fill with Grapefruit Juice.

Most people order this drink by saying, "Give me a vodka and grapefruit juice."

Grit Cocktail

¹/₂ jigger	Irish Whiskey	Shake and then strain.
¹/₂ jigger	Italian Vermouth	

Gunga Din Martini

3 parts	Dry Gin	Shake with ice. Garnish with a
1 part	Dry Vermouth	Pineapple Slice.
	Juice of ¹/₄ Orange	

Gypsy Martini

1¹/₂ oz.	Vodka or Gin	Shake with ice; serve straight
dash	Martini & Rossi	up or on ice. Garnish with a
	Extra Dry Vermouth	Cherry.

Gypsy's Kiss

1 part	Irish Mist	Combine in a highball glass.
1 part	Orange Juice	
1 part	Lemon Juice or Sour Mix	

You can also add a dash of Grenadine.

Half & Half Martini

3 parts	Gin	Shake with ice; serve straight
3 parts	Vodka	up or on ice. Garnish with a
1 part	Dry Vermouth	Lemon Twist.

Harbor Lights #1

1 part	Galliano	Shake with ice and strain into
1 part	Remy Martin Cognac	a shot glass.

Harbor Lights #2

1 part	Chambord	Shake with ice and strain into
1 part	Puerto Rican Rum	a shot glass.
1 part	Orange Juice	

G

Hard Hat

1¼ oz.	Bacardi Silver Rum	In a shaker with ice, combine
1¼ oz.	Fresh Lime Juice	all but the Club Soda. Stir and
1 tsp.	Sugar	strain into a glass with ice. Fill
¼ oz.	Rose's Grenadine	with Club Soda.
	Club Soda	

Harry's Martini

1¾ oz.	Dry Gin	Stir gently with ice; serve
¾ oz.	Sweet Vermouth	straight up or on ice. Garnish
¼ oz.	Pernod	with Mint Sprigs.

Harvey Wallbanger

1/4 oz.	Liquore Galliano	In a tall glass with ice, add
1 oz.	Vodka	Vodka and fill the glass 3/4 full
	Orange Juice	with Orange Juice. Float the
		Galliano on top.

Havana Sidecar

1 1/2 oz.	Puerto Rican Golden Rum	Mix with ice and serve on ice.
3/4 oz.	Lemon Juice	
3/4 oz.	Triple Sec	

Hawaii Five-O

1 1/2 oz.	Finlandia Pineapple Vodka	Shake. Serve in a glass with
1/4 oz.	Blue Curacao	ice. Garnish with a Pineapple
		Spear, Cherry, and umbrella.

Hawaiian

1 part	Cork Dry Gin	Shake with ice. Serve on ice.
1 part	Orange Juice	
Dash	Orange Curacao	

H

Hawaiian Highball

3 oz.	Irish Whiskey	Combine the Whiskey with the
2 tsp.	Pineapple Juice	Juices. Add ice and fill with
1 tsp.	Lemon Juice	Soda. Stir gently.
	Club Soda	

Hawaiian Night

1 oz.	Light Rum	Pour Rum into a tall glass half
1/4 oz.	Cherry-Flavored Brandy	filled with ice. Fill with
	Pineapple Juice	Pineapple Juice and float
		Cherry-Flavored Brandy on top.

Hawaiian Pipeline

1½ oz.	Pineapple Vodka, chilled	Shake. Serve over ice in a tall glass.
2 oz.	Orange Juice	
1 oz.	Cranberry Juice	

Hawaiian Punch

¼ oz.	Southern Comfort	Shake with ice and strain into
¼ oz.	Sloe Gin	a shot glass.
¼ oz.	Cointreau	
¼ oz.	Orange Juice	

Hazelnut Martini

2 oz.	Absolut Vodka	Stir with ice and serve straight up.
splash	Frangelico	Garnish with an Orange Slice.

Invented at the Martini Bar at the Chianti Restaurant in Houston, Texas.

Heartthrob

1¼ oz.	Finlandia Cranberry Vodka, chilled	Shake. Serve in a tall glass with ice.
¼ oz.	Peach Schnapps	
¼ oz.	Grapefruit Juice	

H

Heat Wave

1 oz.	Myers's Dark Rum	Add Rum and Schnapps to a
½ oz.	Peach Schnapps	highball glass with ice. Fill
splash	Grenadine	with Pineapple Juice. Add a
	Pineapple Juice	splash of Grenadine.

The Hennessy Martini

1½ oz.	Hennessy V.S. Cognac	Shake with ice and strain or
dash	Lemon Juice	serve straight up.

Invented at Harry Denton's in San Francisco, California.

Highball

| 1½ oz. | American Whiskey | Combine and stir. |
| 3 oz. | Ginger Ale | |

Hollywood #1

1 oz.	Vodka	Combine ingredients in a tall
1 oz.	Black Raspberry Liqueur	glass with ice. Fill with
	Cranberry Juice	Cranberry Juice.

Hollywood #2

1 part	Stolichnaya Vodka	Shake with ice and strain into
1 part	Chambord	a shot glass.
1 part	Pineapple Juice	

Home Run

1 oz.	Bourbon	Shake with ice and serve over ice.
1 oz.	Light Rum	
1 oz.	Brandy	
2 tsp.	Lemon Juice	

Take a swig at this one.

H

The Honeymooner

2 parts	Bunratty Meade	Shake ingredients and pour
1 part	Amaretto	over ice. Garnish with
1 part	Cream	Cinnamon.

Honolulu Hurricane Martini

4 parts	Dry Gin	Shake with ice and strain.
1 part	French Vermouth	
1 part	Italian Vermouth	
1 tsp.	Pineapple Juice	

Horny Bull

1¼ oz.	Tequila	Add Tequila to a chilled
	Orange Juice	highball glass filled with ice.
		Fill with Orange Juice.

Hot Bomb

⬜	³/₄ oz.	Two Fingers Tequila	Shake with ice; strain into a
	¹/₄ oz.	Cinnamon Schnapps	shot glass.

Hot Irish

🍺	1¹/₂ oz.	Jameson Irish Whiskey	Stud the Lemon Slice with
	2 tsp.	Sugar (brown if	Cloves. Put Lemon, Sugar, and
		available)	Cinnamon into a warm glass.
	¹/₂ slice	Fresh Lemon	Add Boiling Water and Irish
	4	Cloves	Whiskey. Stir well and serve.
	pinch	Cinnamon	
		Boiling Water	

Hot Irish and Port

🍺	1¹/₂ oz.	Bushmills Irish Whiskey	Pour ingredients into a
	2 oz.	Red or Tawny Port	saucepan. Heat to boiling
	2 oz.	Water	point but do not boil. Pour into
			a mug. Add a Cinnamon Stick
			and an Orange Slice.

Hot Lips

⬜	1¹/₂ oz.	Finlandia Cranberry Vodka	Shake with ice and strain into
	¹/₄ oz.	Goldschlager	a shot glass.

Not to kiss and tell.

Hot Mist

🍺	2 parts	Irish Mist	Combine in the glass and
	1 part	Boiling Water	garnish with a slice of Lemon
			and some Cloves.

Hot Pants

⬜	¹/₄ oz.	Absolut Peppar Vodka	Combine over ice.
	1 oz.	Peach Schnapps	

Bottoms up.

Hot Toddy

	1½ oz.	Seagram's V.O. Whisky	Pour Seagram's into Hot Water.
	1 lump	Sugar	Add Sugar and Cloves. Stir.
	2	Cloves	
		Hot Water	

Hula-Hoop

	1½ oz.	Vodka	Combine over ice.
	2 oz.	Pineapple Juice	
	½ oz.	Orange Juice	

Hurricane

	1¼ oz.	Myers's Dark Rum	Combine over ice.
	4 oz.	Pineapple Juice	
	2 oz.	Orange Juice	
	splash	Grenadine	

Ice Breaker

	½ oz.	Myers's Original Dark Rum	Shake with ice and serve in a
	¼ oz.	Crème de Noya	tall glass.
	¼ oz.	Cognac	
	¼ oz.	Gin	
	2 oz.	Lemon Juice	
	1 oz.	Orange Juice	

Iceberg Martini

	2 oz.	Beefeater Gin	Stir with ice and strain.
	splash	White Crème de Menthe	Garnish with Mint.

Created at the Martini Bar at the Chianti Restaurant in Houston, Texas.

Iguana

	½ oz.	Tequila	Combine over ice.
	¾ oz.	Vodka	
	¾ oz.	Coffee Liqueur	

Imperial

1¹/₄ oz.	Bourbon	Mix together all the ingredients
splash	Club Soda	except the Club Soda in
1¹/₄ oz.	Orange Liqueur	a shaker. Strain the mixture into a
splash	Simple Syrup	rocks glass over ice. Top off the
1 scoop	Crushed Ice	glass with Club Soda.

Innisfree Fizz

2 oz.	Irish Whiskey	Mix all ingredients except Club
1 oz.	Lemon Juice	Soda with cracked ice in a
1 oz.	Orange Curacao	shaker or blender. Strain into a
¹/₂ oz.	Sugar Syrup	chilled wine goblet and fill
	Club Soda	with Club Soda.

Inoculation Shot

1 oz.	Jose Cuervo Gold Tequila	Shake with ice and strain into
¹/₄ oz.	Blue Curacao	a shot glass.

Inspiration

¹/₂ oz.	Cork Dry Gin	Combine ingredients with ice.
¹/₂ oz.	Dry Vermouth	
¹/₂ oz.	Calvados	
¹/₂ oz.	Grand Marnier	

I International Coffee

¹/₂ oz.	Devonshire Irish Cream	Pour Devonshire and
¹/₂ oz.	Chambord	Chambord into a cup of hot
5 oz.	Coffee	Coffee.

One of many international coffees.

Irish Angel

1 oz.	Bushmills Irish Whiskey	Mix with ice in a cocktail
¹/₄ oz.	Crème de Cacao	shaker or blender. Strain into a
¹/₄ oz.	White Crème de Menthe	cocktail glass.
¹/₂ oz.	Cream	

Irish Apple

2 parts	Carolans Irish Cream	Stir well with ice.
1 part	Laird's Apple Jack	

Irish Buck

1½ oz.	Irish Whiskey	Pour Irish Whiskey into chilled highball glass with cracked ice. Twist a Lemon Peel over the drink and drop it in. Fill with Ginger Ale.
	Ginger Ale	

Irish Canadian

½ oz.	Irish Mist	In a mixing glass half-filled with ice, combine both of the ingredients. Stir well. Strain into a cocktail glass.
1½ oz.	Canadian Whisky	

Irish-Canadian Sangaree

2 tsp.	Irish Mist	Combine and stir well. Add ice and dust with Nutmeg.
1 ¼ oz.	Canadian Whiskey	
1 tsp.	Orange Juice	
1 tsp.	Lemon Juice	

Irish Candy

3 oz.	Baileys Irish Cream	Build over ice. Stir and serve.
1¼ oz.	Chocolate Raspberry Liqueur	
1 oz.	White Crème de Cacao	

Candy is dandy, but liquor is quicker.

Irish Celebration

1¼ oz.	Bushmills Irish Whiskey	Shake the first two ingredients well with ice and strain. Top up with Champagne.
¼ oz.	Green Crème de Menthe	
splash	Champagne	

Irish Charlie

| 1 part | Irish Cream | Shake with ice and strain into |
| 1 part | White Crème de Menthe | a shot glass. |

You can also layer the Irish Cream over the Crème de Menthe.

Irish Coffee

1¼ oz.	Irish Whiskey	Pour Irish Whiskey in a warm
	Hot Coffee	glass or mug. Fill with Coffee.
	Sugar	Stir in Cream and Sugar to
	Cream	taste.

Irish Collins

2 oz.	Irish Whiskey	Combine the first three
1 tsp.	Powdered Sugar	ingredients in a tall glass
	Juice of a Small Lemon	filled with ice. Fill with Club
	Club Soda	Soda and stir.

A variation on the Tom Collins and Whiskey Collins.

Irish Cooler

1¼ oz.	Irish Whiskey	Pour Whiskey into a highball
6 oz.	Club Soda	glass over ice cubes. Top with
		Soda and stir. Garnish with a
		Lemon Peel Spiral.

Irish Cow

1½ oz.	Irish Whiskey	Pour the Milk into a glass. Add
8 oz.	Hot Milk	the Sugar and Whiskey. Stir well.
1 tsp.	Sugar	

Irish Cowboy

| 1 part | Baileys Irish Cream | Shake or stir over ice. |
| 1 part | Bourbon | |

Irish Cream Stinger

| 3 parts | Carolans Irish Cream | Stir well over ice. |
| 1 part | White Crème de Menthe | |

Irish Delight

| 1¼ oz. | Irish Whiskey | Combine in an ice-filled rocks |
| 1½ oz. | Heavy Cream | glass. Stir. |

Irish Dream

½ oz.	Irish Cream Liqueur	Combine ingredients in a
½ oz.	Hazelnut Liqueur	blender with ice. Blend
½ oz.	Dark Crème de Cacao	thoroughly. Pour into a collins
1 scoop	Vanilla Ice Cream	or parfait glass. Serve with a
		straw.

Irish Eyes

1 oz.	Irish Whiskey	Shake well with crushed ice.
¼ oz.	Green Crème de Menthe	Strain into a chilled cocktail
2 oz.	Heavy Cream	glass. Garnish with Mara-
		schino Cherry.

This will make you smile.

Irish Fix

2 oz.	Irish Whiskey	Fill mixing glass with ice.
½ oz.	Irish Mist	Combine ingredients and stir.
1 oz.	Pineapple Juice	
½ oz.	Lemon Juice	
½ tsp.	Sugar Syrup	

Irish Fizz

2½ oz.	Irish Whiskey	Combine all ingredients except
1½ tsp.	Lemon Juice	the Soda with ice in a shaker
1 tsp.	Triple Sec	and shake. Strain into a collins
½ tsp.	Sugar	glass. Add ice and Club Soda.
	Club Soda	

Irish Flag

	¹/₃ shot	Green Crème de Menthe	Layer this drink in the order
	¹/₃ shot	Irish Cream	listed. Start with Crème de
	¹/₃ shot	Grand Marnier	Menthe on the bottom and
			finish with Grand Marnier on top.

See Chapter 19 for more on layered drinks.

Irish Frog

	³/₄ oz.	Midori	Layer this drink by pouring the
	³/₄ oz.	Baileys Irish Cream,	Midori first and then adding
		chilled	the Irish Cream.

Irish Frost Shooter

	1 shot	Baileys Irish Cream	Shake and strain. Garnish with
	1 splash	Coco Lopez Cream	Cinnamon.
		of Coconut	
	1 splash	Half & Half	

Irish Headlock

	¹/₄ oz.	Brandy	Layer this drink by pouring the
	¹/₄ oz.	Amaretto	Brandy first, then the
	¹/₄ oz.	Irish Whiskey	Amaretto, and so on.
	¹/₄ oz.	Irish Cream	

I

Irish Horseman #1

	1¹/₄ oz.	Bushmills Irish Whiskey	Combine the first three
	¹/₄ oz.	Triple Sec	ingredients in a cordial glass
	¹/₂ oz.	Lime Juice	with crushed ice and stir. Add
	1–2 dashes	Raspberry Liqueur or	one to two dashes of
		Chambord	Raspberry Liqueur on top.

Irish Horseman #2

	³/₄ oz.	Irish Whiskey	Combine Whiskey, Triple Sec,
	¹/₄ oz.	Triple Sec	and Sweet & Sour Mix with
	3 oz.	Sweet & Sour Mix	crushed ice. Shake well. Pour
	8 oz.	Crushed Ice	into a highball glass. Top with
	¹/₄ oz.	Chambord	Chambord.

Irish Kilt

1 oz.	Irish Whiskey	Mix all ingredients with
1 oz.	Scotch	cracked ice in a shaker or
1 oz.	Lemon Juice	blender and strain into a
1½ oz.	Sugar Syrup or to taste	chilled glass.
3–4 dashes	Orange Bitters	

Irish Kiss

¾ oz.	Irish Whiskey	Combine ingredients in an ice
½ oz.	Peach Schnapps	cube-filled collins glass.
4 oz.	Ginger Ale	Garnish with a Lime Wheel.
2 oz.	Orange Juice	

Irish Knight

2 oz.	Bushmills Irish Whiskey	Combine in a rocks glass with
2 dashes	Noilly Prat Dry Vermouth	ice. Add a twist of Orange Peel.
2 dashes	Benedictine	

Irish Lace

1 shot	Irish Mist	Blend and serve in a margarita
2 splashes	Coco Lopez	glass. Garnish with an Orange
	Cream of Coconut	Flag.
2 splashes	Half & Half	
3 splashes	Pineapple Juice	
2 scoops	Ice	

Irish Magic

1 oz.	Irish Whiskey	Pour all ingredients over ice in
¼ oz.	White Crème de Cacao	a glass. Stir.
5 oz.	Orange Juice	

Irish Mist Alexander

1 oz.	Irish Mist	Shake ingredients with cracked
1 oz.	Light Cream	ice and strain. Sprinkle with
1 oz.	Dark Crème de Cacao	Nutmeg.

I

Irish Mist Kiss

1 part	Irish Mist	Serve in a rocks glass over ice.
dash	Blue Curacao	
splash	Soda	

Irish Mist Soda

| 1 part | Irish Mist | Serve with ice and a wedge of |
| 3 parts | Club Soda | Lime or Lemon in a tall glass. |

Irish Mist Sour

| 2 parts | Irish Mist | Shake well over ice. Serve in a |
| 1 part | Lemon Juice or Sour Mix | tall glass. |

Irish Mocha Cooler

2 oz.	Bushmills Irish Whiskey	Combine first two ingredients
1 oz.	Dark Crème de Cacao	over ice in a 14 oz. glass. Fill
	Iced Coffee	with Iced Coffee. Top with
	Whipped Cream	Whipped Cream.

Irish Night Cap

1½ oz.	Bushmills Irish Whiskey	Pour Milk into the glass. Add
4 oz.	Hot Milk	Sugar and Irish Whiskey. Stir well.
1 tsp.	Sugar	

I

Irish Penance

| 1 part | Carolans Irish Cream | Shake slowly and serve over ice. |
| 1 part | Cointreau | |

Irish Prince

1¼ oz.	Bushmills Irish Whiskey	Combine in a rocks glass. Add
3 oz.	Tonic Water	ice cubes and stir gently. Drop
		in a Lemon Peel.

Irish Quaalude #1

¹/₂ oz.	Vodka	Shake with ice and strain.
¹/₂ oz.	Irish Cream	
¹/₂ oz.	Coffee Liqueur	
¹/₂ oz.	Hazelnut Liqueur	

Irish Quaalude #2

¹/₂ oz.	Baileys Irish Cream	Shake with ice and strain.
¹/₂ oz.	Absolut Vodka	
¹/₂ oz.	Frangelico	
¹/₂ oz.	White Crème de Cacao	

Irish Rainbow

1¹/₂ oz.	Irish Whiskey	Mix all ingredients with
3–4 dashes	Pernod	cracked ice in a shaker or
3–4 dashes	Orange Curacao	blender. Pour into a chilled
3–4 dashes	Maraschino Liqueur	rocks glass. Twist an Orange
3–4 dashes	Angostura Bitters	Peel over the drink and drop
		it in.

Irish Raspberry

1 oz.	Devonshire Irish Cream	Blend with ice and serve.
¹/₂ oz.	Chambord	
1 cup	Ice	

Irish Rickey

1¹/₂ oz.	Tullamore Dew	Combine first three ingredients
1 cube	Ice	in a highball glass. Fill with
	Juice of ¹/₂ Lime	Carbonated Water and stir.
	Carbonated Water	Add a Lime Wedge.

Irish Rose Highball

1 jigger	Tullamore Dew	Combine first two ingredients
¹/₃ jigger	Grenadine	in a glass and fill with Club Soda.
	Club Soda	

Irish Russian

1 part	Carolans Irish Cream	Stir well over ice.
1 part	Vodka	

Irish Shillelagh

1½ oz.	Irish Whiskey	Mix all ingredients with
½ oz.	Sloe Gin	cracked ice in a shaker or
½ oz.	Light Rum	blender. Pour into a chilled
1 oz.	Lemon Juice	rocks glass. Garnish with
1 tsp.	Sugar Syrup	Raspberries and a Cherry.
2	Peach Slices, diced	

Irish Sling

1 oz.	Tullamore Dew	Crush Sugar with ice in a
1 oz.	Gin	glass. Add Tullamore Dew and
1 lump	Sugar	Gin. Stir.

Irish Sour

1½ oz.	Irish Whiskey	Shake vigorously with ice until
1 tsp.	Sugar	frothy. Stir into sour glass. Add
	Juice of ½ Lemon	a Maraschino Cherry and an
		Orange Slice.

Irish Spring

1 oz.	Bushmills Irish Whiskey	Combine in a collins glass with
½ oz.	Peach Schnapps	ice and stir well. Garnish with
1 oz.	Orange Juice	an Orange Slice and a Cherry.
1 oz.	Sweet & Sour	

Irish Sting

1½ oz.	Bushmills Irish Whiskey	Shake. Serve straight up or over ice.
¼ oz.	White Crème de Menthe	

Put a bee in your bonnet.

Irish Summer Coffee

1 oz.	Irish Whiskey	Stir first three ingredients with
1/4 oz.	Irish Cream Liqueur	ice and strain. Top with
4 oz.	Cold Coffee	Whipped Cream if desired.
	Whipped Cream	

Irish Surfer

1 1/4 oz.	Irish Mist	Shake Irish Mist, Orange Juice,
3 oz.	Orange Juice	and Sugar. Pour into a glass
	Sugar	and fill it with Club Soda.
	Club Soda	

Irish Whiskey Cooler

1 jigger	Irish Whiskey	Combine in a tall glass with
1 pint	Club Soda	ice. Garnish with Lemon.
1 dash	Angostura Bitters	

Irish Whiskey Sour

1 jigger	Irish Whiskey	Shake ingredients with ice and
1 barspoon	Sugar	strain. Garnish with an Orange
	Juice of 1 Lemon	Slice and a Cherry.

Iron Cross

1 part	Rumple Minze	Layer Brandy over Rumple
1 part	Apricot Brandy	Minze in a shot glass.

I

Isla Grande Iced Tea

1 1/2 oz.	Puerto Rican Dark Rum	Combine the first two
3 oz.	Pineapple Juice	ingredients in a tall glass with
	Unsweetened, Brewed	ice. Fill with Iced Tea.
	Iced Tea	

Island Tea

1¹/₂ oz.	Vodka	Combine with ice and shake.
1 oz.	Grenadine	Strain over ice in a rocks glass
1 tsp.	Lemon Juice	and garnish with a Mint Sprig.

Italian Colada

¹/₄ oz.	Coco Lopez Cream of Coconut	Blend with crushed ice.
1¹/₂ oz.	Puerto Rican White Rum	
¹/₄ oz.	Amaretto	
³/₄ oz.	Sweet Cream	
2 oz.	Pineapple Juice	

Italian Martini

1¹/₂ oz.	Vodka or Gin	Stir with ice. Serve on ice or
dash	Amaretto	strain.

Very similar to a Godmother.

Italian Russian

¹/₂ oz.	Sambuca	Pour over ice cubes in small
1 oz.	Vodka	rocks glass. Stir well. Twist an
		Orange Peel over the glass and
		drop it in.

J.J.'s Shamrock

1 oz.	Irish Whiskey	Mix in a shaker or blender
¹/₂ oz.	White Crème de Cacao	with cracked ice and serve in a
¹/₂ oz.	Green Crème de Menthe	chilled glass.
1 oz.	Milk	

Jack Daniels & Coca-Cola or Jack & Coke

1³/₄ oz.	Jack Daniel's Whiskey	Combine over ice and stir.
3 oz.	Coca-Cola	

Jack Rose

1¹/₂ oz.	Laird's Apple Jack	Shake with ice. Serve with ice
³/₄ oz.	Sour Mix	or strain.
tsp.	Grenadine	

A very special New Jersey drink.

Jackson Martini

1¹/₂ oz.	Absolut Vodka	Stir with ice. Serve with ice or
dash	Dubonnet	strain.
dash	Angostura Bitters	

Jade

1¹/₂ oz.	Puerto Rican White Rum	Shake with ice. Serve over ice.
³/₄ oz.	Lime Juice	
1 barspoon	Sugar	
dash	Triple Sec	
dash	Green Crème de Menthe	

Jager Shake

1 part	Irish Cream	Shake with ice and strain into
1 part	Jagermeister	a cordial glass.
1 part	Root Beer Schnapps	
1 part	Amaretto	
1 part	Cola	

Jalapeñorita

1¹/₄ oz.	Gold Tequila	Rub the rim of the glass with
²/₃ oz.	Grand Marnier	Lime and then dip the rim into
	Juice of ¹/₂ Lime	a saucer of Salt. Fill the glass
¹/₂ tsp.	Tabasco Jalapeño	with ice. Pour first three
	Pepper Sauce	ingredients into an ice-filled
		cocktail shaker or pitcher and
		shake or stir vigorously. Strain
		into the prepared glass. Shake
		in Tabasco and stir. Garnish
		with a Lime Slice.

J

Jamaican Dust

	1 part	Puerto Rican Rum	Shake with ice and strain into
	1 part	Tia Maria	a shot glass.
	1 part	Pineapple Juice	

James Bond Martini #1

	3 parts	Gordon's Gin	Shake ingredients with ice
	1 part	Vodka	until very cold. Pour into a
	1/2 part	Kina Lillet	chilled glass. Then add a large
			thin slice of Lemon Peel.

From the movie Casino Royale.

James Bond Martini #2

	1/2 oz.	Martini & Rossi Extra	Stir with ice and strain.
		Dry Vermouth	Garnish with a Lemon Twist.
	1 1/2 oz.	Smirnoff Vodka	
	1 1/2 oz.	Tanqueray Gin	
	1/2 oz.	Lillet Blanc	

Jamie's Highland Special

	1 part	Green Crème de Menthe	Layer this drink in the order
	1 part	Galliano	listed. Start with Crème de
	1 part	Blackberry Liqueur	Menthe on the bottom and finish
	1 part	Kirschwasser	with Kirschwasser on top.

See Chapter 19 for more info on this type of Pousse-Café drink.

J Jelly Bean #1

	1 part	Anisette	Combine in a rocks glass over ice.
	1 part	Blackberry-Flavored	
		Brandy	

You can also strain this one into a shot glass.

Jelly Bean #2

	1 part	Hiram Walker Blackberry	Shake with ice and strain
		Brandy	into a shot glass.
	1 part	Sambuca Romana	
	1 part	Brandy	

Jellyfish

1 part	Irish Cream	Pour first three ingredients
1 part	White Crème de Cacao	directly into the glass. Pour
1 part	Amaretto	Grenadine in the center of
1 part	Grenadine	the glass.

John Collins

1 oz.	Bourbon or Whiskey	Pour Lemon Juice, Syrup, and
1/2 oz.	Sugar Syrup	Whiskey in a highball glass
	Juice of 1/2 Lime	filled with ice. Squeeze in the
	Club Soda	Juice from 1/2 Lime and save
		the shell. Fill the glass with
		Club Soda. Stir. Decorate with
		the used Lime.

This is Tom's brother.

Jolly Rancher #1

3/4 oz.	Peach Schnapps	Combine in a tall glass with ice.
3/4 oz.	Apple Schnapps	
2 1/2 oz.	Cranberry Juice	

Jolly Rancher #2

3/4 oz.	Midori	Shake with ice and strain into
3/4 oz.	Peach Schnapps	a shot glass.
3/4 oz.	Cranberry Juice	

Journalist Martini

1 1/2 oz.	Dry Gin	Stir with ice. Serve over ice or
1/4 oz.	Sweet Vermouth	strain.
1/4 oz.	Dry Vermouth	
1 dash	Angostura bitters	
1 dash	Lemon Juice	
1 dash	Orange Curacao	

J

Juicy Fruit

1 part	Absolut Vodka	Shake with ice and strain into
1 part	Peach Schnapps	a shot glass.
1 part	Midori	
1 part	Pineapple Juice	

Jump Up and Kiss Me

1¼ oz.	Myers's Dark Rum	Shake with ice and serve over ice.
4 oz.	Pineapple Juice	
½ oz.	Rose's Lime Juice	
dash	Angostura	

Kahlua & Cream

2 oz.	Kahlua	Combine in a highball glass
1 oz.	Cream/Milk	and stir.

The Kahlua Colada

1 oz.	Coco Lopez Cream	Blend with ice and serve
	of Coconut	in a margarita glass.
2 oz.	Pineapple Juice	
1 oz.	Kahlua	
½ oz.	Rum	
1 cup	Ice	

Kahlua Hummer

1 oz.	Kahlua	Blend with ice.
1 oz.	Light Rum	
2 scoops	Vanilla or Chocolate	
	Ice Cream	

Kahlua Iced Cappuccino

1½ oz.	Kahlua	Pour Kahlua and Irish Cream
1 oz.	Carolans Irish	into Coffee and sprinkle with
	Cream Liqueur	Cinnamon.
4 oz.	Cold Coffee	
dash	Cinnamon	

Kahlua Sunset

1 oz.	Kahlua	Combine in a tall glass with ice.
2¹/₂ oz.	Cranberry Juice	
3 oz.	Pineapple Juice	

Kamikazi

1 oz.	Vodka	Shake with ice and strain into
¹/₂ oz.	Cointreau	a shot glass.
¹/₄ oz.	Rose's Lime Juice	

Kandy Kane

1 part	Rumple Minze	Layer Crème de Noya over
1 part	Hiram Walker	Rumple Minze.
	Crème de Noya	

No, you will not find this under "Candy Cane."

Kaytusha Rocket

1 oz.	Vodka	Combine with ice, shake,
¹/₂ oz.	Coffee Liqueur	strain, and serve straight up.
1 dash	Cream	
1 oz.	Pineapple Juice	

Kentucky Cocktail

1 part	Bourbon	Shake with ice and serve over
1 part	Pineapple Juice	ice or strain.

Kentucky Colonel

1¹/₂ oz.	Bourbon	Shake with ice. Strain into
¹/₂ oz.	Benedictine	chilled cocktail glass. Add a
		Lemon Twist.

K

Kentucky Martini

1¹/₂ oz.	Maker's Mark Bourbon	Stir with ice; strain.
¹/₂ oz.	Amaretto	
2 oz.	Orange Slice Soda	

Invented at the Martini Bar at the Chianti Restaurant in Houston, Texas. A Kentucky Martini from a bar in Texas — only in America.

Kerry Cooler

2 oz.	Irish Whiskey	Combine (except the Soda)
1¹/₂ oz.	Sherry	with ice and shake well. Strain
1¹/₄ tbsp.	Crème de Almond	into a glass with ice and add
1¹/₄ tbsp.	Lemon Juice	Soda. Top with a Lemon Slice.
	Club Soda	

Killer Kool-Aid

1 part	Chambord	Combine in a tall glass over ice.
1 part	Vodka	
1 part	Gin	
1 part	Rum	
2 oz.	Cranberry Juice	
1 oz.	Sour Mix	

King Alphonse

1 part	Dark Crème de Cacao	Layer the Cream on top of the
1 part	Cream	Crème de Cacao.

Add a cherry and it's called an Angel Tit.

Kinsale Cooler

1¹/₂ oz.	Irish Whiskey	Mix the first three ingredients
1 oz.	Irish Mist	with cracked ice in a shaker or
1 oz.	Lemon Juice	blender. Pour into a chilled
	Club Soda	collins glass. Fill with equal
	Ginger Ale	parts of Club Soda and Ginger Ale. Stir gently. Twist a Lemon Peel over the drink and drop it in.

K

Kir or Kir Royale

	3 oz.	Champagne	Fill the glass
with Champagne		splash	Crème de Cassis
and add a splash of Crème de			Cassis.

Kiss Me Kate

1 oz.	Saint Brendan's Superior Irish Cream	Shake with ice and strain into a shot glass.
¹/₂ oz.	Crème de Cacao	
¹/₂ oz.	Raspberry Liqueur	

Koala Hug

1¹/₄ oz.	Jameson Irish Whiskey	Shake with ice. Serve in a tall
2 oz.	Lemon Juice	glass with ice cubes. Garnish
1 oz.	Cointreau	with an Orange Slice and
dash	Pernod	straws.

Kool-Aid #1

1 oz.	Vodka	Combine ingredients over ice
1 oz.	Melon Liqueur	in a rocks glass.
2 oz.	Cranberry Juice	

Kool-Aid #2

1 oz.	Absolut	Shake with ice and strain into
¹/₄ oz.	Midori	a shot glass.
¹/₄ oz.	Di Saronno Amaretto	
¹/₄ oz.	Cranberry Juice	

Krazy Kangaroo

K

1¹/₄ oz.	Jameson Irish Whiskey	Pour into a mixing glass with
dash	Pernod	ice. Stir and strain into a glass
2 oz.	Orange Juice	or serve over ice. Decorate
		with Orange Rind.

The Irish created civilization and Australia.

Kretchma

1 oz.	Vodka	Mix all ingredients with
1 oz.	Crème de Cacao	cracked ice in a shaker or
½ oz.	Lemon Juice	blender. Strain into a chilled
½ tsp.	Grenadine	glass.

Kurant Affair

1¼ oz.	Absolut Kurant Vodka	Pour Kurant over ice in a tall
splash	Club Soda	glass. Fill most of the way with
	Cranberry Juice	Cranberry Juice. Top with a
		splash of Soda. Garnish with a
		Lime Wedge.

One of the hot new drinks of the 90s.

Kurant & 7-Up

1¼ oz.	Absolut Kurant Vodka	Pour Kurant over ice in a tall
	7-Up	glass. Fill with 7-Up. Garnish
		with a Lemon Slice and a Lime
		Slice.

Kurant Bon Bon

1 oz.	Absolut Kurant Vodka	Combine Kurant and Godiva in
½ oz.	Godiva Liqueur	a brandy snifter.

Kurant Cosmopolitan

1¼ oz.	Absolut Kurant Vodka, chilled	Pour chilled Kurant into a glass. Add a splash of
splash	Cranberry Juice	Cranberry Juice and a splash
splash	Lime Juice	of Lime Juice.

K

Kurant Martini

1¼ oz.	Absolut Kurant Vodka	Pour Kurant and Vermouth
dash	Extra Dry Vermouth	over ice. Shake or stir well.
		Strain and serve in a cocktail
		glass. Garnish with a Twist or
		an Olive.

You can also serve this one with ice.

Li'l Orphan Annie

1 ½ oz.	Irish Whiskey	Combine all ingredients except
1 oz.	Baileys Irish Cream	the Shaved Chocolate in a
2 tbsp.	Chocolate-flavored	shaker and shake vigorously.
	Ovaltine powder	Strain into a glass. Garnish
	(or 1 tbsp.	with Shaved Chocolate.
	Chocolate Syrup)	
1 tsp.	Shaved Chocolate	

La Bomba

1¼ oz.	Jose Cuervo 1800 Tequila	Shake all ingredients except
¾ oz.	Cointreau	Grenadine. Pour into glass and
1½ oz.	Pineapple Juice	add Grenadine. Garnish with a
1½ oz.	Orange Juice	Lime Wheel.
2 dashes	Grenadine	

La Jollarita

1½ oz.	Jose Cuervo	Shake, strain, and serve.
	Traditional Tequila	
½ oz.	Cointreau	
½ oz.	Chambord	

Ladies' Choice Martini

1½ oz.	Absolut Vodka	Stir with ice and strain.
dash	Martini & Rossi	
	Extra Dry Vermouth	
¼ oz.	Kummel	

If you can ever find Kummel . . .

Latin Lover

1 oz.	Herradura Tequila	Combine in a rocks glass
½ oz.	Amaretto	over ice.

You can also serve this one as a shot (without the ice).

L

Lazer Beam

1 part	Bourbon	Shake with ice and strain into
1 part	Rumple Minze	a shot glass.
1 part	Drambuie	

Lemon Chiffon

1½ oz.	Vodka	Shake ingredients with ice and
¼ oz.	Triple Sec	serve over ice. Squeeze and
1 oz.	Sweet & Sour Mix	drop in a fresh Lemon Wedge.

Lemon Drop #1

2 oz.	Absolut Citron Vodka	Shake. Serve in a sugar-coated
1 oz.	Lemon Juice	chilled cocktail glass with a
	Sugar	squeeze of Lemon.

Lemon Drop #2

1½ oz.	Absolut Citron Vodka	Serve in shot glass whose rim
½ oz.	7-Up	is sugar-coated.
½ oz.	Lemon Juice	

Lemon Ice

1¼ oz.	Vodka	Build over ice and fill with
½ oz.	Triple Sec	7-Up in a 10 oz. glass. Garnish
1½ oz.	Sweet & Sour Mix	with a Lemon Slice.
½ oz.	Lemon Juice	
	7-Up	

Lemontini

2 oz.	Stoli Limonnaya Vodka	Line a cocktail glass with
		Cointreau and pour out excess.
½ oz.	Dry Vermouth	Combine Vodka and Vermouth
	Cointreau	over ice in a mixing glass.
		Strain into the cocktail glass.

Leprechaun

1½ oz.	Irish Whiskey	Put Whiskey and Tonic Water in
3 oz.	Tonic Water	a rocks glass. Add Ice Cubes
3–4	Ice Cubes	and stir gently. Drop in a slice
		of Lemon Peel.

L

Leprechaun's Choice

1¼ oz.	Baileys Irish Cream	Combine in a tall glass. Top
¾ oz.	Smirnoff Vodka	with Club Soda.
	Club Soda	

Leprechaun's Libation

½ oz.	Bushmills Irish Whiskey	Fill blender with Cracked Ice.
½ oz.	Green Crème de Menthe	Add Crème de Menthe and
3½ oz.	Cracked Ice	Bushmills Irish Whiskey. Blend. Pour into a goblet or large wine glass.

Courtesy of Beach Grill in Westminster, Colorado.

Liar's Martini

1½ oz.	Dry Gin	Stir gently with ice and strain.
½ oz.	Dry Vermouth	
¼ oz.	Orange Curacao	
¼ oz.	Sweet Vermouth	

Who lies after a couple of chilled martinis?

Licorice Stick

1 part	Stolichnaya Vodka	Shake with ice and strain into
1 part	Hiram Walker Anisette	a shot glass.
1 part	Triple Sec	

Lifesaver

1 part	Malibu Rum	Shake with ice and strain into
1 part	Absolut Vodka	a shot glass.
1 part	Midori	
1 part	7-Up	

Lime Light Martini

6 parts	Finlandia Vodka	Stir gently with ice and strain
1 part	Grapefruit Juice	into a chilled glass. Garnish
1 part	Midori	with thinly sliced Lemon and Lime Twists.

L

Limp Moose

🥃	1 part	Irish Cream	Shake with ice and strain into
	1 part	Canadian Whisky	a shot glass.

Lizard Slime

🥃	1¹/₂ oz.	Jose Cuervo	In a shot glass, float the
		Mistico Tequila	Midori on top of the Tequila.
		Midori	

Long Island Iced Tea

🥛	¹/₂ oz.	Vodka	Shake the first five ingredients
	¹/₂ oz.	Rum	over ice and strain into a
	¹/₂ oz.	Gin	glass. Fill with Cola.
	¹/₂ oz.	Triple Sec	
	¹/₂ oz.	Tequila	
		Cola	

There are many variations.

What twisted genius created Long Island Iced Tea

FABLES & LORE This drink does hail from Long Island, specifically the Oak Beach Inn in Hampton Bays. Spirits writer John Mariani credits bartender Robert "Rosebud" Butt as the inventor, whose original recipe called for an ounce each of clear liquors (vodka, gin, tequila, light rum), a half ounce of triple sec, some lemon juice, and a splash of cola.

This drink comes in many forms and is still popular with young drinkers, though not with those who have to get up early the next day.

L

Loyal Martini

| 2 oz. | Ketel One Vodka | Stir gently with ice; strain. |
| 3 drops | Expensive Balsamic Vinegar | |

From the Bar D'O in New York, New York.

Lucky Lady

3/4 oz.	Bacardi Light Rum	Blend with crushed ice and
1/4 oz.	Hiram Walker Anisette	serve in a margarita glass.
1/4 oz.	Hiram Walker White Crème de Cacao	
3/4 oz.	Cream	

M&M

| 1 part | Kahlua | Layer the Amaretto over |
| 1 part | Di Saronno Amaretto | the Kahlua. |

Macarena

1 oz.	Jose Cuervo Especial Tequila	Shake and pour over ice into a tall glass. Garnish with Pineapple, Orange, and a Cherry.
1/2 oz.	Malibu Coconut Rum	
3 oz.	Sweet & Sour Mix	
1 oz.	Orange Juice	
1 oz.	Pineapple Juice	
splash	Cranberry Juice	

Madras

1 1/4 oz.	Vodka	Pour Vodka over ice in a tall glass. Fill half way with Orange Juice and top it off with Cranberry Juice.
2 oz.	Cranberry Juice	
2 oz.	Orange Juice	

M

Maiden's Prayer

2 parts	Cork Dry Gin
2 parts	Cointreau
1 part	Orange Juice
1 part	Lemon Juice

Shake with ice and strain into a glass.

Main Squeeze

1½ oz.	Hiram Walker Crème de Strawberry Liqueur
2 oz.	Cranberry Juice
2 oz.	Orange Juice
	Club Soda

Combine first three ingredients in a tall glass and top with Club Soda.

Mai Tai

¾ oz.	Bacardi Light Rum
¼ oz.	Bacardi 151 Rum
½ oz.	Orange Curacao
½ oz.	Rose's Lime Juice
¼ oz.	Orgeat Syrup
¼ oz.	Simple Syrup

Stir with ice. Garnish with Mint, Cherry, and Pineapple.

Malibu Bay Breeze

1½ oz.	Malibu
2 oz.	Cranberry Juice
2 oz.	Pineapple Juice

Combine over ice.

Malibu Beach

1½ oz.	Malibu
1 oz.	Smirnoff Vodka
4 oz.	Orange Juice

Combine over ice.

Malibu Cove

½ oz.	Malibu
½ oz.	Myers's Dark Rum
½ oz.	White Rum
2 oz.	Pineapple Juice
2 oz.	Sweet and Sour Mix

Shake all ingredients with ice and serve over ice.

M

Mai Tai: Out of this world

FABLES & LORE

The Mai Tai was Invented by Vic Bergeron in 1944 at his Polynesian-style Oakland bar. He did not want fruit juices detracting from the two ounces of J. Wray Nephew Jamaican rum he poured as the base for his creation. He merely added a half ounce of French orgeat (an almond-flavored syrup), a half ounce of orange curacao, a quarter ounce of rock candy syrup, and the juice of one lime. Customer Carrie Wright of Tahiti was the first to taste the concoction, to which she responded, "Mai tai . . . roe ae!" (This is Tahitian for "Out of this world . . . the best!")

The Mai Tai became famous, and conflicting stories about its origins aggravated Bergeron so much that he elicited a sworn statement from Mrs. Wright in 1970, testifying to his authorship of the cocktail.

Malibu Orange Colada

1$^{1}/_{2}$ oz.	Malibu	Blend with crushed ice.
1 oz.	Triple Sec	
4 oz.	Coco Lopez Cream of Coconut	

Malibu Rain

1 oz.	Vodka	Shake with ice and serve over ice.
1$^{1}/_{2}$ oz.	Pineapple Juice	
$^{1}/_{2}$ oz.	Malibu	
splash	Orange Juice	

M

Malibu Suntan

| 1½ oz. | Malibu | Combine over ice. Add |
| 5 oz. | Iced Tea | a squeeze of Lemon. |

Mandarin Martini

1 part	Godiva Liqueur	Combine with ice and shake
1 part	Absolut Vodka	well. Strain. Garnish with an
splash	Cointreau or Orange Juice	Orange Slice.

Manhattan

2 oz.	American or Canadian Whisky	Stir. Garnish with a Cherry.
splash	Sweet or Dry Vermouth	
dash	Angostura Bitters	

Manhattan

FABLES & LORE

The Manhattan recipe was created around 1874 at the Manhattan Club, New York, for Lady Randolph Churchill, Winston's mother, on the occasion of a banquet in honor of the lawyer and politician Samuel J. Tilden.

Margarita

1 oz.	Tequila	Blend with crushed ice. Serve
1 oz.	Cointreau or Triple Sec	in a salt-rimmed glass.
1 oz.	Sweet & Sour Mix or Lime Juice	Garnish with a Lime Wheel.

M

The Margarita: Behind every great drink is . . .

This classic drink was invented by Margarita Sames in 1948 in Acapulco, Mexico. She created it using her two favorite spirits: Cointreau and tequila. Her husband gave the drink its name by presenting his wife with glassware etched with "Margarita!"

Margarita Madres

1¼ oz.	Jose Cuervo Gold Tequila	Blend with crushed ice.
½ oz.	Cointreau	Garnish with a Lime.
1 ½ oz.	Sweet & Sour Mix	
1 ½ oz.	Orange Juice	
1 ½ oz.	Cranberry Juice	

Margavero

3 oz.	Agavero Liqueur	Shake with ice or blend and strain into a chilled cocktail glass, the rim of which has been moistened with Lime Juice and dipped in Salt. Garnish with a Lime Wedge.
1 oz.	Fresh Lime Juice	
1 dash	Stolichnaya Ohranj	
	Coarse Salt	

Martini

2 oz.	Gin	Shake or stir Gin and Vermouth over ice. Strain and serve in a cocktail glass straight up or over ice. Garnish with a Twist or an Olive.
dash	Extra Dry Vermouth	

M

Martini mythology

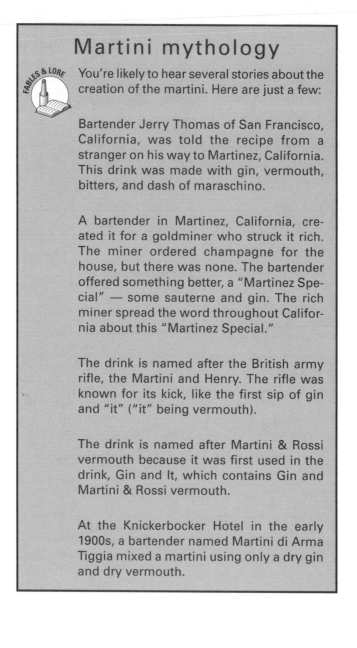

You're likely to hear several stories about the creation of the martini. Here are just a few:

Bartender Jerry Thomas of San Francisco, California, was told the recipe from a stranger on his way to Martinez, California. This drink was made with gin, vermouth, bitters, and dash of maraschino.

A bartender in Martinez, California, created it for a goldminer who struck it rich. The miner ordered champagne for the house, but there was none. The bartender offered something better, a "Martinez Special" — some sauterne and gin. The rich miner spread the word throughout California about this "Martinez Special."

The drink is named after the British army rifle, the Martini and Henry. The rifle was known for its kick, like the first sip of gin and "it" ("it" being vermouth).

The drink is named after Martini & Rossi vermouth because it was first used in the drink, Gin and It, which contains Gin and Martini & Rossi vermouth.

At the Knickerbocker Hotel in the early 1900s, a bartender named Martini di Arma Tiggia mixed a martini using only a dry gin and dry vermouth.

M

Martini Bellini

2 oz.	Vodka or Gin	Shake or stir Vodka or Gin and Schnapps over ice. Strain and serve in a cocktail glass straight up or over ice. Garnish with a Twist.
¹/₄ oz.	Peach Schnapps	

From the Gallery Lounge Sheraton in Seattle, Washington.

Martini Picante

2 oz.	Absolut Peppar Vodka	Stir with ice and strain. Add a Jalapeño and an Olive.
	Jalapeño	
	Olive	

From the Gallery Lounge Sheraton in Seattle, Washington.

Mary Pickford

1¹/₂ oz.	Puerto Rican White Rum	Shake with crushed ice. Serve over ice or strain.
1¹/₂ oz.	Pineapple Juice	
1 splash	Grenadine	

Named after the actress.

Meade Spritzer

2 oz.	Bunratty Meade	Pour Meade into a glass and fill with Club Soda. Garnish with a Lemon Slice.
	Club Soda	

Melon Ball

³/₄ oz.	Midori	Combine in a glass and stir.
1 oz.	Vodka	
4 oz.	Orange Juice	

Metropolitan

1 oz.	Sweet Vermouth	Combine all ingredients except one or two Ice Cubes in a shaker and shake vigorously. Put one or two Ice Cubes in chilled cocktail glass. Strain the drink into the glass.
1¹/₂–2oz.	Brandy	
¹/₂ tsp.	Sugar Syrup	
2 dashes	Angostura Bitters	
4–5	Ice Cubes	

M

Mets Manhattan

1 1/4 oz.	Whiskey	Mix all ingredients with ice
1/4 oz.	Extra Dry Vermouth	and stir well. Strain into a
1/4 oz.	Strawberry Schnapps	chilled cocktail glass.

Mexican Banana

1 1/2 oz.	Sauza Tequila	Pour ingredients into a rocks
3/4 oz.	Crème de Banana	glass filled with ice.

Mexican Berry

1 oz.	Chambord	Shake with ice and strain into
1 oz.	Cuervo Tequila	a shot glass.

Mexican Gold

1 1/2 oz.	Sauza Tequila	In a rocks glass filled with ice,
3/4 oz.	Galliano	pour Sauza Tequila and float
		the Galliano on top.

Mexicarolans

1 part	Carolans Irish Cream	Shake well with ice and serve
1 part	Tequila	over ice.

Mexico Martini

1 1/2 oz.	Gran Centenario Plata Tequila	Shake and strain into an iced glass.
1 tbsp.	Extra Dry Vermouth	
2–3 drops	Vanilla Extract	

Mexico Rose

1/2 oz.	Sauza Tequila	Combine in a rocks glass filled
1 oz.	Lime Juice	with ice.
1/2 oz.	Grenadine (or Crème de Cassis)	

M

Miami Shades

1 oz.	Stoli Ohranj Vodka	Combine over ice.
1/4 oz.	Peach Schnapps	
2 oz.	Grapefruit Juice	

Miami Special

1 oz.	Bacardi Light Rum	Blend with ice.
1/4 oz.	Hiram Walker White Crème de Menthe	
3/4 oz.	Lemon or Rose's Lime Juice	

Mickey Finn Martini

1 1/2 oz.	Absolut Vodka	Stir with ice and strain.
dash	Martini & Rossi Extra Dry Vermouth	Garnish with Mint.
splash	Hiram Walker White Crème de Menthe	

Midnight Martini

1 1/2 oz.	Vodka	Stir with ice and strain.
1/2 oz.	Chambord	Garnish with a Lemon Twist.

From the Gallery Lounge Sheraton in Seattle, Washington.

Midnight Orchid

1 1/2 oz.	Finlandia Cranberry Vodka, chilled	Shake. Serve over crushed ice or blend with ice.
1/4 oz.	Chambord	
2 oz.	Pineapple Juice	
1/2 oz.	Half & Half	

Midnight Sun Martini

5 parts	Finlandia Cranberry Vodka	Stir with ice and strain.
1 part	Classic Finlandia Vodka	
1 part	Kahlua	

M

Midori Cheap Shades

³/₄ oz.	Midori	Shake with ice and serve over
³/₄ oz.	Peach Schnapps	ice in a tall glass.
3 oz.	Orange Juice	
3 oz.	Pineapple Juice	
1¹/₂ oz.	Margarita Mix	

Midori Green Iguana Margarita

¹/₂ oz.	Midori	Blend and pour into a salt-
1 oz.	Tequila	rimmed glass.
2 oz.	Sweet & Sour Mix	

Midori Pearl Diver

1¹/₄ oz.	Midori	Combine over ice in a tall
¹/₄ oz.	Hiram Walker CocoRhum	glass.
2 oz.	Pineapple Juice	

Midori Skinny Dipper

2 oz.	Midori	Combine over ice in a tall
3 oz.	Cranberry Juice	glass.

Midori Sun of a Beach

1 oz.	Midori	Combine over ice in a tall
1 oz.	Beefeater Gin	glass.
6 oz.	Orange Juice	

Milk & Honey

1 part	Irish Mist	Combine in a rocks glass on ice.
1 part	Carolans Irish Cream	

Mimosa

3 oz.	Champagne	Combine in a champagne flute
2 oz.	Orange Juice	and stir.

A great brunch drink.

The Mimosa: A French creation

The Mimosa was created around 1925 at the Ritz Hotel Bar in Paris, France. It took its name from the mimosa flowering plant, whose color it resembles.

Mind Eraser

1 part	Vodka	Shake with ice and strain into
1 part	Kahlua	a shot glass.
1 part	Club Soda	

Mingling of the Clans

1¼ oz.	Bushmills Irish Whiskey	Combine in a mixing glass
½ oz.	Scotch Whisky	with ice. Strain into a cocktail
2 tsp.	Lemon Juice	glass.
3 dashes	Orange Bitters	

Mint Cooler

1 oz.	Bombay Gin	In a tall glass with ice,
¼ oz.	Peppermint Schnapps	combine the first two
	Club Soda	ingredients. Fill the glass
		with Club Soda.

Mint Julep

2 oz.	Makers Mark Bourbon	In a silver cup, mash four Mint
¼ oz.	Sugar Syrup	Leaves with Sugar Syrup. Fill
5	Mint Leaves	the cup with crushed ice. Add
		Bourbon and garnish with
		a Mint Leaf.

Don't forget that it's served in a silver cup.

M

Mint Martini

1 part	Godiva Liqueur	Combine with ice and shake
1 part	Absolut Vodka	well. Serve straight up. Garnish
splash	White Crème de Menthe	with a Mint Leaf.

Mintini or Gin Stinger

2 parts	Bombay Gin	Stir gently with ice and strain.
1 part	White Crème de Menthe	

Mist Old Fashioned

1¼ oz.	Irish Mist	Muddle the Orange, Cherry
	Orange Slice	Bitters, and Sugar. Add Irish
	Cherry Bitters	Mist. Top with Club Soda or
	Sugar	Water.
	Club Soda or Water	

Mister Murphy

1 part	Irish Mist	Combine in a rocks glass over
1 part	White Rum	ice with a dash of Angostura
1 part	Orange Juice	Bitters.
dash	Angostura Bitters	

Mistic Beach

1¼ oz.	Jose Cuervo Mistico	Combine over ice in a tall
¾ oz.	Cointreau	glass. Stir. Garnish with a
3 oz.	Cranberry Juice	Lemon Wedge.

Mistic Chocklic

¾ oz.	Jose Cuervo Mistico	Shake and strain into a rocks
¾ oz.	Kahlua Coffee Liqueur	glass with ice.
1 oz.	Orange Juice	

Mistic Merlin

¾ oz.	Jose Cuervo Mistico	Shake with ice and strain.
¾ oz.	Orange Liqueur	
½ oz.	Lime Juice	

Mistic Shandy

1¹/₄ oz.	Jose Cuervo Mistico	Combine Jose Cuervo Mistico
7 oz.	Draft Beer	and Beer in a glass.

Mistical Mayan

1¹/₄ oz.	Jose Cuervo Mistico	Stir the first two ingredients
3 oz.	Orange Juice	with ice in a tall glass. Fill with
	7-Up	7-Up. Garnish with a Lime Wedge.

Mistico Bandito

1 oz.	Jose Cuervo Mistico	Shake and serve in a shot glass.
1 oz.	Cranberry Juice	
1 oz.	Black Cherry Juice	

Mistico Berry

1 oz.	Jose Cuervo Mistico	Combine first five ingredients
1 oz.	Cabernet Wine	in a tall glass with ice. Fill with
splash	Triple Sec	Sweet & Sour Mix and garnish
splash	Lime Juice	with a Lemon Wedge.
splash	7-Up	
	Sweet & Sour Mix	

Mistico Caliente

2 oz.	Jose Cuervo Mistico	Combine in a shot glass and
splash	Tabasco Sauce	drop into a Draft Beer.

Mistico Caribbean Sea

1¹/₄ oz.	Jose Cuervo Mistico	Combine first three ingredients
³/₄ oz.	Blue Curacao	in a tall glass over ice. Fill with
¹/₂ oz.	Peach Schnapps	Sweet & Sour Mix.
	Sweet & Sour Mix	

Mistico Desert Berry

1¹/₂ oz.	Jose Cuervo Mistico	Stir and strain into a shot glass.
dash	Chambord	

Mistico Lemonade

1 oz.	Jose Cuervo Mistico	Serve in a tall glass over ice.
1 oz.	Orange Curacao	
1 oz.	Club Soda	
1 oz.	Cranberry Juice	
	Juice from $1/2$ Lemon	

Mistico Martini

1 oz.	Jose Cuervo Mistico	Stir with ice and strain into a
1 oz.	Chambord	martini glass.
1 oz.	Sweet & Sour Mix	

Mistico Mirage

$1^{1}/_2$ oz.	Jose Cuervo Mistico	Stir with ice and garnish with
$1^{1}/_2$ oz.	Orange Juice	a Lime Wedge.
$1^{1}/_2$ oz.	Tonic Water	

Mistico Missile

1 oz.	Jose Cuervo Mistico	Shake and strain. Serve in a
$1/2$ oz.	Peach Schnapps	shot glass.
splash	Grapefruit Juice	

Mistico Morning

1 oz.	Jose Cuervo Mistico	Combine first four ingredients.
1 oz.	Pineapple Juice	Float Grenadine on top.
1 oz.	Orange Juice	Garnish with Lime.
splash	Triple Sec	
	Grenadine	

Mistico Mystery

1 oz.	Jose Cuervo Mistico	Shake and strain into a shot glass.
1 oz.	Triple Sec	
1 oz.	Pineapple Juice	

M

Mistico Slide

1/2 oz.	Kahlua	Layer ingredients in order
1/2 oz.	Baileys Irish Cream	listed, starting with Kahlua,
1/2 oz.	Jose Cuervo Mistico	in a shot glass.

Mistico Spike

1 1/2 oz.	Jose Cuervo Mistico	Stir with ice. Garnish with an
3 oz.	Ruby Red Grapefruit Juice	Orange Wedge.
dash	Bitters	

Mistico Vertigo

1 1/4 oz.	Jose Cuervo Mistico	Stir with ice. Garnish with an
2 oz.	Sweet & Sour Mix	Orange Wheel.
1 oz.	Cranberry Juice	
	Juice from 1/2 Lemon	

Misty Mist

1 1/4 oz.	Irish Mist	Serve on shaved ice.

Misty-Eyed Irishman

3/4 oz.	Bushmills Irish Whiskey	Combine first three ingredients
1 oz.	Peppermint Schnapps	in the glass. Fill with Coffee
1 pkg.	Hot Chocolate Mix	and stir well. Top with
	Hot Coffee	Whipped Cream.
	Whipped Cream	

Optional: Sprinkle with Candy Mint Shavings.

Mocha Melt

1 oz.	Jose Cuervo Gold Tequila	Combine ingredients in a glass
5 oz.	Freshly Brewed Strong,	and stir. Top with Whipped Cream.
	Hot Coffee	
1 pkg.	Hot Cocoa Mix	
	(single-serving envelope)	
1/2 oz.	Coffee Brandy	
	Whipped Cream	

M

Mocha Mint

³/₄ oz.	Coffee-Flavored Brandy	Combine ingredients in a glass
³/₄ oz.	White Crème de Menthe	and stir. Strain into a cocktail
³/₄ oz.	White Crème de Cacao	glass.

Mockingbird

1¹/₄ oz.	Tequila	Combine in a shaker and shake
2 tsp.	White Crème de Menthe	vigorously. Strain into a chilled
1 oz.	Fresh Lime Juice	cocktail glass with ice.

Monkey See Monkey Do

1 part	Baileys Irish Cream	Shake with ice and strain.
1 part	Rhum Barbancort	
1 part	Banana Liqueur	
1 part	Orange Juice	

Monsoon

¹/₄ oz.	Vodka	Shake with ice; serve over ice.
¹/₄ oz.	Coffee Liqueur	
¹/₄ oz.	Amaretto	
¹/₄ oz.	Irish Cream	
¹/₄ oz.	Hazelnut Liqueur	

Monster Mash

¹/₂ oz.	Two Fingers Tequila	Shake with ice. Strain into shot
¹/₂ oz.	Du Bouchett Tequila Monster	glass.
¹/₂ oz.	Du Bouchett Blue Curacao	
¹/₄ oz.	Du Bouchett Melon Liqueur	

Monster on the Beach

1¹/₂ oz.	Du Bouchett Tequila Monster	Combine over ice.
2 oz.	Cranberry Juice	
splash	Lime Juice	
splash	Grenadine	

M

Montego Margarita

1½ oz.	Appleton Estate Rum	Blend with ice and serve.
½ oz.	Triple Sec	
1 oz.	Lemon or Lime Juice	
1 scoop	Crushed Ice	

Moonlight Margarita

1½ oz.	Jose Cuervo Gold Tequila	Rub the rim of a margarita
1 oz.	Blue Curacao	glass with Lime Rind and dip
1 oz.	Lime Juice	it into Salt. Blend ingredients
	Salt	and serve in the prepared
		glass. Garnish with a Lime Slice.

Morgan's Madras

1¼ oz.	Captain Morgan Spiced Rum	Combine over ice in a tall glass.
5 oz.	Orange Juice	
splash	Cranberry Juice	

Morgan's Red Rouge

1 oz.	Captain Morgan Spiced Rum	Stir with ice and serve over ice.
½ oz.	Blackberry Brandy	
2 oz.	Pineapple Juice	
½ oz.	Lemon Juice	

Morgan's Spiced Rum Alexander

1 oz.	Captain Morgan Spiced Rum	Shake and strain. Dust with Nutmeg.
½ oz.	Crème de Cacao	
1 oz.	Heavy Cream	

Morgan's Wench

¾ oz.	Captain Morgan Spiced Rum	Shake Rum and Amaretto with ice and strain into a shot glass.
¾ oz.	Amaretto	Float Crème de Cacao on top.
¾ oz.	Dark Crème de Cacao	

M

Moscow Chill

1¹/₂ oz.	Vodka	Pour Vodka over shaved ice in
4 oz.	Dr. Pepper	a champagne glass. Fill with
		Dr. Pepper. Garnish with a Lime
		Wedge.

Moscow Mule

| 1¹/₂ oz. | Smirnoff Vodka | Stir with ice. Garnish with a |
| 4 oz. | Ginger Beer | Lime Wedge. |

Should be served in a bronze cup or mug.

Mountain Melter

1 oz.	Jose Cuervo Gold Tequila	Combine ingredients in a glass
¹/₂ oz.	Triple Sec	and stir. Top with Whipped
5 oz.	Hot Water	Cream and Ground Cinnamon.
1 pkg.	Hot Cocoa Mix	
	(single-serving envelope)	

The Mount Gay Grinder

1¹/₂ oz.	Mount Gay Rum	Combine in a tall glass.
2 oz.	Cranberry Juice	
splash	7-Up	

Ms. Tea

| 1¹/₄ oz. | Irish Mist | Mix with ice; serve over ice. |
| 3 oz. | Iced Tea | |

Mudslide #1

¹/₄ oz.	Coffee Liqueur	Combine first three ingredients
1 oz.	Vodka	in a glass with ice and
¹/₄ oz.	Irish Cream	fill with Cola.
	Cola	

Mudslide #2

| ³/₄ oz. | Coffee Liqueur | Pour over ice in a rocks glass. |
| ³/₄ oz. | Irish Cream | |

Murphy's Dream

1 part	Irish Mist	Shake. Serve straight up or
1 part	Gin	over ice.
1 part	Lemon Juice	
	Sugar	

Myers's Heatwave

³/₄ oz.	Myers's Dark Rum	Pour Rum and Schnapps
¹/₂ oz. Peach Schnapps		over ice. Fill with Pineapple
6 oz.	Pineapple Juice	Juice and add a splash of
1 splash	Grenadine	Grenadine.

Myers's Madras

1¹/₄ oz.	Myers's Dark Rum	Serve in a tall glass over ice.
1¹/₂ oz.	Orange Juice	
1¹/₂ oz.	Cranberry Juice	

Myers's Sharkbite

1¹/₄ oz.	Myers's Dark Rum	Add Rum to a tall glass with
	Orange Juice	ice. Fill with Orange Juice. Add
splash	Grenadine	a splash of Grenadine.

Myers's Strawberry Daiquiri

1¹/₄ oz.	Myers's Dark Rum	Blend with crushed ice.
¹/₂ oz.	Triple Sec	
	Juice of ¹/₂ Lime	
¹/₂ cup	Strawberries	
1 tsp.	Bar Sugar	

Myers's Sunset

1¹/₄ oz.	Myers's Dark Rum	Combine over ice and stir.
4 oz.	Pineapple Juice	
2 oz.	Orange Juice	
2 oz.	Cranberry Juice	
dash	Rose's Grenadine (optional)	

M

Mystical Martini

1 oz.	Encantado Mezcal	Shake over ice and strain into
1/4 oz.	Lillet	a martini glass. Add a long
		Lemon or Orange Twist.

Invented at Stars in San Francisco, California.

Naked Glacier Martini

2 oz.	Classic Finlandia Vodka	Frost the rim of the martini
splash	Peppermint Schnapps	glass with Sugar. Shake
		ingredients with ice and
		strain into the prepared glass.

Naked Martini

2 oz.	Vodka or Gin	Serve over ice.

Nation Cocktail

1 1/2 oz.	Jose Cuervo Gold Tequila	Combine first three ingredients
1 1/2 oz.	Pineapple Juice	over ice. Float Blue Curacao.
1 1/2 oz.	Orange Juice	
1/4 oz.	Blue Curacao	

You can also serve this one without ice.

Negroni

1/2 oz.	Dry Vermouth	Combine in a rocks glass over ice.
1/2 oz.	Bombay Gin	
1/2 oz.	Campari	

Nellie Jane

1 1/4 oz.	Irish Mist	Mix all but the Ginger Ale.
1/4 oz.	Hiram Walker	Float the Ginger Ale on top.
	Peach Schnapps	
3 oz.	Orange Juice	
1 oz.	Ginger Ale	

Neon Tequila Monster

1 oz.	Burnett's Vodka
1 oz.	Tequila
3 oz.	Orange Juice

Combine over ice.

Nervous Breakdown

1½ oz.	Vodka
½ oz.	Chambord
splash	Cranberry Juice
	Soda

Combine the first three ingredients in a tall glass. Fill with Soda.

Neva

1 ½ oz.	Vodka
½ oz.	Tomato Juice
½ oz.	Orange Juice

In a shaker, mix all ingredients. Pour over ice into a stemmed glass.

New Life

1½ oz.	Sauza Tequila
1 lump	Sugar
3 dashes	Angostura Bitters

Muddle Sugar and Bitters in a rocks glass and fill with crushed ice. Add Tequila. Garnish with a Lemon Twist.

1951 Martini

2 oz.	Gordon's Gin
splash	Cointreau
	Anchovy Stuffed Olive

Rinse glass with Cointreau. Add the Gin and Olive.

The return to another classic with a rinse.

Nut House

1½ oz.	Finlandia Cranberry Vodka
¼ oz.	Amaretto

Combine over ice.

Nut 'n' Holli

1 part	Irish Mist	Shake. Serve straight up in a
1 part	Amaretto	shot glass.
1 part	Carolans Irish Cream	
1 part	Frangelico	

Nuts & Berrys

¹/₂ oz.	Vodka	Combine with ice and shake.
¹/₂ oz.	Hazelnut Liqueur	Strain and serve straight up in
¹/₂ oz.	Coffee Liqueur	a rocks glass.
¹/₄ oz.	Cream	

Nutty Irishman

1 part	Irish Cream	Layer Irish Cream over
1 part	Hazelnut Liqueur	Hazelnut Liqueur in a
	(Frangelico)	shot glass.

Nutty Martini

1 part	Godiva Liqueur	Combine with ice; shake well.
1 part	Absolut Vodka	Serve chilled. Garnish with
splash	Frangelico or	three Almonds.
	Amaretto Liqueur	

Nutty Professor

1 part	Irish Cream	Combine over ice.
1 part	Hazelnut Liqueur	
	(Frangelico)	
1 part	Grand Marnier	

You can also serve this one straight up in a shot glass.

O'Casey's Scotch Terrier

1 part	Baileys Irish Cream	Stir well over ice.
1 part	J&B Scotch	

O

O.J. Mist

| 1 part | Irish Mist | Combine in a tall glass over ice. |
| 3 parts | Orange Juice | |

O.J. Morgan

| 1½ oz. | Captain Morgan Spiced Rum | Combine in a tall glass over ice. |
| 5 oz. | Orange Juice | |

Oatmeal Cookie #1

1 part	Baileys Irish Cream	Layer with Schnapps on the
1 part	Goldschlager	bottom, then the Goldschlager,
1 part	Butterscotch Schnapps	and then the Irish Cream.

Oatmeal Cookie #2

³/₄ oz.	Baileys Irish Cream	Shake with ice and serve over ice.
³/₄ oz.	Butterscotch Schnapps	
¹/₂ oz.	Jagermeister	
¹/₄ oz.	Cinnamon Schnapps	

You can also strain this one into a shot glass.

Ohranj Julius

1 oz.	Stoli Ohranj Vodka	Combine in a tall glass with ice.
1 oz.	Cointreau	Garnish with an Orange Slice.
1 oz.	Sour Mix	
1 oz.	Orange Juice	

Ohranj Martini

1½ oz.	Stoli Ohranj Vodka	Shake with ice. Serve straight
splash	Triple Sec	up or over ice. Garnish with
		an Orange Peel.

Oil Slick

| 1 part | Rumple Minze | Shake with ice and strain into |
| 1 part | Bourbon | a shot glass. |

Old Etonian

1 oz.	Cork Dry Gin	Mix with ice; serve over ice.
1 oz.	Lillet	Garnish with a Twist of Orange
2 dashes	Orange Bitters	Peel.
2 dashes	Crème de Noyeaux	

Old Fashioned

1¹/₂ oz.	American or Canadian Whisk(e)y	Muddle the Cherry (without stem), Orange Slice, Sugar, and
¹/₄ tsp.	Superfine Sugar	a splash of Club Soda. Add the
2 dashes	Angostura Bitters	remaining ingredients and
splash	Club Soda	stir.
	Cherry and Orange Slice	

You can also use Scotch, Brandy, or just about any other spirit in this drink.

Opening Cocktail

¹/₂ oz.	Canadian Whisky	Mix all ingredients in a shaker
¹/₂ oz.	Sweet Vermouth	with crushed ice. Strain the
¹/₂ oz.	Grenadine	mixture into a chilled cocktail glass.

Orange Blossom

1 ¹/₄ oz.	Absolut Vodka	Stir with ice in a tall glass.
3 oz.	Orange Juice	
1 tsp.	Superfine Sugar	

Orange Crush

1¹/₄ oz.	Vodka	Shake with ice. Strain or serve
³/₄ oz.	Triple Sec	over ice.
2 oz.	Orange Juice	

Orange Margarita

1¹/₂ oz.	Jose Cuervo Gold Tequila	Blend. Garnish with Strawberries.
¹/₂ oz.	Triple Sec	
3 oz.	Orange Juice	
¹/₂ oz.	Sweet & Sour Mix	

O

Orange Sunset

1 oz.	Bombay Gin	Combine over ice.
1/4 oz.	Banana Liqueur	
1 oz.	Sweetened Lemon Mix	
1 oz.	Orange Juice	

Orangetini

1 1/2 oz.	Absolut Vodka	Stir gently and strain over ice.
dash	Martini & Rossi Extra Dry Vermouth	Garnish with an Orange Peel.
splash	Hiram Walker Triple Sec	

Orgasm #1

1 part	Irish Cream	Shake with ice and strain into
1 part	Amaretto	a shot glass.
1 part	Coffee-Flavored Liqueur (Kahlua)	

Orgasm #2

1 part	Di Saronno Amaretto	Shake with ice and strain into
1 part	Kahlua	a shot glass.
1 part	Baileys	
1 part	Cream	

Oriental Rug

1 part	Irish Cream	Stir with ice and strain into
1 part	Hazelnut Liqueur (Frangelico)	a shot glass.
1 part	Jagermeister	
1 part	Coffee-Flavored Liqueur (Kahlua)	
dash	Cola	

Outrigger

1 oz.	Vodka	Combine with ice in a shaker
1/2 oz.	Peach Schnapps	and shake. Strain over ice into
1 dash	Lime Juice	a rocks glass.
2 oz.	Pineapple Juice	

Oyster Shooter

1 oz.	Vodka	Pour Vodka over the Oyster
1	Raw Oyster	and Sauce in a small rocks
1 tsp.	Cocktail Sauce	glass and stir. Add a squeeze
		of Lemon.

You can also add a dash of horseradish if you dare.

Paddy Cocktail

1½ oz.	Irish Whiskey	Mix all ingredients with
¾ oz.	Sweet Vermouth	cracked ice in a shaker or
3–4 dashes	Angostura Bitters	blender. Serve in a chilled
		glass.

Paddy O'Rocco

1½ oz.	Irish Mist	Mix Irish Mist and Orange
3 oz.	Orange Juice	Juice. Top with a splash of
splash	Amaretto	Amaretto.

Paddy's Wagon

1½ oz.	Irish Whiskey	Combine all ingredients in
1½ oz.	Sweet Vermouth	shaker and shake. Serve
1–2 dashes	Angostura Bitters	straight up or over ice in a
1–2 dashes	Southern Comfort	chilled glass.

Parisian Pousse-Café

2 parts	Orange Curacao	Layer this drink in the order
2 parts	Kirschwasser	listed. Start with Curacao on
1 part	Chartreuse	the bottom and finish with
		Chartreuse on top.

Parknasilla Peg Leg

1½ oz.	Irish Whiskey	Mix Whiskey, Coconut Syrup,
1 oz.	Coconut Syrup	and Fruit Juices in a shaker or
3 oz.	Pineapple Juice	blender with cracked ice and
1 tsp.	Lemon Juice	pour into a chilled highball
	Club Soda	glass along with several ice
		cubes. Fill with Club Soda.
		Stir gently.

Patty's Pride

1¼ oz.	Bushmills Irish Whiskey	Combine in a shot glass.
¼ oz.	Peppermint Schnapps	

You can also serve this one with Club Soda in a highball glass.

Peach Banana Daiquiri

P

1½ oz.	Puerto Rican Light Rum	Blend with crushed ice.
½	Medium Banana, diced	
1 oz.	Fresh Lime Juice	
¼ cup	Sliced Peaches (fresh, frozen, or canned)	

Peach Irish

1 ½ oz.	Irish Whiskey	Blend with crushed ice.
1	Ripe Peach (peeled, pitted, and sliced)	
½ cup	Fresh Lime Juice	
1 oz.	Apricot Brandy	
1 Tbsp.	Superfine Sugar	
dash	Vanilla Extract	

Peach Margarita

1½ oz.	Jose Cuervo Gold Tequila	Blend. Garnish with Peach Slices.
1 oz.	Triple Sec	
1 oz.	Lime Juice	
½ cup	Peaches (canned)	

Peach Melba

½ oz.	Captain Morgan Spiced Rum	Blend with crushed ice. Top with Raspberry Syrup.
¾ oz.	Raspberry Liqueur	
2 oz.	Peach Cocktail Mix	
1 oz.	Heavy Cream	
2	Peach Halves	
	Raspberry Syrup	

Peaches 'n' Cream

3 oz.	Coco Lopez Cream of Coconut	Blend with crushed ice.
2 oz.	Pineapple Juice	
1 oz.	Coffee Liqueur	
1/2 oz.	Rum	

P

Pear Martini

2 parts	Stolichnaya Vodka	Stir gently with ice and strain.
1 part	Perle de Brillet Liqueur	Garnish with a Pear Half.

Pearl Diver

1 1/2 oz.	Midori	Combine in a tall glass over ice.
1/2 oz.	Coconut Rum	
4 oz.	Orange Juice	

Peppar Manhattan

1 1/2 oz.	Absolut Peppar Vodka	Mix Vodka and Sweet Vermouth in a cocktail shaker over ice and stir. Strain into a stemmed glass. Add a Cherry for garnish.
1/2 oz.	Sweet Vermouth	

Peppar Martini

2 oz.	Absolut Peppar Vodka	Stir gently with ice and strain. Garnish with a Jalapeño Stuffed Olive.
dash	Dry Vermouth	

Peppar Salty Dog

1 1/4 oz.	Absolut Peppar Vodka Grapefruit Juice	Salt the rim of a rocks glass. Fill with ice. Pour in Vodka and fill with Grapefruit Juice.

Peppermint Patti #1

³/₄ oz.	Peppermint Schnapps	Combine over ice in a rocks
¹/₂ oz.	Green Crème de Menthe	glass.

Peppermint Patty #2

¹/₂ oz.	Rumple Minze	Shake with ice and strain into
¹/₂ oz.	Kahlua	a shot glass.
¹/₂ oz.	Dark Crème de Cacao	
¹/₂ oz.	Cream	

P

Peppertini

1¹/₂ oz.	Absolut Peppar Vodka	Mix Vodka and Dry Vermouth
¹/₂ oz.	Vermouth	in a cocktail shaker over ice. Stir and pour into rocks glass. Add an Olive for garnish.

Picadilly

2 parts	Cork Dry Gin	Mix with ice. Serve over ice.
1 part	Dry Vermouth	
dash	Pernod	
dash	Grenadine	

Piña Colada

1¹/₄ oz.	Light or Dark Rum	Mix in a shaker and serve over
2 oz.	Unsweetened Pineapple Juice	ice, or blend with crushed ice.
2 oz.	Coco Lopez Cream of Coconut	

Piñata

1¹/₂ oz.	Jose Cuervo Gold Tequila	Combine in a collins glass.
5 oz.	Pineapple Juice	Garnish with fresh Pineapple.

Pineapple Bomb

1 part	Malibu Rum	Shake with ice and strain into
1 part	Bacardi Black	a shot glass.
1 part	Pineapple Juice	

Pineapple Pie

1¼ oz.	Finlandia Pineapple Vodka, chilled	Shake with ice. Strain into a rocks glass and add a dollop
¼ oz.	White Crème de Cacao	of Whipped Cream.
	Whipped Cream	

Pineapple Twist

1½ oz.	Appleton Estate Rum	Shake and pour into a tall
6 oz.	Pineapple Juice	glass over ice.
splash	Lemon Juice	

Pink Cadillac with Hawaiian Plates

1¼ oz.	Jose Cuervo 1800 Tequila	Combine in a rocks glass.
2 oz.	Pineapple Juice	Garnish with a Lime Wedge.
2 oz.	Cranberry Juice	
½ oz.	Sweet & Sour Mix	

Pink Diamond Martini

1 part	Finlandia Cranberry Vodka	Stir gently with ice and strain.
2 parts	Finlandia Pineapple Vodka	Garnish with a perfect Cherry
3 parts	Classic Finlandia Vodka	or Rose Petals floated on top.
1 part	Peach Schnapps	

Pink Gin (a.k.a. Gin & Bitters)

| 1¾ oz. | Gin | Rinse a chilled glass with |
| dash | Angostura Bitters | Bitters. Add Gin. |

Pink Lady

1¼ oz.	Gin	Shake with ice and strain into a
2 tsp.	Grenadine	cocktail glass or serve over ice.
3 oz.	Half & Half	

The ori-gins of Pink Gin

In 1824, Dr. Johan G. B. Siegert created Angostura bitters as a remedy for stomach complaints suffered by the Venezuelan army. He named this concoction after the town on the Orinoco River where he had worked.

The British Navy added this product to its medicine chest but soon discovered that it added a whole new dimension to Plymouth gin, and thus Pink Gin came to be.

Pink Lemonade

1¼ oz.	Vodka	Combine Vodka, Sugar, Sweet &
1 oz.	Cranberry Juice	Sour Mix, and Cranberry Juice in
1¼ oz.	Sweet & Sour Mix	a tall glass. Stir to dissolve Sugar.
½ tsp.	Sugar	Add ice and top with Club Soda.
	Club Soda	Add a squeeze of Lime.

Pink Mustang

1 part	Finlandia Cranberry Vodka	Serve on ice.
1 part	Rumple Minze	

Pink Panther #1

1½ oz.	Sauza Tequila	Blend with crushed ice
½ oz.	Grenadine	and strain into a chilled
2 oz.	Cream or Half & Half	glass.

Pink Panther #2

1¼ oz.	Bacardi Light Rum	Blend with crushed ice and strain.
¾ oz.	Lemon Juice	
¾ oz.	Cream	
½ oz.	Rose's Grenadine	

Pink Squirrel

1 oz.	Crème de Almond	Shake all ingredients over
1 oz.	Crème de Cacao	cracked ice. Strain.
4 oz.	Cream	

Pirate's Punch

1³/₄ oz.	Rhum Barbancort	Shake with ice and serve
¹/₄ oz.	Sweet Vermouth	over ice.
dash	Angostura Bitters	

Planter's Punch

1³/₄ oz.	Rum	Shake or blend all ingredients
2 tsp.	Sugar	except the Dark Rum and pour
2 oz.	Orange Juice	into glass. Top with Dark Rum.
dash	Rose's Grenadine	
splash	Myers's Dark Rum	

Planter's Punch

FABLES & LORE

In 1879, Fred L. Myers founded the Myers's Rum distillery in Jamaica and celebrated by creating what he named a Planter's Punch. This concoction became the house specialty at Kelly's Bar in Sugar Wharf, Jamaica, and its popularity spread soon after.

Poet's Punch

1 oz.	Irish Mist	Heat the Milk, Cinnamon Stick,
1 stick	Cinnamon	and Lemon and Orange Twists
twist	Lemon	to boiling point. Add Vanilla
twist	Orange	and Irish Mist. Strain. Sprinkle
¹/₂ tsp.	Vanilla	with Nutmeg.
¹/₂ cup	Milk	

Port Royal

1¹/₂ oz.	Appleton Estate Rum	Shake with ice and strain into
¹/₂ oz.	Sweet Vermouth	large rocks glass over ice
	Juice of ¹/₄ Orange	cubes. Garnish with Orange or
	Juice of ¹/₄ Lime	Lime Wedge.

Pot o' Gold

1 part	Goldschlager	Combine in a shot glass.
1 part	Baileys Irish Cream	

Pousse-Café #1

1 part	Grenadine	Layer this drink in the order
1 part	Yellow Chartreuse	listed. Start with Grenadine on
1 part	White Crème de Menthe	the bottom and finish with
1 part	Sloe Gin	Brandy on top.
1 part	Green Chartreuse	
1 part	Brandy	

See Chapter 19 for more on layered drinks.

Pousse-Café #2

1 part	Benedictine	Layer this drink by pouring the
1 part	White Crème de Cacao	Benedictine first, then the
1 part	Remy Martin Cognac	Creme de Cacao, and then
		Cognac.

Pousse-Café à la Francaise

1 part	Green Chartreuse	Layer this drink in the order
1 part	Maraschino Liqueur	listed. Start with Green
1 part	Cherry Brandy	Chartreuse on the bottom and
1 part	Kummel	finish with Kummel on top.

Pousse-Café Standish

¹/₂ oz.	Grenadine	Layer this drink in the order
¹/₂ oz.	White Crème de Menthe	listed. Start with Grenadine on
¹/₂ oz.	Galliano	the bottom and finish with
¹/₂ oz.	Kummel	Brandy on top.
¹/₂ oz.	Brandy	

Prairie Fire

1½ oz.	Tequila	Combine in a shot glass.
2 or 3 drops	Tabasco	

Presbyterian

2–3 oz.	Bourbon or American Whiskey	Pour the Bourbon into a chilled highball glass. Add ice cubes.
	Ginger Ale	Top off the glass with equal
	Club Soda	parts of Ginger Ale and Soda.

Presidente

¼ oz.	Dry Vermouth	Mix with ice and serve.
¾ oz.	Sweet Vermouth	
1½ oz.	Puerto Rican White Rum	
1 splash	Grenadine	

Princess Mary

1 part	Cork Dry Gin	Shake with ice and serve in a
1 part	Crème de Cacao	margarita glass.
1 part	Fresh Cream	

Puerto Rican Rum Cappuccino

1½ oz.	Puerto Rican Dark Rum	Combine the Rum and Sugar
1 tsp.	Sugar	in a glass. Add equal parts
	Hot Coffee	Coffee and Milk. Top with
	Steamed Milk	Cream and Cinnamon.
	Ground Cinnamon	
	Whipped Cream	

Pulco

2 oz.	Jose Cuervo 1800 Tequila	Combine over ice.
½ oz.	Cointreau	
1½ oz.	Lime Juice	

Purple Gecko

1¹/₂ oz.	Jose Cuervo Especial Tequila	Shake all ingredients and pour into a large, salt-rimmed margarita glass. Garnish with a Lime Wedge.
¹/₂ oz.	Blue Curacao	
¹/₂ oz.	Bols Red Curacao	
1 oz.	Cranberry Juice	
1 oz.	Sweet & Sour Mix	
¹/₂ oz.	Lime Concentrate	

Purple Haze

1 part	Chambord	Combine in a shot glass.
1 part	Vodka	
1 part	Cranberry Juice or Sour Mix	

Q

Purple Hooter

¹/₂ oz.	Vodka	Shake and strain Vodka, Black Raspberry Liqueur and Cranberry Juice. Top with a splash of Club Soda.
¹/₂ oz.	Black Raspberry Liqueur	
¹/₂ oz.	Cranberry Juice	
splash	Club Soda	

Purple Orchid

1 part	White Crème de Cacao	Combine in a shot glass.
1 part	Blackberry Brandy	
1 part	Cream	

Purple Passion

1¹/₄ oz.	Vodka	Combine ingredients and stir. Chill and add Sugar to taste. Serve in a collins glass.
2 oz.	Grapefruit Juice	
2 oz.	Grape Juice	

Quarter Deck

1 oz.	Puerto Rican Light Rum	Shake with ice.
¹/₂ oz.	Puerto Rican Dark Rum	
¹/₂ oz.	Cream Sherry	
¹/₂ oz.	Lime Juice	

Queen Elizabeth Martini

1¹/₂ oz.	Absolut Vodka	Stir gently with ice and strain.
dash	Martini & Rossi Extra Dry Vermouth	
splash	Benedictine	

R & B

1¹/₄ oz.	Captain Morgan Original Spiced Rum	Pour ingredients over ice.
2 oz.	Orange Juice	
2 oz.	Pineapple Juice	
1 splash	Grenadine	

R.A.C.

1¹/₂ oz.	Cork Dry Gin	Combine ingredients and stir
¹/₄ oz.	Dry Vermouth	with ice. Garnish with a Cherry
dash	Angostura Bitters	and an Orange Slice.
dash	Grenadine	

Racer's Edge

1¹/₂ oz.	Bacardi Light Rum	Pour Rum into a glass half
¹/₄ oz.	Green Crème de Menthe	filled with ice. Fill with
	Grapefruit Juice	Grapefruit Juice and float Crème de Menthe.

Raffles Bar Sling

¹/₄ oz.	Benedictine	Combine Gin, Bitters, Lime
³/₄ oz.	Gin	Juice, and Cherry-Flavored
¹/₄ oz.	Cherry-Flavored Brandy	Brandy with ice in a highball
2 dashes	Bitters	glass. Stir in Ginger Beer. Float
¹/₂ tsp.	Lime Juice	Benedictine on top. Garnish
	Ginger Beer	with Mint.

Q

Rainbow Pousse-Café

1/2 oz.	Dark Crème de Cacao	Layer this drink in the order
1/2 oz.	Crème de Violette	listed. Start with Crème de
1/2 oz.	Yellow Chartreuse	Cacao on the bottom and
1/2 oz.	Maraschino Liqueur	finish with Cognac on top.
1/2 oz.	Benedictine	
1/2 oz.	Green Chartreuse	
1/2 oz.	Cognac	

Ramos Fizz

1 1/2 oz.	Gin	Mix ingredients in the order
1 tbsp.	Powdered Sugar	given. Add crushed ice. Shake
3–4 drops	Orange-Flower Water	for long time, until the mixture
	Juice of 1/2 Lime	acquires body. Strain into a
	Juice of 1/2 Lemon	tall glass.
1	Egg White	
1 1/2 oz.	Cream	
1 squirt	Seltzer	
2 drops	Vanilla Extract (optional)	

R

Raspberry Martini

1 part	Godiva Liqueur	Combine with ice and shake
1 part	Absolut Vodka	well. Serve in a glass whose
splash	Chambord or	rim has been dipped in
	Raspberry Liqueur	powdered sugar.

A very sweet, sweet drink.

Razz-Ma-Tazz

1 1/2 oz.	Vodka	Serve over ice in a tall glass,
1/2 oz.	Chambord	chilled.
1 1/2 oz.	Club Soda	

Real Gold

1 part	Stolichnaya Vodka	Combine in a shot glass.
1 part	Goldschlager	

Red Devil

2 oz.	Irish Whiskey	Combine with ice and shake
1½ oz.	Clam Juice	gently. Strain straight up.
1½ oz.	Tomato Juice	
1 tsp.	Lime Juice	
few drops	Worcestershire Sauce	
	Pinch Pepper	

Red Hot Mama

1¼ oz.	Bacardi Silver Rum	Combine over ice.
4 oz.	Cranberry Juice	
2 oz.	Club Soda	

R

Red Monster

1 part	Du Bouchett Tequila Monster	Combine in a shot glass.
1 part	Orange Juice	
1 part	Tomato Juice	

You can also serve this one over ice in a rocks glass.

Red Snapper

1 oz.	Crown Royal Canadian Whisky	Combine ingredients with ice in a shaker and shake well.
¼ oz.	Amaretto	Strain into a shot glass.
¾ oz.	Cranberry Juice	

You can also serve this drink in a rocks glass with ice.

Ring of Kerry

1½ oz.	Irish Whiskey	Mix all ingredients except
1 oz.	Baileys Irish Cream	Shaved Chocolate with
½ oz.	Kahlua or Crème de Cacao	cracked ice in a shaker or blender. Strain into a chilled
	Shaved Chocolate	glass. Sprinkle with Shaved Chocolate.

Road Kill

1 part	Irish Whiskey	Combine in a shot glass.
1 part	Wild Turkey Bourbon	
1 part	Bacardi 151 Rum	

Rob Roy

2 oz.	Scotch	Stir over ice and strain.
dash	Sweet or Dry Vermouth	

You can also serve it with ice.

Rocket Fuel

1 oz.	Rumple Minze	Combine in a shot glass.
1 oz.	Bacardi 151 Rum	

Root Beer

1 part	Kahlua	Combine in a shot glass.
1 part	Galliano	
1 part	Cola	
1 part	Beer	

R

Rosalind Russell Martini

1¹/₂ oz.	Absolut Vodka	Stir gently with ice and strain.
dash	Aquavit	

Named after Rosalind Russell. You can also serve this drink over ice.

Royal Cape

1³/₄ oz.	Crown Royal	Combine over ice.
1 oz.	Cranberry Juice	
¹/₂ oz.	Lime Juice	

Royal Romance

2 parts	Cork Dry Gin	Stir with ice and serve over ice.
1 part	Grand Marnier	
1 part	Passion Fruit Juice	
dash	Sugar Syrup	

Royal Smile

2 parts	Cork Dry Gin	Shake with ice and strain.
1 part	Calvados	
3 dashes	Sugar Syrup	
3 dashes	Lemon Juice	

You can also serve this one over ice.

Ruby Slippers

| 1 part | Finlandia Cranberry Vodka | Shake and pour over ice. |
| 1 part | Goldschlager | |

Ruddy McDowell

1½ oz.	Irish Whiskey	Combine all ingredients in a
2 oz.	Tomato Juice	shaker and shake vigorously.
1 dash	Tabasco Sauce	Strain into a glass with ice.
6–8	Ice Cubes	
dash	Freshly Ground Pepper	

Rum & Coke

| 1½ oz. | Rum | Stir ingredients with ice. |
| 3 oz. | Cola | |

Rum Yum

1 oz.	Baileys Irish Cream	Blend with ice and serve.
1 oz.	Malibu Rum	
1 oz.	Cream or Milk	

This drink also looks nice in a margarita glass.

Rusty Nail (a.k.a. Nail Drive)

| 1 oz. | Scotch | Combine in a rocks glass, add |
| 1 oz. | Drambuie | ice, and stir. |

S.O.S.

| 1 part | Stoli Ohranj Vodka | Combine over ice. |
| 1 part | Sambuca | |

Sakitini

1¹/₂ oz.	Absolut Vodka	Gently stir with ice and strain.
dash	Sake	

Salt and Peppar

1¹/₄ oz.	Absolut Peppar Vodka, chilled	Pour Vodka into a salt-rimmed cocktail glass. Garnish with a Cucumber Spear.

Salt Lick

1¹/₄ oz.	Vodka	Pour ingredients over ice in a salt-rimmed wine glass.
2 oz.	Bitter Lemon Soda	
2 oz.	Grapefruit Juice	

Salty Dog

1¹/₂ oz.	Gin or Vodka	Mix with ice and pour into a salt-rimmed glass.
3 oz.	Grapefruit Juice	

S

San Francisco

1 part	Cork Dry Gin	Mix ingredients with ice. Garnish with a Cherry.
1 part	Dry Vermouth	
1 part	Sweet Vermouth	
dash	Orange Bitters	
dash	Angostura	

San Juan Irishman

1 part	Baileys Irish Cream	Shake with ice and serve over ice.
1 part	Puerto Rican Rum	

Santa Fe Maggie

1¹/₄ oz.	Jose Cuervo Gold Tequila	Combine ingredients over ice and garnish with a Lime Wedge.
¹/₂ oz.	Triple Sec	
2 oz.	Sweet & Sour Mix	
2 oz.	Cranberry Juice	

Savoy Hotel

	¹/₂ oz.	White Crème de Cacao	Layer this drink in the order
	¹/₂ oz.	Benedictine	listed. Start with Crème de
	¹/₂ oz.	Brandy	Cacao on the bottom and
			finish with Brandy on top.

Sazerac Cocktail

	2 oz.	Bourbon	Shake ingredients with ice.
	1 tsp.	Ricard/Pernod	Garnish with a Lemon Twist.
	¹/₂ tsp.	Superfine Sugar	
	2 dashes	Angostura Bitters	
	1 tsp.	Water	

Scarlett O'Hara

	1¹/₂ oz.	Southern Comfort	Combine with ice and stir.
	3 oz.	Cranberry Juice	

Gone with the Cranberry Juice.

Schnappy Shillelagh

	2 parts	Carolans Irish Cream	Stir well over ice.
	1 part	Peppermint Schnapps	

Scorpion

	¹/₂ part	Vodka	Combine in a shot glass.
	¹/₂ part	Blackberry Brandy	
	1 part	Rose's Grenadine	

Scorpion's Sting

	1¹/₄ oz.	Absolut Peppar Vodka	Combine in a glass over ice.
	¹/₄ oz.	White Crème de Menthe	

Scotch 'n' Soda

	1¹/₂ oz.	Scotch	Stir with ice.
	3 oz.	Club Soda	

Scotch 'n' Water

1¹/₂ oz.	Scotch	Stir with ice.
3 oz.	Water	

Scotch Irish

1 part	Baileys Irish Cream	Shake or stir over ice.
1 part	J&B Scotch	

Scotch Smoothie

1 oz.	Coco Lopez Cream of Coconut	Blend with crushed ice.
1¹/₄ oz.	Scotch	
¹/₂ oz.	Baileys Irish Cream	
¹/₂ oz.	Almond Liqueur	
2 scoops	Vanilla Ice Cream	

Scotch Sour

1¹/₄ oz.	Scotch	Stir ingredients in a mixing
1 oz.	Lemon Juice	glass and pour into a rocks
1 tsp.	Sugar	glass with ice. Garnish with a Cherry and an Orange Slice.

You can also shake this drink with cracked ice.

Scotch Swizzle

1³/₄ oz.	Chivas Regal Scotch	Combine first three ingredients
¹/₄ oz.	Lime Juice	in a glass and fill with Club Soda.
dash	Angostura Bitters	
	Club Soda	

Scotty Dog

1¹/₄ oz.	Scotch	Shake with ice and strain into
1¹/₂ oz.	Lime Juice	a glass. Garnish with a Lime Slice.

Screaming Orgasm

1 part	Irish Cream	Combine in a shot glass.
1 part	Kahlua	
1 part	Vodka	
1 part	Amaretto	

Screwdriver

1¼ oz.	Vodka	Add Vodka to a tall glass with
4 oz.	Orange Juice	ice and fill with Orange Juice.

Seabreeze

1¼ oz.	Vodka	Pour Vodka over ice. Fill half way
	Cranberry Juice	with Grapefruit Juice and top it off
	Grapefruit Juice	with Cranberry Juice.

S

Sea Dipper

1½ oz.	Puerto Rican Rum	Shake with ice and serve
1 oz.	Pineapple Juice	over ice.
¼ oz.	Rose's Lime Juice	
1 tsp.	Powdered Sugar	

Secret Place

1½ oz.	Puerto Rican Dark Rum	Stir with crushed ice and serve.
½ oz.	Cherry Brandy	
2 tsp.	Dark Crème de Cacao	
4 oz.	Cold Coffee	

See-Thru

1¼ oz.	Gin	Pour over lots of ice.

Serpent's Smile

³/₄ oz.	Irish Whiskey	Combine all ingredients except
1¹/₂ oz.	Sweet Vermouth	two to three Ice Cubes and the
³/₄ oz.	Lemon Juice	Lemon Peel in a shaker and
1 tbsp.	Kummel	shake vigorously. Place remaining
2 dashes	Angostura Bitters	Ice Cubes in a glass and strain
5–7	Ice Cubes	drink into the glass. Twist the
1 strip	Lemon Peel	Lemon Peel over the drink to
		release oil and drop it in.

Serpent's Tooth

1 oz.	Irish Whiskey	Stir well and strain into a
2 oz.	Sweet Vermouth	small wine glass.
¹/₂ oz.	Kummel	
1 oz.	Lemon Juice	
dash	Angostura Bitters	

S

7 & 7

1¹/₂ oz.	Seagram's 7 Blended Whiskey	Combine over ice.
3 oz.	7-Up	

7 Seas

1¹/₂ oz.	Seagram's 7 Blended Whiskey	Combine over ice.
¹/₂ oz.	Melon Liqueur	
¹/₂ oz.	Pineapple Juice	

Sex on the Beach #1

³/₄ oz.	Chambord	Combine in a mixing glass.
³/₄ oz.	Midori	Shake or stir. Pour in a shot
2 oz.	Pineapple Juice	glass.
splash	Cranberry Juice	

You can also serve this one over ice in a rocks glass.

Sex on the Beach #2

¹/₄ oz.	Chambord	Combine in a shaker. Shake
¹/₄ oz.	Midori	or stir. Serve straight up
1 oz.	Vodka	or over ice.
1 oz.	Pineapple Juice	

Shady Lady

1 oz.	Two Fingers Tequila	Combine all ingredients in a
1 oz.	Melon Liqueur	shaker and shake. Serve over ice.
3 oz.	Grapefruit Juice	

Shamrock Cocktail #1

1¹/₂ oz.	Irish Whiskey	Stir well with cracked ice and
¹/₂ oz.	French Vermouth	strain or serve over ice.
¹/₄ oz.	Green Crème de Menthe	Garnish with an Olive.

Shamrock Cocktail #2

1¹/₂ oz.	Irish Whiskey	Mix all ingredients in a
³/₄ oz.	Green Crème de Menthe	blender at high speed until
4 oz.	Vanilla Ice Cream	smooth. Pour into a chilled
		wine goblet.

Shetland Pony

1¹/₂ oz.	Scotch	Mix all ingredients with
³/₄ oz.	Irish Mist	cracked ice in a mixing glass
dash	Orange Bitters (optional)	and strain into a chilled
		cocktail glass.

You can also serve this drink over ice.

Shore Breeze

1¹/₂ oz.	Puerto Rican Light Rum	Shake with ice and serve in a
3 oz.	Pineapple Juice	rocks glass.
2 oz.	Cranberry Juice	
2 dashes	Angostura	

Siberian Sunrise

1½ oz.	Vodka	Mix all ingredients with
4 oz.	Grapefruit Juice	cracked ice in a shaker
½ oz.	Triple Sec	or blender.

Sicilian Kiss

| 1 oz. | Southern Comfort | Shake with ice and strain into |
| 1 oz. | Di Saronno Amaretto | a shot glass. |

Sidecar

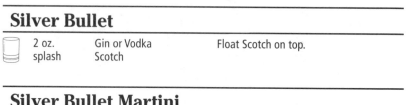

½ oz.	Cointreau	Combine all ingredients in a
½ tsp.	Fresh Lemon Juice	shaker and shake vigorously.
1 oz.	Brandy	Strain into chilled cocktail
3–4	Ice Cubes	glass.

S

Siesta

1½ oz.	Sauza Tequila	Blend or shake with ice
¾ oz.	Lime Juice	and strain into a chilled
½ oz.	Sloe Gin	cocktail glass.

Silk Panties

| 1 part | Stolichnaya Vodka | Combine in a shot glass. |
| 1 part | Peach Schnapps | |

Created by Sandra Gutierrez of Chicago, Illinois.

Silver Bullet

| 2 oz. | Gin or Vodka | Float Scotch on top. |
| splash | Scotch | |

Silver Bullet Martini

1½ oz.	Vodka	Stir the first two ingredients
dash	Extra Dry Vermouth	gently over ice and strain.
splash	Scotch	Float Scotch on top.

Silver Shamrock

2 parts	Bunratty Meade	Stir with ice.
1 part	Vodka	

Silver Splinter

1/2 oz.	Sambuca	Combine over crushed ice.
1 oz.	Dark Rum	
2 oz.	Heavy Cream	

Simply Bonkers

1 part	Chambord	Combine in a shot glass.
1 part	Puerto Rican Rum	
1 part	Cream	

Singapore Sling

1 1/2 oz.	Gin	Shake first five ingredients and pour into a tall glass. Top with Club Soda.
1/2 oz.	Cherry-Flavored Brandy	
3 dashes	Benedictine	
dash	Rose's Grenadine	
dash	Sweetened Lemon Mix	
	Club Soda	

Sling this . . .

The Singapore sling was invented by Ngiam Tong Boon, a bartender at the Long Bar in Singapore's Raffles Hotel around 1915. The Raffles Bar Sling, a variation of the Singapore Sling, gets its name from the very same Raffles Hotel.

Sixty-Ninth Regiment Punch

3 oz.	Irish Whiskey
3 oz.	Scotch Whisky
1 tsp.	Sugar
2–3 dashes	Lemon Juice
10 oz.	Hot Water

Pour the Whiskeys into Hot Water. Add Sugar and Lemon Juice and stir.

Should be served in a warm glass.

Skibbereen Tonic

2 oz.	Irish Whiskey
	Tonic Water

Pour Irish Whiskey into a chilled rocks glass with several ice cubes. Fill with Tonic Water. Twist a Lemon Peel over the drink and drop it in.

Slim Gin

1¼ oz.	Gin
	Diet Soda

Pour Gin in a glass filled with ice. Fill with your favorite Diet Soda.

Slippery Elf

1 part	Baileys Irish Cream
1 part	Smirnoff Vodka

Combine in a shot glass.

Slippery Nipple

1 part	Romana Sambuca
1 part	Baileys

Shake with ice and strain into a shot glass.

Slippery Nut

1½ oz.	Saint Brendan's Irish Cream
2 oz.	Roncoco Rum Liqueur

Combine in a shot glass.

Sloe Gin Fizz

1½ oz.	Sloe Gin	Shake Gin and Lemon Mix and
3 oz.	Sweetened Lemon Mix	pour into a glass. Top with
	Club Soda	Club Soda.

A popular drink of the '60s.

Snowshoe

1 oz.	Rumple Minze	Shake with ice and strain into
1 oz.	Brandy	a shot glass.

Sol-a-Rita

1¼ oz.	Jose Cuervo Gold Tequila	Combine over ice.
¾ oz.	Cointreau	
1½ oz.	Orange Juice	
2 dashes	Grenadine	

Sombrero

1½ oz.	Coffee Liqueur	Combine in a snifter with ice.
½ oz.	Half & Half	

This drink is also known as a Muddy River.

Southern Sour

¼ oz.	Bourbon	Shake with ice and strain or
¾ oz.	Southern Comfort	serve over ice. Garnish with a
3 oz.	Sweetened Lemon Mix	Cherry and an Orange Slice.

Southern Traditional Margarita

1½ oz.	Jose Cuervo Gold Tequila	Combine in a tall glass over
⅝ oz.	Southern Comfort	ice. Garnish with a Lime
5 oz.	Sweet & Sour Mix	Wedge.
½ oz.	Fresh Lime Juice	

Soviet Cocktail

1¹/₂ oz.	Vodka	Shake or blend all ingredients
¹/₂ oz.	Dry Vermouth	with cracked ice in a shaker or
¹/₂ oz.	Dry Sherry	blender and strain into a chilled
		glass. Twist a Lemon Peel over the
		drink and drop it in.

Spanish Moss

¹/₂ oz.	Herradura Tequila	Shake ingredients with ice
³/₄ oz.	Kahlua	and strain or serve over ice.
¹/₂ oz.	Green Crème de Menthe	

Spanish Town Cocktail

2 oz.	Rhum Barbancort	Stir ingredients and serve
1 tsp.	Triple Sec	straight up or over ice in a
		cocktail glass.

S

Sparks

1 oz.	Absolut Peppar Vodka	Combine in a champagne glass.
3 oz.	Champagne	

Spearamisty

1 oz.	Irish Mist	Stir ingredients and serve
¹/₄ oz.	Spearmint Schnapps	straight up or over ice.

Spike

1¹/₂ oz.	Jose Cuervo Gold Tequila	Combine in a highball glass.
4 oz.	Grapefruit Juice	

Spinner

1½ oz.	Bourbon	Combine all ingredients in a
1 oz.	Orange Juice	shaker. Shake briskly and
1 tbsp.	Lime Juice	strain the mixture into a
1 tsp.	Superfine Sugar	cocktail glass. Garnish with
1 scoop	Crushed Ice	an Orange Slice.

You can also serve this one over ice in a rocks glass.

Spritzer

3 oz.	Dry White Wine	Pour Wine in a glass and fill
	Club Soda	with Soda. Garnish with a
		Lemon Twist.

Spyglass

1 oz.	Captain Morgan Spiced Rum	Blend until smooth.
2 scoops	Vanilla Ice Cream	
1 tbsp.	Honey	
dash	Milk	

St. Patrick's Day Cocktail

¾ oz.	Irish Whiskey	Stir well with cracked ice and
¾ oz.	Green Crème de Menthe	strain into a cocktail glass.
¾ oz.	Green Chartreuse	
1 dash	Angostura Bitters	

St. Petersburg

2 oz.	Vodka	Stir with ice. Garnish with an
¼ tsp.	Orange Bitters	Orange Peel.

Steamboat Special

¼ oz.	Orange Liqueur or Triple Sec	Float Orange Liqueur or Triple Sec over Scotch
1 oz.	Scotch	in a shot glass.

Stinger

1³/₄ oz.	Cognac/Brandy	Shake well with ice.
¹/₄ oz.	White Crème de Menthe	

Stoli Oh What a Night Martini

1¹/₂ oz.	Stoli Ohranj Vodka	Shake ingredients and strain
splash	Caffe Sport Espresso	into a cocktail glass. Garnish
	Liqueur	with an Orange Slice.

You can also serve this one over ice.

Stoli Power Martini

1¹/₂ oz.	Stoli Ohranj Vodka	Pour ingredients into a mixing
¹/₂ oz.	Lemon Juice	glass, add ice, and shake well.
3 oz.	Orange Juice	Strain into a chilled glass and
1 oz.	Raspberry Syrup	garnish with an Orange Peel.

S

Stoli Sunset

1¹/₂ oz.	Stoli Limonnaya Vodka	Combine in a tall glass
4 oz.	Cranberry Juice	with ice.
1–2 oz.	Grapefruit Juice	

Stolichnaya Lemonade

1¹/₄ oz.	Stoli Limonnaya Vodka	Combine in a tall glass
¹/₄ oz.	Grand Marnier	with ice.
¹/₂ oz.	Sweet & Sour Mix	
¹/₂ oz.	Lemon Soda	

Stolichnaya Paradise Martini

2 parts	Stoli Ohranj Vodka	Shake ingredients with ice.
1 part	Orange Juice	Pour into a martini glass.
		Garnish with an Orange Slice.

Sunshine Frosty Punch

1¹/₄ oz.	Vodka	Blend until smooth and serve
2 scoops	Vanilla Ice Cream	in a 12 oz. brandy snifter.

Sunsplash

³/₄ oz.	Coco Lopez Cream of Coconut	Shake with ice and serve.
1¹/₄ oz.	Frangelico Liqueur	
³/₄ oz.	Captain Morgan Spiced Rum	
5 oz.	Orange Juice	

Sunstroke

1¹/₂ oz.	Vodka	Pour Vodka and Grapefruit
3 oz.	Grapefruit Juice	Juice into a rocks glass filled
splash	Triple Sec	with ice. Add a little Triple Sec and stir.

Swedish Bear

S

³/₄ oz.	Absolut Vodka	Pour ingredients over ice in a
¹/₂ oz.	Dark Crème de Cacao	chilled rocks glass and stir.
1 tbsp.	Heavy Cream	

Sweet Irish Storm

1¹/₂ oz.	Bushmills Irish Whiskey	Mix ingredients with cracked
³/₄ oz.	Noilly Prat Sweet French Vermouth	ice in a shaker or blender. Pour into a chilled rocks glass.
3–4 dashes	Angostura Bitters	
3–4 dashes	Southern Comfort	

Sweet Tart

1 oz.	Absolut Vodka	Shake with ice and strain into
¹/₄ oz.	Chambord	a shot glass.
¹/₄ oz.	Rose's Lime Juice	
¹/₄ oz.	Pineapple Juice	

Taboo

1¹/₂ oz.	Finlandia Pineapple Vodka, chilled	Blend with crushed ice. Serve in a tall glass. Garnish with
¹/₂ oz.	Cranberry Juice	a Pineapple Wedge and a
¹/₂ oz.	Sour Mix	Cherry.
splash	Triple Sec	

Tailgate

1½ oz.	Don Q Cristal Rum	Combine the first three
½ oz.	Grenadine	ingredients in a tall glass
½ oz.	Fresh Lime Juice	with ice. Fill with Cola.
	Coca Cola	

Tangerine

1¼ oz.	Stoli Ohranj Vodka	Shake with ice and serve.
2 oz.	Orange Juice	
dash	Grenadine	

Tango

2 parts	Cork Dry Gin	Shake with ice and serve.
1 part	Sweet Vermouth	
1 part	Dry Vermouth	
2 dashes	Orange Curacao	
dash	Orange Juice	

You'll dance all night.

Tanqueray & Tonic

1½ oz.	Tanqueray Gin	Pour Gin in a glass with ice. Fill
3 oz.	Tonic Water	with Tonic. Garnish with a
		Lime Wedge.

Tarzan O'Reilly

1 oz.	Baileys Irish Cream	Build in a shot glass over ice. Stir.
½ oz.	Smirnoff Vodka	
½ oz.	Crème de Banana	

You'll swing from trees.

Taxi

| 1 part | Stoli Ohranj Vodka | Combine in a shot glass. |
| 1 part | Coffee Liqueur | |

You can also serve this drink over ice in a highball glass.

Tear Drop

| | 1¼ oz. | Absolut Peppar Vodka | Combine in a shot glass. Drop in |
| | ¼ oz. | Orange Liqueur or Triple Sec | a Cherry. |

Not on your head.

Tequador

	1½ oz.	Tequila	Shake the first three
	2 oz.	Pineapple Juice	ingredients with crushed ice.
	1 dash	Rose's Lime Juice	Strain. Add a few drops of
		Grenadine	Grenadine.

Tequila Gimlet

	1½ oz.	Tequila	Blend Tequila and Lime Juice
	1½ oz.	Rose's Lime Juice	with crushed ice and pour
			into a glass. Garnish with a
			Lime Wheel or Green Cherry.

Tequila Julep

	1¼ oz.	Tequila	Crush three Mint Leaves with
	1 tsp.	Superfine Sugar	Sugar in a chilled highball glass
	2 sprigs	Fresh Mint	and fill with ice. Add Tequila
		Club Soda	and top with Club Soda. Garnish
			with a Sprig of Mint.

Tequila Sunrise

	1½ oz.	Tequila	Pour Grenadine into a tall glass
	½ oz.	Grenadine	first. Then add Tequila and fill
		Orange Juice	with ice and Orange Juice.
			Garnish with an Orange Slice.

Tequila Teaser

	1½ oz.	Tequila	Pour ingredients into a tall glass
	½ oz.	Triple Sec	filled with ice.
	1½ oz.	Orange Juice	
	½ oz.	Grapefruit Juice	

Tequina

	2 oz.	Tequila	Stir Tequila and Vermouth with
	1/2 oz.	Dry Vermouth	ice in a mixing glass until
			chilled. Strain into a chilled
			cocktail glass and garnish with
			a Lemon Twist.

Terminator #1

	1 part	Bacardi 151 Rum	Combine in a shot glass.
	1 part	Hiram Walker Blackberry	
		Brandy	
	1 part	Cranberry Juice	

I'm back.

Terminator #2

	1 part	Vodka	Layer. Pour the Vodka first,
	1 part	Grand Marnier	then the Grand Marnier,
	1 part	Sambuca	and so on.
	1 part	Coffee-Flavored Liqueur	
	1 part	Irish Cream	

I'm back again.

The Ultimate Tea

	1 1/2 oz.	Irish Mist	Pour Irish Mist in a warm
		Hot Tea	glass. Fill with Hot Tea. Garnish
			with a Lemon Slice.

The Wave Cutter

	1 1/2 oz.	Mount Gay Rum	Shake with ice and serve
	1 oz.	Cranberry Juice	over ice.
	1 oz.	Orange Juice	

Three Barrels of Monkeys

	1 oz.	Myers's Dark Rum	Combine over ice and stir.
	1/4 oz.	Banana Liqueur	
	1/4 oz.	Irish Cream	

Three-Leaf Shamrock Shaker

1 oz.	Bushmills Irish Whiskey	Shake ingredients with cracked
1 oz.	Light Rum	ice. Strain into a chilled glass.
1 oz.	Brandy	
1 tsp.	Lemon Juice	
dash	Sugar Syrup	

Thunder and Lightning

1 part	Rumple Minze	Combine in a shot glass.
1 part	Bacardi 151 Rum	

Thunderbolt

2 parts	Herradura Tequila	Stir over ice in a rocks glass.
1 part	Dr. McGillicuddy's	
	Mentholmint Schnapps	

Tidy Bowl

1¹/₂ oz.	Ouzo	Combine in a shot glass.
splash	Blue Curacao	

It's blue.

Tijuana Tea

³/₄ oz.	Jose Cuervo 1800 Tequila	Combine ingredients in the
³/₄ oz.	Jose Cuervo Gold Tequila	glass and stir. Garnish with a
¹/₂ oz.	Triple Sec	Lime Slice and a Maraschino
1 oz.	Sweet & Sour Mix	Cherry.
3 oz.	Cola	

Tinker's Tea

1¹/₂ oz.	Baileys Irish Cream	Pour Irish Cream in a glass and
	Hot Tea	fill with Hot Tea.

Tipperary Cocktail

³/₄ oz.	Irish Whiskey	Stir well with cracked ice and
³/₄ oz.	Green Chartreuse	strain into cocktail glass.
³/₄ oz.	Italian Vermouth	

To the Moon

1 part	Irish Cream	Combine in a shot glass.
1 part	Amaretto	
1 part	Coffee-Flavored Liqueur	
1 part	151-proof Rum	

Toasted Almond

1 oz.	Coffee Liqueur	Pour over ice and stir.
1/2 oz.	Amaretto	
1 oz.	Cream or Milk	

Tom Collins

1 1/2 oz.	Gin	Shake first two ingredients
	Juice of 1 lemon	and pour over ice. Top with
	Club Soda	Club Soda.

John or Tom Collins?

This drink was invented by John Collins, a waiter at Lipmmer's Old House on Coduit Street in Hanover Square, England. The name Tom was used instead of John because the drink was made with Old Tom Gin. Today, a John Collins is made with whiskey.

T

Tootsie Roll #1

1 part	Kahlua	Combine in a shot glass.
1 part	Vodka	
1 part	Orange Juice	

Tootsie Roll #2

1/2 oz.	Baileys Irish Cream	Top Root Beer Schnapps with
1 oz.	Root Beer Schnapps	Irish Cream in a shot glass.

Top Ten

1¼ oz.	Captain Morgan Spiced Rum	Blend with crushed ice.
2 oz.	Cola	
1 oz.	Coco Lopez Cream of Coconut	
1 oz.	Heavy Cream	

Topaz Martini

1¾ oz.	Bacardi Limón	Combine in a cocktail glass.
¼ oz.	Martini & Rossi Extra Dry Vermouth	
splash	Blue Curacao	

Invented at the Heart and Soul in San Francisco, California.

Traffic Light

⅓ oz.	Green Crème de Menthe	Layer this drink in the order
⅓ oz.	Crème de Banana	listed. Start with Crème de
⅓ oz.	Sloe Gin	Menthe on the bottom and finish with Sloe Gin on top.

Transfusion

1½ oz.	Stolichnaya Vodka	Combine over ice and stir.
3 oz.	Grape Juice	

Tres Martini

1½ oz.	Tres Generaciones	Rinse a chilled martini glass with a
splash	Cointreau	splash of Cointreau and discard. Place Tres Generaciones in a shaker. Fill with ice, shake, and strain into the prepared glass. Garnish with Orange Zest.

T

Trilby

³/₄ oz.	Scotch	Mix all ingredients with
³/₄ oz.	Sweet Vermouth	cracked ice in a shaker or
³/₄ oz.	Parfait Amour	blender. Pour into a chilled
3–4 dashes	Pernod	rocks glass.
3–4 dashes	Angostura Bitters	

Trip to the Beach

¹/₂ oz.	Malibu	Combine over ice.
¹/₂ oz.	Peach Schnapps	
¹/₂ oz.	Smirnoff Vodka	
3 oz.	Orange Juice	

Tropical Breeze

1 oz.	Coco Lopez Cream of Coconut	Blend with crushed ice. Garnish with a Pineapple Slice.
2 oz.	Orange Juice	
1 oz.	Rum	
¹/₂ oz.	Crème de Banana	

Tropical Iceberg

1¹/₂ oz.	Finlandia Pineapple Vodka, chilled	Blend ingredients and serve in a margarita glass.
¹/₂ oz.	Banana Liqueur or	
¹/₂	Banana	
¹/₂ oz.	Cream of Coconut	
dash	Cream or Half & Half	

Tuaca Frizzante

1¹/₂ oz.	Tuaca	Pour Tuaca over ice in a rocks glass.
splash	San Pellegrino Mineral Water	Stir in a splash of Mineral Water to taste. Garnish with a Lemon Peel.

Tuaca Rocca

1 oz.	Tuaca	Combine with ice in a rocks
1 oz.	Peach Schnapps	glass.
1 oz.	Vodka	

Turbo

	¹/₄ oz.	Vodka	Combine in a shot glass.
	¹/₄ oz.	Peach Schnapps	
	¹/₄ oz.	Apple Schnapps	
	¹/₄ oz.	Cranberry Juice	

You can also combine the ingredients with ice in a rocks glass.

Turkey Shooter

	³/₄ oz.	Bourbon	Shake in cocktail shaker. Strain
	¹/₄ oz.	White Crème de Menthe	into a brandy snifter.

This drink is also known as a Bourbon Stinger.

24 Karat Nightmare

	1 part	Goldschlager	Combine in a shot glass.
	1 part	Rumple Minze	

Twilight Zone

	1¹/₂ oz.	Puerto Rican Light Rum	Shake with ice and strain into
	¹/₂ oz.	Myers's Rum	a shot glass.
	splash	Rose's Grenadine	

U-Z

	³/₄ oz.	Irish Mist	Shake ingredients and strain
	³/₄ oz.	Baileys Irish Cream	into shot glass.
	³/₄ oz.	Kahlua	

Under the Volcano Martini

	2 oz.	Mezcal	Stir over ice in a cocktail glass.
	¹/₂ oz.	Martini & Rossi Vermouth	Garnish with a Jalapeño-Stuffed Olive.

Invented at Harry Denton's in San Francisco, California.

Vanilla Koke

1¹/₂ oz.	Stoli Vanil Vodka	Combine in a collins glass
3 oz.	Cola	and stir.

Vesper Martini

1¹/₂ oz.	Gin	Stir gently with ice and strain
dash	Blonde Lillet	into a cocktail glass.

Vicious Sid

1¹/₂ oz.	Puerto Rican Light Rum	Shake ingredients with ice and
¹/₂ oz.	Southern Comfort	serve over ice.
¹/₂ oz.	Cointreau or Triple Sec	
1 oz.	Lemon Juice	
1 dash	Bitters	

Viking

1 oz.	Liquore Galliano	Float Akvavit on top of the
¹/₄ oz.	Akvavit (ice cold)	Galliano in a shot glass.

Violetta Martini

5 parts	Classic Finlandia Vodka	Stir gently over ice and strain.
1 part	Cranberry Juice Cocktail	
splash	Blue Curacao	

You can also serve this drink over ice.

V

Vodka & Tonic

1¹/₂ oz.	Vodka	Stir ingredients with ice in a
3 oz.	Tonic	glass. Garnish with a Lime
		Wheel.

Vodka Martini

2 oz.	Vodka	Stir ingredients with ice and
dash	Dry Vermouth	strain. Garnish with a Lemon
		Twist or an Olive.

You can also serve a Vodka Martini on ice.

Vulcan Mind Probe #1

1 oz.	Ouzo	Shake with ice and strain into
1 oz.	Bacardi 151 Rum	a shot glass.

Vulcan Mind Probe #2

1 part	Irish Cream	Layer in a shot glass by first pour-
1 part	Peppermint Schnapps	ing the Rum, then the Schnapps,
1 part	151-proof Rum	and then the Irish Cream. Serve
		with a large straw.

You drink this one by sucking the drink down through the straw in one gulp.

Ward Eight

1¹/₄ oz.	Whiskey	Shake ingredients with cracked
4 dashes	Grenadine	ice and strain into a glass with
	Juice of ¹/₂ Lemon	finely cracked ice.

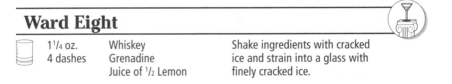

The origins of the Ward Eight

This drink is named after Boston's Ward Eight, known years ago for its bloody po-litical elections. The drink is basically a Whiskey Sour with a splash of grenadine. Locke-O-Ber's in Boston is a great place to try one.

Watermelon

1 oz.	Vodka	Combine ingredients in a glass
1 oz.	Midori	over ice.
2 oz.	Orange Juice	
2 oz.	Cranberry Juice	

Wet Spot

1 oz.	Cuervo Tequila	Shake with ice and strain into
1 oz.	Baileys Irish Cream	a shot glass.

Whiskey Collins

1¼ oz.	Whiskey	Shake the first three ingredients
	Juice of 1 lemon	with cracked ice and strain in a
1 tsp.	Sugar	glass over ice. Fill with Club
	Club Soda	Soda and stir. Decorate with a
		Cherry and an Orange Slice.

Whiskey Sour

1½ oz.	Whiskey	Shake with ice. Serve straight
¾ oz.	Sweetened Lemon Juice	up or over ice.
1 tsp.	Superfine Sugar	

White Chocolate Martini

1½ oz.	Vodka	Stir gently with ice and strain
½ oz.	White Crème de Cacao	into a chocolate-rimmed
		cocktail glass.

Invented at the Continental Cafe in Philadelphia, Pennsylvania.

White Lady

1½ oz.	Gin	Shake and strain into a frosted
½ oz.	Cointreau	glass.
1½ oz.	Lemon Juice	

The lowdown on the White Lady

The White Lady was created by Harry MacElhone in 1919 at Ciro's Club in London, England. In 1923, he took over a bar in Rue Daunou, Paris, renaming it Harry's New York Bar. In 1929, he altered the original White Lady recipe by using gin in place of white crème de menthe, and this concoction became a worldwide favorite.

W

White Russian

	1¹/₂ oz.	Vodka	Shake and serve over ice.
	¹/₂ oz.	Kahlua	
	¹/₂ oz.	Cream	

White Spider

	1 part	Stolichnaya Vodka	Combine in a shot glass.
	1 part	Rumple Minze	

Wicklow Cooler

	1¹/₂ oz.	Irish Whiskey	Mix all ingredients except
	1 oz.	Jamaican Dark Rum	Ginger Ale with cracked ice in
	¹/₂ oz.	Lime Juice	a shaker or blender. Pour into a
	1 oz.	Orange Juice	chilled collins glass. Fill with
		Ginger Ale	Ginger Ale.

Wild Irish Rose

	1¹/₂ oz.	Irish Whiskey	Fill a highball glass with ice.
	1¹/₂ tsp.	Grenadine	Add Irish Whiskey, Grenadine,
	¹/₂ oz.	Lime Juice	and Lime Juice. Stir well. Fill
		Club Soda	with Club Soda.

Wolfhound

	1 oz.	Bushmills Irish Whiskey	Stir ingredients with ice and
	³/₄ oz.	Dark Crème de Cacao	serve over ice.
	¹/₂ oz.	Half & Half	
	splash	Club Soda	

Woo Woo #1

	³/₄ oz.	Vodka	Combine in a glass with ice.
	³/₄ oz.	Peppermint Schnapps	

Woo Woo #2

	1 oz.	Vodka	Combine ingredients over ice.
	¹/₂ oz.	Peach Schnapps	
	2 oz.	Cranberry Juice	

Xiantha

1 part	Cork Dry Gin	Mix with ice and strain in a
1 part	Yellow Chartreuse	cocktail glass.
1 part	Cherry Brandy	

Yellow Bird

³/₄ oz.	Bacardi Rum	Shake with ice. Serve over ice.
¹/₄ oz.	Liquore Galliano	
¹/₄ oz.	Hiram Walker Crème de Banana	
2 oz.	Pineapple Juice	
2 oz.	Orange Juice	

Yellow Morning

1 part	Crème de Banana	Layer this drink in the order
1 part	Cherry Heering	listed. Start with Crème de
1 part	Cognac	Banana on the bottom and finish with Cognac on top.

Zipperhead

1 part	Stolichnaya Vodka	Combine in a shot glass with
1 part	Chambord	the Club Soda on top.
1 part	Club Soda	

Zombie

³/₄ oz.	Bacardi Light Rum	Mix the first two Rums and all
¹/₄ oz.	Bacardi Dark Rum	Juices with ice in a shaker or
¹/₄ tsp.	Bacardi 151 Rum	blender and pour into a tall
1 oz.	Pineapple Juice	glass. Garnish with a Pineapple
1 oz.	Orange Juice	Spear and a Red Cherry. If desired,
1 oz.	Lemon or Rose's Lime Juice	float ¹/₄ tsp. Bacardi 151 on top
1 tsp.	Powdered Sugar (optional)	with 1 tsp. Powdered Sugar.

Zorbatini

| 1¹/₂ oz. | Stolichnaya Vodka | Stir gently with ice and strain. |
| ¹/₄ oz. | Metaxa Ouzo | Garnish with a Green Olive. |

Z

Chapter 19
Those Famous Pousse-Cafés

*P*ousse-Cafés are layered speciality drinks that first became popular with bartenders in New Orleans in the 1840s and became a fad throughout the United States in the early 1900s. Pousse-Café is French for *push down the coffee*. Pouring this sort of drink is a true test for bartenders (so if you ask a bartender to make one for you, be sure to tip him or her well).

It's All about Specific Gravity

To produce a nicely layered drink, you need a steady hand, a spoon, and some knowledge of the specific gravities of cordials, syrups, brandies, and other spirits. Basically, you have to carefully pour "lighter" liquids on top of "heavier" liquids in order for them to stay separate. The result is a colorful rainbow effect.

Easier said than done. You can help your effort immensely if you pour the liquids that you're layering over the back of a spoon. The spoon brakes the fall of the liquids, enabling them to layer more easily.

If you get everything right, the drink will amaze your friends and win you influence. If you plan to serve Pousse-Cafés at a party, you can avoid performance anxiety and the accompanying shaky hands by making your Pousse-Cafés ahead of time. They will keep for at least an hour in the refrigerator.

Some Helpful Charts

Table 22-1, from Hiram Walker Cordials, lists the specific gravity index of its various liqueurs, syrups, and so on. (If you use other brands, the specific gravities may vary.)

Table 22-2 lists a layering order based on my own experience, testing, and tasting.

For best results, layer ingredients that have a ranking at least four spaces apart on the chart. It's unlikely that Crème de Cacao (6) will float on Praline (5), but Blue Curacao (12) certainly will.

Table 22-1   Hiram Walker Pousse-Café Specific Gravity Index

No.	Proof	Product	Specific Gravity	Color
1	40	Crème de Cassis	1.1833	Light brown
2	25	Grenadine	1.1720	Red
3	54	Crème de Cacao, Brown	1.1561	Brown
4	48	Hazelnut Schnapps	1.1532	Tawny
5	40	Praline	1.1514	Brown
6	54	Crème de Cacao, White	1.1434	White
7	56	Crème de Noyaux	1.1342	Red
8	48	Licorice Schnapps	1.1300	Clear
9	54	Chocolate Cherry	1.1247	Brown
10	56	Crème de Banana	1.1233	Yellow
11	54	Chocolate Mint	1.1230	Brown
12	48	Blue Curacao	1.1215	Blue
13	54	Swiss Chocolate Almond	1.1181	Brown
14	60	Crème de Menthe, White	1.1088	Clear
15	60	Crème de Menthe, Green	1.1088	Green
16	60	Orange Curacao	1.1086	Tawny
17	60	Anisette, White and Red	1.0987	White/Red
18	48	Crème de Strawberry	1.0968	Red
19	48	Wild Strawberry Schnapps	1.0966	Clear
20	48	Red Hot Schnapps	1.0927	Red

No.	Proof	Product	Specific Gravity	Color
21	60	Triple Sec	1.0922	White
22	60	Rock & Rye	1.0887	Yellow
23	40	Cranberry Cordial	1.0872	Red
24	50	Amaretto	1.0842	Tawny
25	48	Old Fashioned Root Beer Schnapps	1.0828	Tawny
26	84	Sambuca	1.0813	White
27	40	Country Melon Schnapps	1.0796	Pink
28	70	Coffee-Flavored Brandy	1.0794	Brown
29	48	Red Raspberry Schnapps	1.0752	Clear
30	48	Snappy Apricot Schnapps	1.0733	Tawny
31	48	Cinnamon Schnapps	1.0732	Red
32	48	Spearmint Schnapps	1.0727	Clear
33	60	Shamrock Schnapps	1.0617	Green
34	60	Peppermint Schnapps	1.0615	Clear
35	48	Jubilee Peach Schnapps	1.0595	Clear
36	70	Raspberry-Flavored Brandy	1.0566	Red
37	70	Apricot-Flavored Brandy	1.0548	Tawny
38	70	Peach-Flavored Brandy	1.0547	Tawny
39	70	Cherry-Flavored Brandy	1.0542	Red
40	70	Blackberry-Flavored Brandy	1.0536	Purple
41	90	Peach Schnapps	1.0534	Clear
42	90	Root Beer Schnapps	1.0441	Brown
43	50	Amaretto and Cognac	1.0394	Tawny
44	90	Cinnamon Spice Schnapps	1.0358	Reddish
45	60	Sloe Gin	1.0241	Red
46	70	Ginger-Flavored Brandy	0.9979	Light brown
47	90	Kirschwasser	0.9410	Clear

Table 22-2   The Foley-Cowan-Zazzali Layering Guide

No.	Product	Color
1	Crème de Cassis	Red
2	Crème de Cacao, Brown	Brown
3	Kahlua	Brown
4	Peach Schnapps	Clear
5	Crème de Banana	Yellow
6	Anisette	Clear
7	Crème de Menthe, Green	Green
8	Crème de Menthe, White	Clear
9	Melon	Green
10	Tia Maria	Brown
11	Cherry Brandy	Red
12	Apricot Brandy	Gold
13	Sambuca	Clear
14	Galliano	Yellow
15	Amaretto	Tawny
16	Drambuie	Gold
17	Benedictine	Gold
18	Peppermint Schnapps	Clear
19	Frangelico	Gold
20	Spearmint Schnapps	Clear
21	Baileys Irish Cream	Cream
22	Irish Mist	Gold
23	Cointreau	Clear
24	Grand Marnier	Gold
25	Malibu Rum	Clear
26	Sloe Gin	Red
27	B & B	Gold
28	Southern Comfort	Gold

No.	Product	Color
29	Chartreuse	Green
30	Ouzo	Clear
31	Pernod	Yellow

Pousse-Café Recipes

You'll find all of the following Pousse-Café recipes in the recipes section (Chapter 18) of this book.

- Angel's Delight
- Champerelle
- Champs Elysses
- Fifth Avenue
- Fourth of July
- Gravure
- Irish Flag
- Jamie's Highland Special
- Parisian Pousse-Café
- Pousse-Café #1
- Pousse-Café #2
- Pousse-Café à la Française
- Pousse-Café Standish
- Rainbow Pousse-Café
- Savoy Hotel
- Traffic Light
- Yellow Morning

Chapter 20

Punches

In This Chapter

▶ A little background

▶ Several recipes

*P*unch may have come from the word *puncheon,* a cast made to hold liquids such as beer. The word may also have come from the Hindu word *pantsh,* which means five. What does five have to do with anything? British expatriates in India in the 17th century made a beverage consisting of five ingredients: tea, water, sugar, lemon juice, and a fermented sap called *arrack.*

Regardless of the history or origin, punches of all kinds are an expected beverage at many of today's social gatherings. Whether you're an aspiring bartender or just someone who wants to be a good host (and the life of the party), you need to have at least a few of the following punches in your repertoire.

Ambrosia Punch

20 oz. can	Crushed Pineapple, undrained	In a blender, puree the Pineapple and Cream of Coconut until smooth. In a punch bowl, combine the pureed mixture, Nectar, Juice, and Rum (if desired). Mix well. Just before serving, add Club Soda and serve over ice.
15 oz.	Coco Lopez Cream of Coconut	
2 cups	Apricot Nectar, chilled	
2 cups	Orange Juice, chilled	
1¹/₂ cups	Light Rum, optional	
1 liter	Club Soda, chilled	

This recipe serves about 24.

Bacardi Confetti Punch

750 ml.	Bacardi Light Rum	
6 oz. can	Frozen Lemonade Concentrate	
6 oz. can	Frozen Grapefruit Juice Concentrate	
6 oz. can	Fruit Cocktail, drained	
2 liters	Club Soda, chilled	

Combine the first four ingredients in a large container and chill for two hours, stirring occasionally. To serve, pour the mixture over ice in a punch bowl and add two liters of chilled Club Soda. Stir gently.

This recipe makes 8 servings.

Champagne Punch Royale

1 bottle	Chantaine Sparkling Wine, chilled
¹/₃ cup	Royale Montaine Cognac and Orange Liqueur
1 cup	Sliced Strawberries
1 cup	Orange Juice
1 small bottle	Club Soda
2 tbsp.	Sugar

Place Sliced Strawberries in large bowl and sprinkle with Sugar. Add Orange Juice and Royale Montaine Cognac and Orange Liqueur. Macerate for 1 hour. Add the chilled Sparkling Wine and Club Soda.

This recipe serves 8.

Cointreau Punch

1 bottle	Cointreau
1 bottle	Vodka
3 quarts	Club Soda
6 oz. can	Orange Juice Concentrate
6 oz. can	Pineapple Juice Concentrate

Place a clear block of ice in a large punch bowl. Combine ingredients and stir. Garnish with Orange Slices decorated with Cranberries and studded with Cloves.

This recipe makes enough for 40 punch-cup drinks.

Double Berry Coco Punch

20 oz.	Frozen Strawberries in Syrup, thawed
15 oz.	Coco Lopez Cream of Coconut
48 oz.	Cranberry Juice Cocktail, chilled
2 cups	Light Rum, optional
1 liter	Club Soda, chilled

In a blender, puree the Strawberries and Cream of Coconut until smooth. In large punch bowl, combine the pureed mixture, Cranberry Juice, and Rum (if desired). Just before serving, add Club Soda and serve over ice.

This recipe serves about 32.

Formula #21

1 bottle	Smirnoff Vodka	Mix the ingredients in a punch
1 bottle	White Wine	bowl.
2 quarts	Pineapple Juice	
$^1/_2$ cup	Lime Juice	
2 quarts	Chilled Club Soda	
	Sugar, to taste	

This recipe serves 12–20.

Malibu Party Punch

1 bottle	Malibu	Combine ingredients in a punch
48 oz.	Cranberry Juice	bowl and stir. Garnish with Lemon,
6 oz.can	Frozen Orange Juice Concentrate	Orange Slices, and Cloves.
6 oz.can	Frozen Lemonade or Limeade Concentrate	

This recipe serves 12–20.

M&R Hot Spiced Wine Punch

1.5 liters	Martini & Rossi Red Vermouth	Combine all ingredients except
2 dashes	Angostura Bitters	Orange Slices in a heavy saucepan
6	Cloves	and heat but don't boil. Strain into
3	Cinnamon Sticks	a punch bowl. For added effect,
3 tsp.	Superfine Sugar	heat a poker and dip it into the
pinch	Allspice	punch before serving. Garnish with
pinch	Ground Clove	Orange Slices.
	Orange Slices	

This recipe serves 6–12.

Metaxa Fruit Punch

$^1/_2$ gallon	Orange Sherbet	Mix all ingredients except the
3 bottles	7-Up	Raspberry Sherbet and Orange
16 oz.	Metaxa Manto Liqueur	Slices. Chill for one hour. Place
6–8 scoops	Raspberry Sherbert	scoops of Raspberry Sherbet atop
1	Orange, sliced thin	the punch. Add Orange slices.

This recipe serves 10–15.

Myers's Planter's Punch

3 oz.	Orange Juice	Shake or blend until frothy. Serve
	Juice of ¹/₂ lemon or lime	over shaved ice in a highball glass.
1¹/₂ oz.	Myers's Rum	If desired, garnish with an Orange
1 tsp.	Superfine Sugar	Slice and a Cherry.
dash	Grenadine	

This recipe only makes one drink, so you'll have to do some multiplying to make enough to serve a bunch of people.

Open House Punch

750 ml.	Southern Comfort	Chill ingredients. Mix the first four
6 oz.	Lemon Juice	ingredients in punch bowl. Add
6 oz. can	Frozen Lemonade	7-Up or Sprite. Add drops of Red
6 oz. can	Frozen Orange Juice	Food Coloring as desired and stir.
3 liters	7-Up or Sprite	Float a block of ice and garnish
	Red Food Coloring	with Orange and Lemon Slices. Note
		that the first four ingredients may
		be mixed in advance. Add 7-Up or
		Sprite and ice when ready to serve.

This recipes makes 32 4-oz. servings.

Patio Punch

750 ml.	Southern Comfort	Mix ingredients and add ice. Serve
16 oz.	Grapefruit Juice	from a punch bowl or pitcher. Note
8 oz.	Fresh Lime Juice	that the first three ingredients can
2 liters	7-Up or Ginger Ale	be mixed in advance and refriger-
		ated. Add the 7-Up or Ginger Ale
		and ice when ready to serve.

This recipe serves 15–20.

Peach-E-Vino Punch

¹/₃ cup	Sugar	In a large pitcher, combine Sugar
¹/₂ cup	Fresh Lemon Juice	and Lemon Juice. Stir until
1 bottle	Dry White Wine	dissolved. Add Wine and Schnapps.
¹/₄ cup	DeKuyper Peachtree Schnapps	Just before serving, add Club Soda,
¹/₄ cup	DeKuyper Apple Barrel Schnapps	Sliced Fruit (Apples, Peaches,
1 quart	Club Soda	Cherries, Limes, Oranges, Lemons),
	Ice Cubes	and Ice Cubes.
	Fresh Fruit	

This recipe serves 15–20.

Chapter 21
Non-Alcoholic Drinks

In This Chapter

▶ Several recipes for non-alcoholic beverages

A good number of your guests may choose not to drink alcohol, but this decision doesn't mean that they're stuck with boring soft drinks. Any of the following recipes are sure to impress.

Cranberry Collins

¹/₂ cup	Ocean Spray Cranberry Juice Cocktail	Mix Cranberry Juice Cocktail and Lime Juice. Stir in Club Soda. Add Ice Cubes and Lime Slices.
¹/₂ tbsp.	Lime Juice	
1 cup	Club Soda, chilled	
	Ice Cubes	
	Lime Slices	

Chocolate Banana Colada Shake

¹/₃ cup	Coco Lopez Cream of Coconut	Mix in a blender until smooth. Serve immediately.
¹/₂ cup	Milk	
1 tbsp.	Chocolate Syrup	
1¹/₂ cups	Chocolate or Vanilla Ice Cream	
¹/₂ cup	Sliced Bananas	

Chocolate Colada Shake

¹/₃ cup	Coco Lopez Cream of Coconut	Mix in a blender until smooth. Serve immediately.
¹/₂ cup	Milk	
1 tbsp.	Chocolate Syrup	
1¹/₂ cups	Chocolate or Vanilla Ice Cream	

Clamato Cocktail

1 oz.	Rose's Lime Juice	Stir together in a highball
6 oz.	Mott's Clamato Juice	glass filled with ice.

Coco Lopez Shake

2¹/₂ oz.	Coco Lopez Cream of Coconut	Mix in a blender until smooth.
1 scoop	Vanilla Ice Cream	
1 cup	Ice	

Dust Cutter

³/₄ oz.	Rose's Lime Juice	Combine over ice in a tall
6 oz.	Schweppes Tonic Water	glass.

Grapefruit Cooler

8 oz.	Grapefruit Juice	Pour Grapefruit Juice into a
3 dashes	Angostura Bitters	tall glass filled with ice. Add Bitters and stir.

Kona Coast

1 oz.	Rose's Lime Juice	Stir together and serve
¹/₄ oz.	Rose's Grenadine	over ice in a tall glass.
5 oz.	Mott's Apple Juice	
2 oz.	Schweppes Ginger Ale	

New Orleans Day

2 oz.	Coco Lopez Cream of Coconut	Mix in a blender until smooth.
1 oz.	Butterscotch Topping	
1 oz.	Half & Half	
1 cup	Ice	

Nada Colada

1 oz.	Coco Lopez Cream of Coconut	Mix in a blender until smooth.
2 oz.	Pineapple Juice	
1 cup	Ice	

Orange Smoothie

2¹/₂ oz.	Coco Lopez Cream of Coconut	Mix first four ingredients in a blender until smooth.
3 oz.	Orange Juice	Sprinkle with Nutmeg.
1 scoop	Vanilla Ice Cream	
1 cup	Ice	
	Nutmeg	

Piña Colada Shake

¹/₂ cup	Unsweetened Pineapple Juice	Mix in a blender until smooth. Serve immediately.
¹/₃ cup	Coco Lopez Cream of Coconut	
1¹/₂ cups	Vanilla Ice Cream	

Red Racket

¹/₂ cup	Ocean Spray Cranberry Juice Cocktail, chilled	In a blender, combine Cranberry Juice Cocktail, Grapefruit Juice and Ice Cubes. Blend on high speed till frothy. Pour into a tall glass.
¹/₂ cup	Ocean Spray Grapefruit Juice, chilled	
	Ice Cubes	

Ruby Cooler

1 cup	Ocean Spray Cranapple Cranberry Apple Drink	Mix together Cranapple Juice and Tea. Pour over ice into two tall glasses with Lemon Wedge garnishes.
1 tsp.	Instant Tea	
	Lemon Wedges	

Shirley Temple

1 oz.	Rose's Lime Juice	Pour ingredients over ice in
1 oz.	Rose's Grenadine	a tall glass. Garnish with a
	6 oz.	Schweppes Ginger Ale
		Cherry.

Virgin Mary

4 oz.	Tomato Juice	In a glass filled with ice, add
dash	Worcestershire Sauce	Tomato Juice. Add a dash or
dash	Tabasco Sauce	two of Worcestershire Sauce,
dash	Salt and Pepper	Tabasco, Salt, and Pepper.
		Garnish with a Celery Stalk.

Part IV

The Part of Tens

In this part. . .

Chapter 22 contains roughly ten cures for hiccups and hangovers. Chapter 23 lists many more than ten bartending-related Web sites and other resources.

At Least Ten Cures and Lores

. . . .

In This Chapter

▶ Hiccup cures

▶ Hangover cures

. . . .

*P*art of being a bartender is settling arguments, mending broken hearts, and curing two primary medicinal problems: hiccups and hangovers.

Hiccups

Hiccups are caused by the involuntary contraction of the diaphragm followed by the rapid closure of the vocal cords. Here are some cures:

✔ Slice a lemon and remove the pits. Top the slices with sugar and Angostura bitters and eat the whole thing. This is the sure cure.

✔ Mix Angostura bitters and club soda and sip slowly.

✔ Drink a glass of water backwards. This can be a very wet cure!

✔ Hold your nose and breath. Then count to 10 or 20, or to be certain, count to 100.

✔ Blow into a paper bag.

Hangovers

Cause: Take a guess.

Cures: There are only two real cures.

✔ A little prevention: Do not over-indulge or let yourself be overserved. Someone told me once that even in moderation, I am excessive.

✔ Sleep. Drink plenty of fluids (water-based, not alcohol-based). Get some peace and quiet.

Here are a few more possible cures:

- Drink two ounces Fernet Branca or Fernet Branca Menta (Italian digestives) on the rocks.
- Drink one small bottle of Underberg (a German digestive).
- From my friends in Puerto Rico (Gere and Linda), rub a half of a lemon under each armpit!
- Drink a bottle of flat beer left out open overnight.
- Hair of the Dog: One shot of whatever you were drinking!
- Try using a few dashes of Angostura aromatic bitters with either water or soda. It should relieve your upset stomach.

Chapter 23

Ten Thousand Web Sites and Other Resources

I've loaded this chapter with Web sites to visit and resources to contact. Have fun.

Web Sites

Go to mine first:

BARTENDER Magazine: http://www.bartender.com

Beer-related sites

Amstel (Van Munching's Amstel Riversite Cafe): http://www.amstel.nl

Bass Ale (Guinness Imports): http://www.bassale.com

The Beer and Brewing Index: http://www.mindspring.com

Beer Games Guide: http://www.realbeer.com

Black Star Premium Lager: http://www.blackstarbeer.com

Boddingtons: http://www.labatt.com

Budweiser: http://www.budweiser.com

Budweiser (Bud Ice): http://www.budice.com

Budweiser Specialty Brewing Group: http://www.hopnotes.com

Cream City Suds: http://www.creamcitysuds.com

Fischer Beverages Int'l.: http://www.aaweb.com

Foster's: http://www.fostersbeer.com

Grolsch: http://www.grolsch.com

Hacker-Pschorr: http://www.paulaner.com/bier

Hart Brewing: http://www.HartBrew.com

Hatuey Beer (Bacardi-Martini USA): http://www.hatuey.com

Heineken (Heineken USA): http://www.heineken.com

Labatt: http://www.labatt.com

Leinenkugel: http://www.leinie.com

Miller: http://www.mgdtaproom.com

Molson (Molson USA): http://www.molson.com

Molson Ice: http://www.molsonice.com

Paulaner: http://www.paulaner.com/bier

Pilgrim Brewery: http://www.pilgrimale.com

Red Dog Beer (Miller Brewing): http://www.reddog.com

Spoetzl Brewery, Shiner, Tx: http://www.shiner.com

Virtual Brewery: http://www.portola.com/TR/VBA/index.html

Witbeer: http://www.interport.net/witbeer

Zima: http://www.zima.com

Spirit-related sites

Absolut Vodka (Seagram Americas): http://www.absolutvodka.com

Allied Domecq: http://www.whereitsat.com

Appleton Rum: http://www.appletonrum.com

Bacardi (Bacardi-Martini USA): http://www.bacardi.com

Ballantine's: http://www.ballantines.com

Beefeater: http://beefeatergin.co.uk

Bombay: http://www.stoli.com

Brown-Forman: http://www.brown-forman.com

Bushmills: http://www.bushmills.com

Canadian Mist: http://www.canadianmist.com

Captain Morgan: http://www.rum.com

Chivas Regal (Seagram Americas): http://www.careertoolbox.com

Chinaco Tequila (Jim Beam Brands): http://www.realtequila.com

Classic Malts (Schieffelin & Somerset): http://www.scotch.com

Courvoisier: http://www.courvoisier.com

Goldschlager (IDV North America): http://www.schlager.com

Glenmorangie (Brown-Forman): http://www.glenmorangie.com

Harveys: http://www.harveysbc.com

Jack Daniels: http://www.jackdaniels.com

Jim Beam Brands: http://www.jimbeam.com

Jim Beam (The Small Batch Bourbon Collection): http://www.smallbatch.com

Jose Cuervo (IDV North America): http://www.cuervo.com

Johnnie Walker & Classic Malts Scotch: http://scotch.com

Malibu Rum: http://www.malibu-rum.com

Niche Marketing Corp.: http://www.ourniche.com

Sauza: http://www.tequila-sauza.com

Scotch Email Cards: http://www.scotch.com/postcards

Sidney Frank Importing Co. (Jagermeister): http://www.jagermeister.com

Smirnoff Vodka (IDV North America): http://www.purethrill.com

Southern Comfort: http://www.SouthernComfort.com

Stolichnaya (Spirits of the World): http://www.stoli.com

Wine-related sites

Antinori (The Wine of Tuscany): http://www.telemaco.it/telemaco/antinori

Beringer Vineyards (Wine World Estates): http://www.beringer.com/index.html

Bolla Wines (Brown-Forman Beverages): http://www.bolla.com

Fontana Candida: http://www.fontanacandida.com

Matanzas Creek Winery, Santa Rosa, CA: http://www.winery.com

Moët & Chandon: (Schieffelin & Somerset) http://www.moet.com

Napa Valley: http://www.freerun.com/napavalley/winetxt/

Pellegrini Vineyards: http://pellegrinivineyards.com

R.J. Dube & Associates (wine racks): http://www.ashtabula.net/Northcoast

Robert Mondavi Winery: http://www.mondavi.com/index.html

Roederer Estate: http://www.winery.com/roederer

Sonoma: http:www.sonoma.com

Sutter Home (Sutter Home Winery): http://www.sutterhome.com

The Wine Institute: http://www.wineinstitute.org

Wines on the Internet: http://www.wines.com

Non-alcoholic beverage sites

Coca-Cola: http://www.cocacola.com

LaChoy (Hunt Wesson): http://www.lachoyfoodservice.com

Pepsi-Cola: http://www.pepsi.com

Perrier: http://www.perrier.com

Snapple: http://www.snapple.com

Restaurant and bar sites

Crazy Horse Saloon: http://www.sherms.com/crazyhorse

Cyber Pub in England: http://www.netropolis.co.uk/

Empty Glass Bar (Jon Steel): http://www.citynet.net.net/davids/glass.html

Great Lost Bear Bar, Maine: http://www.mainelink.net/bear

Rainforest Cafe: http://www.rainforestcafe.com

Sheffield Pub: Bershire Co. of Wellsley, MA: http://www.sheffield-pub.com

Other sites

American Dj Supply: http://www.american-dj-supply.com

Autofry: http://www.autofry.com

Coldelite Corporation: http://www.mindspring.com~coldelite

FOX Sports Direct: http://www.foxsportsdirect.com

Imperial Drink Distributors: http://www.nerds.net/Imperial/eye popping neons.look@mycopy

Internet Restaurant Delivery: http://www.ird.net/cgi/get?ird/index

Manitowoc Ice Machines: http://www.Manitowoc.com

McIlhenny Company (Tabasco): http://www.TABASCO.com

National Fisheries Institute (NFI): http://www.nfi.org

Bartending Resources

American Beverage Institute
1775 Pennsylvania Avenue NW, Suite 1200
Washington, DC 20006
800-843-8877; 202-463-7110; Fax 202-463-7107
John Doyle, Director of Media Relations

American Council on Alcoholism, Inc. (ACA)
2522 St. Paul Street
Baltimore, MD 21218
410-889-0100
Bruce Cotter, Executive Director

American Hotel and Motel Association (AH&MA)
1201 New York Avenue, NW, Suite 600
Washington, DC 20005-3931
202-289-3100
Marni Dacy, Manager of Media Relations

American Institute of Wine and Food (AWF)
1550 Bryant Street, Suite 700
San Francisco, CA 94103
415-255-3000
Roberta Klugman, Executive Director

American Irish Bartenders Association
34-15 32nd Street
Long Island City, NY 11106
718-706-1585
Sean Patrick Flynn, President

American Wine Alliance for Research and Education (AWARE)
P.O. Box 765
Washington, DC 20044-0765
800-700-4050
John Juergens, Ph.D, Chairman

***BARTENDER* Magazine**
Foley Publishing Corp.
P.O. Box 158
Liberty Corner, NJ 07938
908-766-6006; Fax 908-766-6607
Raymond P. Foley, Publisher
http://www.bartender.com
e-mail: barmag@aol.com

Beer Institute
122 C Street, NW, Suite 750
Washington, DC 20001
202-737-2337; Fax 202-737-7004
Raymond McGrath, President

Bureau of Alcohol, Tobacco, and Firearms (ATF)
Department of Treasury
650 Massachusetts Avenue
Washington, DC 20226
202-927-8100
Jerry LaRusso, Division Chief

California Association of Winegrape Growers (CAWG)
555 University Avenue, Suite 250
Sacramento, CA 95825
916-448-2676
Karen Ross, President

The Century Council
550 South Hope Street, Suite 1950
Los Angeles, CA 90071-2604
213-624-9898; Fax 213-624-9012
The Honorable John C. Lawn, Chairman of the Board

Champagne Wines Information Bureau
KCSA Public Relations
820 Second Avenue
New York, NY 10017
800-64 CHAMPagne; Fax 212-697-0910

Club Managers Association of America (CMAA)
1733 King Street
Alexandria, VA 22314
703-739-9500
Karen Miller, Information, Research & Publications

Distilled Spirits Council of the United States, Inc. (DISCUS)
1250 I Street NW, Suite 900
Washington, DC 20005
202-628-3544; Fax 202-682-8888
F.A. Meister, President/CEO

The Educational Foundation
Foodservice, Management, Professional
250 S. Wacker Drive, Suite 1400
Chicago, IL 60606-5834
800-765-2122 Ext. 725

Food and Wines From France
215 Park Avenue South, 16th Floor
New York, NY 10003
212-477-9800; Fax 212-473-4315

National Alcoholic Beverage Control Association (NABCA)
4216 King Street West
Alexandria, VA 22302
703-578-4200; Fax 703-820-3551
James Sgueo, Executive Director

National Association of Beverage Importers, Inc. (NABI)
1025 Vermont Avenue NW, Suite 1066
Washington, DC 20005
202-638-1617; Fax 202-638-3122
Robert Maxwell, President

National Association of Beverage Retailers (NABR)
5101 River Road, Suite #108
Bethesda, MD 20816
301-656-1494; Fax 301-656-7539
John B. Burcham, Jr., Executive Director

National Association of Wholesaler-Distributors (NAW)
1725 K Street NW Suite 300
Washington, DC 20006
202-872-0885; Fax 202-785-0586
Kimberly Morgan, Director-Communications

National Beer Wholesalers Association, Inc. (NBWA)
1100 South Washington Street, First Floor
Alexandria, VA 22314-4494
703-683-4300; Fax 703-683-8965
Gary Galanis, Public Affairs

National Conference of State Liquor Administrators (NCSLA)
Lewis L. Goldstein Treasury Building
80 Calvert Street, Room 310
Annapolis, MD 21401
410-974-3319; Fax 410-974-3201
Aaron L. Stansbury, Executive Secretary

National Licensed Beverage Association (NLBA)
4214 King Street West
Alexandria, VA 22302
703-671-7575; Fax 703-845-0310
Debra Leach, Executive Director

National Restaurant Association (NRA)
1200 17th Street NW
Washington, DC 20036
800-424-5156
Lynn Reiner, Information Services

Roundtable for Women in Foodservice, Inc. (RWF)
3022 W. Eastwood
Chicago, IL 60625
800-898-2849; 312-463-3396; Fax 312-463-3397
Erin Davey Jordan, Executive Director
E-Mail: EJordan@msn.com

Texas Alcoholic Beverage Commission (TABC)
P.O. Box 13127
Austin, TX 78711
512-458-2500
Randy Yarborough, Assistant Administrator

United States Bartenders Association (USBA)
1920 Sherry Lane #59
Santa Ana, CA 92705
714-542-4241
Fred Ireton, President

Wine Institute
425 Market Street, Suite 1000
San Francisco, CA 94105
415-512-0151; Fax 415-442-0742
John A. DeLuca, President & General Manager

Wine Market Council
100 Lincoln Village Circle, #107
Larkspur, CA 94939
415-925-1116; Fax 415-925-1117

Wine and Spirits Shippers Association, Inc. (WSSA)
11800 Sunrise Valley Drive, Suite 332
Reston International Center
Reston, VA 20191
703-860-2300; Fax 703-860-2422

Wines and Spirits Wholesalers of America, Inc. (WSWA)
805 Fifteenth St., NW, Suite 430
Washington, DC 20005
202-371-9792; Fax 202-789-2405
David Dickerson, Director of Communications

Women for Winesense
1925 Vintner Court
Yountville, CA 94599
800-204-1616
Lynn Garvey, Executive Director

Women Chefs & Restauranteurs
110 Sutter Street, Suite 210
San Francisco, CA 94104
415-362-7336; Fax 415-362-7335
Frankie Whitman, Executive Director

World Association of Alcohol Beverage Industries (WAABI)
1250 I Street NW, Suite 900
Washington, DC 20005
202-628-3544; Fax 202-682-8844
Peggy Donovan, National President
Helen Gatewood, Executive Director

Zinfandel Advocates & Producers (ZAP)
P.O. Box 1487
Rough & Ready, CA 95975
916-432-8964
Rebecca Robinson, Executive Director

Drinks Index

Chambord/Raspberry Liqueur Drinks

Curacao Drinks

Galliano Drinks

Irish Cream Drinks

Irish Whiskey Drinks

Midori/Melon Liqueur Drinks

Rum Drinks

Vermouth Drinks

Whiskey Drinks

Topics Index